# 100 to Dinner

# Better Cooking for

CLUBS, CAMPS & RESORTS

INSTITUTIONS

INDUSTRIAL PLANTS and all

PUBLIC DINING PLACES

# IOO TO DINNER

by

**Elspeth Middleton**

**Muriel Ransom Carter**

**Albert Vierin**

UNIVERSITY OF TORONTO PRESS

TYPOGRAPHIC DESIGN BY ANTJE LINGNER

DRAWINGS BY BUDGE WILSON

# Preface

This recipe manual is planned to serve as a guide to better cooking in clubs, schools, camps, factories, offices, institutions, tourist resorts—in fact, wherever large numbers of people are served. It is the result of work done by the authors during World War II. At that time they were attempting to provide attractive, nourishing meals to large numbers and realized that it was essential to have accurate recipes with simple directions that were easy to follow. Every recipe in this volume is the fruit of prolonged testing, and the quantities specified for preparing servings of 100-125 portions may be relied on.

The first edition was submitted for publication in the hope that those just entering the field of food service would find it helpful and that even experienced cooks would value it for its concise directions and convenient size. That this has been the case is proven by the request for a second, enlarged edition.

E.M.
M.R.C.
A.V.

# Contents

# Miscellaneous Information

## TABLE OF WEIGHTS AND MEASURES

The following table gives the weight in ounces per imperial quart (40 oz.) of the foodstuffs as listed. The imperial quart is the basic measure used for all recipes in this book.

In the use of this table it must be noted that the measuring cup commonly found on the Canadian market today and used throughout this book is an eight-ounce (wine measure) cup, while the larger measuring equipment (pint, quart, gallon) is based on the forty-ounce quarts (imperial measure), making five eight-ounce cups per quart.

A table showing the American equivalents for the imperial pint, quart and gallon measures will be found on page 3.

To calculate the weight of one cup of the following, one-fifth of the quart weight must be taken.

| ITEM | OZ. PER QT. | ITEM | OZ. PER QT. |
|---|---|---|---|
| Almonds, shelled | 24 | Eggs, hard-cooked, chopped | 29 |
| Apples, diced | 20 | raw, whole (25) | 42 |
| sliced | 20 | yolks (66) | 42 |
| cooked | 40 | whites (40) | 42 |
| Apricots, dried, A.P. | 27 | Figs, dried, chopped | 28 |
| Baking powder | 32 | Fish, flaked | 32 |
| Bread crumbs, | | Flour | |
| dry sifted | 16 | Cake & Pastry, sifted | 16 |
| fresh | 10 | unsifted | 20 |
| Bran | 8 | All Purpose and Bread, sifted | 20 |
| Butter | 40 | unsifted | 23 |
| Cheese, grated | 16 | Flour, soya, sifted | 14 |
| Cherries, glacée | 32 | Gelatine | 24 |
| Chicken, cooked, diced | 26 | Honey or Jam | 50 |
| Cinnamon | 16 | Jelly powder | 36 |
| Citron, chopped | 24 | Lard | 36 |
| Cocoa | 16 | Lemon juice | 40 |
| Coconut, shredded | 12 | Lemon rind | 16 |
| Coffee | 13 | Macaroni, raw | 20 |
| Corn flakes | 4 | cooked | 32 |
| Corn meal | 28 | Mayonnaise | 40 |
| Corn starch | 24 | Meat, cooked, diced | 26 |
| Corn syrup | 55 | raw, minced | 40 |
| Cranberries, raw | 16 | Milk, whole, fluid | 40 |
| Cream of wheat | 30 | skim, powdered | 28 |
| Currants, dried | 28 | Molasses | 56 |
| Dates, chopped | 28 | Mustard | 12 |

| ITEM | OZ. PER QT. | ITEM | OZ. PER QT. |
|---|---|---|---|
| Nutmeg | 20 | Sago | 32 |
| Nuts, chopped | 21 | Shortening | 32 |
| Oil, salad | 38 | Soda, baking | 36 |
| Orange juice | 40 | Tapioca, pearl | 28 |
| Parsley, chopped | 15 | minute | 26 |
| Peanut butter | 46 | Tea | 12½ |
| Peanuts, skin off, salted | 24 | Walnuts, broken | 20 |
| Peel, chopped | 24 | | |
| Pepper, white | 20 | **VEGETABLES** | |
| Pecans, broken | 20 | Beans, dried | 32 |
| Pimentos, chopped | 40 | Beets, cooked, diced | 32 |
| Prunes, as purchased | 30 | Cabbage, shredded, raw | 12 |
| Raisins, Texas seeded | 24 | Carrots, diced, raw | 24 |
| sultanas | 26 | shredded, raw | 20 |
| currants | 28 | Cauliflower, diced, raw | 16 |
| Rice, cooked | 32 | Celery, diced, raw | 20 |
| Rice or barley | 40 | Cucumbers, diced, raw | 24 |
| Rolled oats | 16 | Mushrooms, sliced, raw | 16 |
| Sage | 10 | Onions, diced, raw | 24 |
| Savoury | 8 | Potatoes, diced, cooked | 28 |
| Sugar, granulated | 32 | diced, raw | 24 |
| brown | 28 | mashed | 36 |
| fruit | 36 | Peas, split | 32 |
| icing | 22 | Peppers, green, diced, raw | 24 |
| Suet, chopped | 20 | Spinach, shredded, raw | 8 |
| Salt | 50 | Turnips, diced, raw | 24 |

## SPICES

| | |
|---|---|
| 1 oz. Ground allspice, cloves, curry powder, mace, nutmeg, pepper | 4½ tbsp. |
| 1 oz. Ground cinnamon, ginger, mustard | 5 tbsp. |
| 1 oz. Salt | 5 tsp. |

## U.S. EQUIVALENTS OF IMPERIAL MEASURES

| Imperial Measure | Weight | U.S. Measure |
|---|---|---|
| 1 pint | 20 oz. | 1 pint + ½ cup (16 oz. + 4 oz.) |
| 1 quart | 40 oz. | 1 quart + 1 cup (32 oz. + 8 oz.) |
| 1 gallon | 160 oz. | 1 gallon + 1 quart (128 oz. + 32 oz.) |

## OVEN TEMPERATURES

When thermometers are not used for determining the temperature of an oven, a simple test may be made with flour.

Place a tablespoonful of flour on a pie plate or piece of paper. Put it in the centre of the oven.

Leave for 5 minutes and then remove.

A creamy-coloured flour indicates a slow oven of temperature 250°-325°F.

A light-brown flour indicates a moderate oven of temperature 350°-375°F.

A golden-brown flour indicates a hot oven of temperature 400°-425°F.

A dark brown flour indicates a very hot oven above 425°F.

## ABBREVIATIONS

| | |
|---|---|
| A.P. | As Purchased |
| E.P. | Edible Portion |
| lb. | pound |
| oz. | ounce |
| bus. | bushel |
| gal. | gallon |
| qt. | quart |
| pt. | pint |
| c. | cup |
| tbsp. | tablespoon |
| tsp. | teaspoon |

## EQUIVALENTS

| | |
|---|---|
| 3 tsp. | 1 tbsp. |
| 16 tbsp. | 1 c. |
| 2 c. (10 oz.) | 1 pt. |
| 2½ c. (8 oz.) | 1 pt. |
| 2 pts. | 1 qt. |
| 4 qts. | 1 gal. |
| 1 pt. | 20 oz. |
| 1 qt. | 40 oz. |
| 1 gal. (water) | 10 lbs. |
| 1 bu. | 4 pecks |

## GENERAL INFORMATION FOR BAKING

### HOW TO SUBSTITUTE SOUR FOR SWEET MILK IN A RECIPE

If the milk is but slightly soured, no alteration in the recipe is necessary.
The following changes apply only when using thick (clabbered) sour milk or buttermilk.

1. Beat the sour milk until smooth.
2. Substitute an equal quantity of sour milk for the sweet.
3. Add 1 tsp. of soda per quart of sour milk.
4. Use ¾ of the amount of baking powder given in the recipe.

### HOW TO SUBSTITUTE BAKING POWDER FOR EGGS IN A RECIPE

Add ½ tsp. baking powder for each egg omitted.

### HOW TO SUBSTITUTE DRIED EGGS FOR FRESH EGGS

Dried eggs may be used successfully in flour mixtures.
1 lb. dried eggs = 3 doz. eggs.

### HOW TO GREASE PANS FOR BAKING

Brush lightly and evenly with pan-grease. If too much grease is used, it will fry the outer surface of the product.

## PAN-GREASE FOR BAKING

| 1½ qts. | Fat | 3 lbs. |
| 1½ pts. | Flour | 1 lb. |

**METHOD**

1. Whip together at # 2 speed or mix to a paste by hand.
2. Use for greasing all baking tins.

**NOTE**

The fat used should be flavourless.

## FLAVOURINGS

Under this term are included fruit juices and rind as well as flavouring extracts, caramel, chocolate, cocoa and coffee.

When there is a choice, use the fruit juice and rind in preference to the extract, as it has a more natural and agreeable flavour.

Extracts are very concentrated, should be used sparingly and should be carefully measured. A better taste is obtained with a small than with a large amount.

Greater variety will be given to meals if a wider use is made of the many flavourings obtainable. For example, almond or maple extract, grated orange or lemon rind, should be used occasionally to replace the vanilla called for in desserts or plain cake, cookies, etc.

### MONOSODIUM GLUTAMATE

Monosodium Glutamate enhances the natural flavour of some foods and may be added to fish, meats, gravies, sauces and soups.

#### QUANTITY REQUIRED

Use 1 oz. (3 tbsp.) Monosodium Glutamate to

        45 lbs. beef or poultry
        35 lbs. other meats
        35 lbs. oily fish (such as mackerel)
        60 lbs. dry fish (cod)
        8 gals. soup
        7 gals. cream or other mild sauces
        2 gals. highly flavoured sauces
        5 gals. brown gravy.

#### HOW TO USE

1. Steaks, chops, fish fillets, chicken breasts etc.; sprinkle on both sides. Let stand for 10 minutes before cooking.
2. Roasts, whole turkeys, chickens etc.; sprinkle on surface before roasting. Sprinkle cavity of poultry as well.
3. Minced meat; mix with the other seasonings.
4. Gravies, sauces, soups and stews; mix with other seasonings or add just before serving.

## HERBS AND SPICES

Herbs and spices lose their flavour when they are stored for a long time, or if they are not kept in covered containers.

By using a variety of herbs and a variety of spices much greater interest can be added to meals. For example, do not always add sage to dressings, do not always add cinnamon to desserts, but try one or more of the other herbs and spices listed. Add both herbs and spices sparingly. They are intended to bring out the flavour of the food in which they are used, not to hide it.

## HERBS AND THEIR USES

| LEAVES—FRESH OR DRIED | USE |
| --- | --- |
| Basil | Tomato dishes, cheese dishes, cream soups, pork and poultry dressing. |
| Bay | Use very sparingly. Particularly suitable for tomato, dried bean and split pea soup. Used in tomato sauce, simmered meat or fish, fish sauces. |
| Chervil | Fresh in salad. Fresh or dried in soups, meat loaf, creamed chicken, stews. |
| Chives | Fresh in soups, stews, salads, salad dressings, sandwiches, egg dishes. It gives a delicate flavour of onion. |
| Dill | Tomato soup, tomato sauce, creamed chicken, cream cheese and fish sauces.<br>Note: dried seeds may also be used. |
| Marjoram | Fresh: chopped fine and sprinkled on green peas, beans, spinach, tomatoes. Dried: meat and poultry dressing, gravies, sausages. |
| Mint | Fresh: in vinegar, mint sauce, jellied salads, iced beverages, fruit cup, on new potatoes. Dried: mint sauce, pea soup. |

## HERBS AND THEIR USES (cont'd)

| | |
|---|---|
| Parsley | Salads, scrambled eggs, meat loaf, meat balls, hamburgers, fish and poultry dressing. Sauces for vegetables. As a garnish. |
| Sage | Meat loaf and meat balls, sausages, pork, duck and goose dressing. |
| Savoury | Meat loaf, meat balls, hamburgers, croquettes, soups, poultry and meat dressings. |
| Thyme or Oregano | Poultry or meat dressings, and soups. Chop fine and sprinkle on carrots. |

**BULBS AND ROOTS**

| | |
|---|---|
| Garlic (bulb: each section is called a clove) | Salads—rub a piece around the inside of the bowl before mixing the salad. On mutton or lamb—rub over the raw meat before roasting. |
| Horse-radish (fresh or dried—grated) | In sauces for fish or meat, Harvard or pickled beets. |

## SPICES

Ground spice should be mixed with sugar or some other ingredient that will separate the grains, before it is added to any mixture. This is particularly important when it is used for flavouring fruit desserts such as apple pie.

When possible, tie whole spices in a thin piece of cotton when they are used in soups or sauces that do not require straining.

| SPICE | | USE |
|---|---|---|
| Allspice | Berries | Soups, meat and fish sauces, simmered meat or fish. |
| | Ground | Cakes, cookies. |

Cassia (substitute for Cinnamon)
|  | Buds | Stewed fruits, pudding sauces. |
|  | Ground | Puddings, cakes, cookies, apple pie. |

| Cayenne | Ground | Use very sparingly in salad dressing, meat and fish dishes. |
|  | Whole Fruit (dried) | In pickles. |

| Cinnamon | Sticks | Stewed fruits, sauces, soups, pickles. |
|  | Ground | Cakes, cookies, puddings, apple pie. |

| Cloves | Whole | Tomato soup, sauce, or jelly, dessert sauces, baked apples or pears, stewed fruit. |
|  | Ground | Cakes, cookies, steamed puddings. |

| Curry Powder (a mixture of many spices) | | Sauces such as tomato or curry, soups, mutton or lamb stew, French, mayonnaise dressings. |

| Ginger | Dried Root | Syrups for cooked fruit, pudding sauces. |
|  | Ground | Cakes, cookies. |
|  | Preserved | Cakes, cookies, fillings and icings, pudding sauces. |

| Mace | In pieces | Stewed fruits, sauces. |
|  | Ground | Curries, cakes, French dressing, mayonnaise. |

| Mustard · | Ground | Meat and fish dishes, sauces, cheese dishes, sandwich fillings. |

| Nutmeg | Ground | Cakes, cookies, pies, pudding sauces, green beans, spinach. |

| Pepper | Whole | Soups, sauces, pickles. |
|  | Ground | Soups, sauces, meat, fish, cheese and egg dishes. |
|  |  | Note: Black pepper is stronger than white. |

## CAN SIZES, WEIGHT AND VOLUME

| Size of can | Average net weight of contents | Average drained weight of fruits and vegetables | Volume of contents (net) | Approx. no. of cans required to make 1 gal. | Approx. no. of cans required to make 1 gal. of drained fruit or vegetable |
|---|---|---|---|---|---|
| #1 Tall | 1 lb. | | $\frac{4}{5}$ pt. | 10 | |
| #2 | 1 lb., 3 oz. | 12 oz. | 1 pt. | 8 | $13\frac{1}{3}$ |
| #$2\frac{1}{2}$ | 1 lb., 12 oz. | 17 oz. | $1\frac{2}{5}$ pts. | $5\frac{3}{4}$ | $9\frac{1}{2}$ |
| #3 | 3 lbs. | | $2\frac{2}{5}$ pts. | $3\frac{1}{2}$ | |
| #10 | 6 lbs., 9 oz. | 3 lbs., 14 oz. | $5\frac{1}{4}$ pts. | $1\frac{1}{2}$ | $2\frac{1}{2}$<br>$1\frac{1}{2}$ (solid pack) |

## CAN EQUIVALENTS (Approx.)

| No. 10 can | | No. 1 can | | No. 2 can | | No. $2\frac{1}{2}$ can | | No. 3 can |
|---|---|---|---|---|---|---|---|---|
| 1 | = | 7 | = | 5 | = | 4 | = | $2\frac{1}{4}$ |
| 3 | | 20 | | 16 | | 11 | | 7 |
| 5 | | 33 | | 26 | | 19 | | $11\frac{1}{2}$ |

# Beverages

## GENERAL RULES FOR MAKING TEA OR COFFEE

1. Tea and coffee should not be boiled.
2. Both tea and coffee should be made with freshly boiling water. Water that has been boiling for a long time will not give as good a flavour.
3. Keep one pot for tea only and reserve another one for coffee.
4. Both pots must be washed and rinsed very thoroughly after using. When not in use, the lids should be left off.
5. Keep tea bags and coffee bags separate. Rinse in clear hot water after using. Keep in clear cold water until needed again. Do **not** wash them with soap.
6. Tea or coffee should be prepared only a few minutes before serving time. Make in relays when serving large numbers.
7. Keep tea and coffee hot and at an even temperature.

## TEA

|  |  |
|---|---|
| ½ lb. | Tea |
| 6 gals. | Water |

**METHOD**

1. Put the tea in a thin cotton bag and tie the bag tightly at the top. (The dry tea should occupy only one-third of the bag in order to allow for expansion.)
2. Bring cold fresh water to a full rolling boil in a perfectly clean pot. Add the tea.
3. Remove from the heat at once. Cover. Let stand in a warm place for 3 to 4 minutes. Move the bag around in the water, lift out, drain thoroughly.
4. Keep the tea covered.
5. Tea should be made just before it is to be served as it deteriorates very rapidly on standing.

**NOTE**

When no thin cotton bag is available, place tea in a dry, heated pot, pour freshly boiling water over it. Allow to steep 3 to 4 minutes in a warm place. Strain immediately into another dry, heated pot.

## CARE OF URNS

1. Scour the urns thoroughly each day with baking soda and rinse well. Do not use any other cleansing agent. Clean the faucets with a small brush.
2. Whenever urns are not in use, leave a small amount of water in the inner lining.
3. When in constant use, keep the leach bags clean by washing in hot water (never use soap). When not in use, keep the bags in a bowl of cold water.

## RULES FOR MAKING COFFEE IN URNS

1. Always use fresh water for making coffee. This means that all of the water should be drained from the water urn every night. Have the fresh water boiling hard and use at once.
2. Never use water out of the jacket for making the coffee.
3. Do not allow the water in the jacket to leak into the urn. Look into the urn each day before making coffee to see that no water has leaked in.
4. Always keep plenty of water in the jacket of the urn and be sure that it is near the boiling point. Coffee will not hold its flavour if allowed to get cool.
5. The urn and all utensils must be hot from start to finish.
6. When using a new leach bag—wash in cold water before putting it in urn.
7. If using new urns, boil well with coffee before using, to eliminate the taste of lead from the joints.

## URN COFFEE

**METHOD**

1. Fill the water urn with fresh water. Heat.
2. Check the jacket around the coffee urn to make sure that it is well filled. Heat.
3. If the coffee bag is dry, rinse it in cold water.
4. Weigh or measure the coffee accurately, put it in the bag and place the bag in the urn.
5. Run the correct measure of freshly boiling water slowly through the coffee. Do not allow the coffee to bubble over the top of the bag or work under the ring.
6. Repour about $\frac{1}{4}$ of the brew through the coffee grounds.

### PROPORTIONS FOR MAKING COFFEE

10 oz. Coffee to 1 gallon Water
16 ,,      ,,     ,, 2  ,,      ,,
20 ,,      ,,     ,, 3  ,,      ,,
30 ,,      ,,     ,, 5  ,,      ,,
6 oz. Coffee to each additional gallon.

## STEEPED COFFEE

| | |
|---|---|
| **2½ lbs.** | **Coffee** |
| **6 gals.** | **Water** |

**METHOD**

1. Have water freshly boiling in a perfectly clean pot.
2. Remove from the heat to let the water go off the boil.
3. Put in the coffee bag as when making tea. Cover.
4. Let stand 10 minutes. Press the bag thoroughly with a spoon, as you lift it out.
5. Cover the coffee and keep it hot.

**YIELD**

5 gallons.

## COCOA

| | | |
|---|---|---|
| 1½ qts. | Cocoa | 1 lb., 8 oz. |
| 1½ pts. | Sugar | 1 lb., 8 oz. |
| 1 tsp. | Salt | |
| 3 gals. | Water | |
| 3 gals. | Milk | |

**METHOD**

1. Mix cocoa, sugar, salt and water.
2. Simmer for 5 minutes.
3. Add milk and reheat.

**YIELD**

6 gallons.


## COCOA PASTE

| | | |
|---|---|---|
| 1½ gals. | Water | 15 lbs. |
| 1 tbsp. | Salt | |
| 3 qts. | Granulated Sugar | 6 lbs. |
| 6 qts. | Cocoa | 6 lbs. |

**METHOD**

1. Boil water, salt and sugar until latter is dissolved.
2. Add cocoa, stirring until smooth and thick. Cook for 5 minutes.
3. Keep covered in a cool place until used. Add paste to hot milk to taste.

**YIELD**

Paste for 24 gallons cocoa.

# Cakes

## GENERAL INFORMATION ABOUT CAKES

If a cake has been properly made, it will double in volume while baking, will be golden-brown in colour and will have a flat surface which is neither crusty nor cracked.

The texture of the cake will be fine and even with no tunnels or large holes. The crumb will be tender and moist and have a good flavour.

Such cake can be produced only when suitable ingredients are used, the formula properly balanced and the greatest care taken in regard to temperature, weighing and mixing.

### GENERAL PREPARATION

1. Remove eggs, milk and fat from the refrigerator long enough ahead of time to ensure that they will be at 73-75°F. when mixing starts. This improves the texture of the cake and prevents curdling when the milk is added.
2. Consult the chart as to the temperature required for baking the type of cake being made (page 19). Regulate the oven until it remains at this temperature.
3. Grease the pans (page 5).
4. Weigh all the ingredients very accurately before starting to mix.

### BAKING

1. Do not put the cakes in the oven until the temperature is correct.
2. Do not overcrowd the ovens.
3. As far as possible, place the cakes in the centre of the oven.
4. Do not open the oven doors until the cakes have been baking for at least half the time required for cooking them.
5. Do not bang the door, when closing it.
6. If the cakes have to be moved in order to be evenly cooked, wait until they have stopped rising.
7. If it is difficult to prevent the oven from becoming too hot, put a pan of water on the bottom and place a piece of brown paper over the cakes.
8. A cake is cooked:
   (a) When it begins to shrink from the sides of the pan.
   (b) If the surface springs back when pressed lightly with the finger-tip.
   (c) When a toothpick thrust into the centre comes out dry.

# OVEN TEMPERATURES FOR CAKES

| Kind | Depth | Temperature | Time |
|---|---|---|---|
| Plain or Spice | ½"-¾" (layer cake) | 360° | 20 to 25 min. |
| Plain or Spice | 1" | 360° | 20 to 30 min. |
| Plain or Spice | Loaf tins ⅔ full | 325°-350° | 50 to 55 min. |
| Plain or Spice | Cup cakes or muffin tins ⅔ full | 375° | 15 to 20 min. |
| White | ½"-¾" (layer cake) | 375° | 20 min. |
| White | 1" | 360° | 20 to 25 min. |
| White | Loaf tins ⅔ full | 325°-350° | 50 to 55 min. |
| Chocolate | ½"-¾" (layer cake) | 360° | 20 min. |
| Chocolate | 1" | 350° | 20 to 25 min. |
| Chocolate | Loaf tins ⅔ full | 325°-350° | 50 to 55 min. |
| Gingerbread | 1" | 350° | 20 to 25 min. |
| Gingerbread | Loaf tins ⅔ full | 325°-350° | 50 to 55 min. |
| Fruit Cake (Christmas Cake) | Square, round or loaf tins ⅔ full | 275° | 2 to 6 hours depending on depth and weight |
| Sponge Cakes | ¾"-9" tins | 325° | 45 to 60 min. |

## CAKES MADE WITH FAT

### MACHINE MIX

1. Sift the flour, baking powder and salt into the bowl of the mixer and add the shortening and sugar.
2. Beat the eggs sufficiently to mix them and add them to the milk and flavouring. Pour about half of this mixture into the dry ingredients.
3. Turn on the beater and mix for 2 minutes at low speed.
4. Add half the remaining milk and egg gradually—mix for 1 minute on low speed. Stop the machine, scrape down the bowl.
5. Add the remainder of the milk and egg. Mix for 4 minutes on low speed.
6. Scale off.
7. Consult chart for time required for baking.

**NOTE**

Since there is considerable variation in the amount of liquid required for different flours, it is advisable, when starting on a new bag, to mix only $\frac{3}{4}$ of the milk with the eggs. The rest of the milk can be added with the last lot of the milk and egg mixture should it be needed. This will prevent the use of too much liquid and ensure that all the eggs will be added.

### HAND MIX

1. Mix and sift the flour, baking powder and salt.
2. Cream the fat well.
3. Add the sugar—a little at a time and continue creaming until the sugar is dissolved.
4. Add the eggs—two at a time and beat until light and creamy after each addition.
5. Add the flavouring. Scrape down the side of the bowl.
6. Add a small amount of the dry ingredients to the creamed mixture and stir smooth.
7. Add all the milk and the remainder of the dry ingredients and then stir smooth.
8. Scale off.
9. Consult chart (page 19) for time required for baking.

## APPLE SAUCE CAKE

### A

| | | |
|---|---|---|
| 3½ pts. | Shortening | 3 lbs., 8 oz. |
| 4 qts. | Brown Sugar | 7 lbs. |

### B

| | | |
|---|---|---|
| 3 qts. | Raisins | 5 lbs. |
| 3 qts. | Currants | 5 lbs. |
| 1 gal. | Dry Apple Sauce | 10 lbs. |

### C

| | | |
|---|---|---|
| 5½ qts. | Unsifted Pastry Flour | 7 lbs. |
| 2 tbsp. | Baking Soda | 1 oz. |
| 6 tbsp. | Baking Powder | 2½ oz. |
| 3 tbsp. | Salt | 2 oz. |
| 4 tbsp. | Cinnamon | 1 oz. |
| 2 tbsp. | Nutmeg | |

**METHOD**

1. Combine A according to general cake method.
2. Add ingredients in B.
3. Mix and sift C—add to A and B.
4. Bake in a slow oven (250°-300°F.) until cooked, approximately 2 hours.

**YIELD**

100 orders.

## CHOCOLATE CAKE

| | | |
|---|---|---|
| 3½ pts. | Shortening | 3 lbs., 8 oz. |
| 3½ qts. | Sugar | 7 lbs. |
| 24 | Eggs | 2 lbs., 8 oz. |
| | Cocoa or Chocolate | 1 lb. |
| 5 qts. | Unsifted Pastry Flour | 6 lbs., 4 oz. |
| ¾ c. | Baking Powder | 5 oz. |
| 2 tbsp. | Salt | |
| 2½ qts. | Milk | 6 lbs., 4 oz. |
| 3 tbsp. | Vanilla | |

**METHOD**

1. Make according to the general cake method.
2. Bake in a moderate oven (350°F.) for 30-45 minutes.

**YIELD**

100 large pieces.

## LIGHT FRUIT CAKE

| | | |
|---|---|---|
| 3¾ qts. | **Raisins** | 6 lbs. |
| 1¾ qts. | **Currants** | 3 lbs. |
| 2 qts. | **Cherries** | 4 lbs. |
| 3 qts. | **Peel** | 4 lbs., 8 oz. |
| 2½ qts. | **Unsifted Pastry Flour** | 3 lbs. |
| 1 tbsp. | **Baking Powder** | |
| 1 tbsp. | **Finely Grated Lemon Rind** | |
| ½ c. | **Lemon Juice** | 5 oz. |
| 3 pts. | **Butter** | 3 lbs., 12 oz. |
| 3 pts. | **White Sugar** | 3 lbs. |
| 28 | **Eggs** | 3 lbs. |

**METHOD**

1. Line the sides and bottom of bread tins, empty jam tins from which the brim has been trimmed, tomato cans or deep cake tins, with three layers of brown paper.
2. Brush the inner layer with melted butter or line with waxed paper.
3. Regulate the heat so that the oven will be slow (250°F.).
4. Pick over and wash the raisins and currants; drain well. Dry between perfectly clean towels or absorbent paper, if possible. When dry place in a large bowl or pot.
5. Cut the cherries in half or chop rather coarsely. Slice the peel very thin. Add these to the other fruit.
6. Weigh or measure the sifted flour and sift about 1 qt. of it over the dried fruit. Mix well, so that all the fruit is coated.
7. Mix and sift the remaining flour with the baking powder.
8. Cream the butter until very soft (low speed).
9. Add the sugar gradually and beat well (low speed).
10. Add the egg yolks two at a time and beat after each addition (low speed).
11. Beat the egg whites until stiff but not dry, add to the mixture and beat until light (low speed).
12. Add the sifted dry ingredients by hand, and when partially mixed, add the fruit ⅓ at a time.
13. Fill the tins ¾ full.
14. Bake until the surface of the cake does not retain the pressure of the finger (1½ to 3 hrs. depending on the size of the cakes).
15. Keep a pan of water in the oven during the baking.

**NOTE**

All ingredients must be at 73°-75°F. before mixing starts.

**YIELD**

29 lbs. of cake.

## DARK FRUIT CAKE

| | | |
|---|---|---|
| 3 qts. | Raisins, seeded | 4 lbs., 8 oz. |
| 4 qts. | Raisins, seedless | 6 lbs., 8 oz. |
| 1 qt. | Cherries | 2 lbs. |
| 2½ pts. | Almonds | 1 lb., 10 oz. |
| 2 qts. | Citron Peel | 3 lbs. |
| 2 qts. | Dates | 3 lbs., 8 oz. |
| 2½ qts. | Unsifted Pastry Flour | 3 lbs. |
| 2 tbsp. | Cinnamon | |
| 1 tbsp. | Nutmeg | |
| ½ tbsp. | Mace | |
| 3 pts. | Butter | 3 lbs., 12 oz. |
| 1¾ qts. | Brown Sugar | 3 lbs. |
| 1¼ qts. | (31) Eggs | 3 lbs., 4 oz. |
| ¼ pt. | Molasses | 7 oz. |
| ½ pt. | Jam (Grape or Strawberry) | 12 oz. |
| ¼ pt. | Grape Juice | 5 oz. |

**METHOD**

1. Follow the directions given for making Light Fruit Cake.
2. Sift the spices with the flour.
3. Add the jam, molasses and grape juice to the creamed sugar and eggs.
4. Finish and bake as Light Fruit Cake.

**YIELD**

33 lbs.

## GINGERBREAD

| 5 qts. | Unsifted Pastry Flour | 6 lbs., 4 oz. |
| 1¼ tbsp. | Baking Powder | ½ oz. |
| 4½ tbsp. | Baking Soda | 2 oz. |
| 1 tbsp. | Cinnamon | |
| 10 tbsp. | Ginger | 2 oz. |
| 5 tsp. | Salt | 1 oz. |
| 2½ pts. | Shortening | 2 lbs., 8 oz. |
| 1½ qts. | Brown Sugar | 2 lbs., 10 oz. |
| 10 | Eggs | 1 lb., 2 oz. |
| 2½ pts. | Water | 3 lbs. |
| 3½ pts. | Molasses (light) | 6 lbs. |

**METHOD**

1. Combine by the cake method.
2. Bake in a moderate oven (350°F.) for 25 to 30 minutes.
3. Serve plain or iced, or serve hot with Orange or Butterscotch Sauce for dessert.

**NOTE**

1. 4 lbs. 11 oz. of bread flour (3¾ qts.) may be used in place of pastry flour.
2. 5 oz. dried eggs (1 cup) and 1 cup of water may be used in place of fresh eggs.

**YIELD**

100 3-oz. servings.

## ORANGE AND RAISIN CAKE

| | | |
|---|---|---|
| 4¾ qts. | Unsifted Pastry Flour | 6 lbs. |
| 6 tbsp. | Baking Powder | 2½ oz. |
| 2¼ tbsp. | Baking Soda | 1 oz. |
| 5 tsp. | Salt | 1 oz. |
| 2½ pts. | Shortening | 2 lbs., 8 oz. |
| 2¾ qts. | Sugar | 5 lbs., 8 oz. |
| 8 | Medium Oranges | |
| 2½ qts. | Raisins | 4 lbs. |
| 1 qt. | (25) Eggs | 2 lbs., 10 oz. |
| 1½ qts. | Milk | 3 lbs., 12 oz. |

**METHOD**

1. Combine the ingredients by the cake method. Put the oranges and raisins through the mincer and collect the orange juice. Add the fruit and juice when the first lot of eggs and milk is poured in. When mixing by hand, add 1 pt. of sifted flour to the creamed shortening, eggs and sugar, before adding the fruit.
2. Baking in a slow oven (325°F.) for 40 minutes.

**YIELD**

100 4-oz. servings.

## ORANGE AND DATE CAKE

5 lbs. of dates may be substituted for the raisins.

## PLAIN CAKE

| | | |
|---|---|---|
| 4¾ qts. | **Unsifted Pastry Flour** | 6 lbs. |
| ¾ c. | **Baking Powder** | 5 oz. |
| ¼ c. | **Salt** | 2½ oz. |
| 2¾ pts. | **Shortening** | 2 lbs., 12 oz. |
| 3 qts. | **Sugar** | 6 lbs. |
| 2¼ pts. | **(28) Eggs** | 3 lbs. |
| 3 pts. | **Milk** | 3 lbs., 12 oz. |
| 2 tbsp. | **Flavouring** | 1 oz. |

**METHOD**

1. Follow the general method for mixing cakes.
2. Consult chart for oven temperature and time required for baking.

**YIELD**

100 3-oz. servings.

**VARIATIONS**

1. **Chocolate:** Add 2 lbs. of cocoa or chocolate and omit 1 lb. of flour.
2. **Spice:** Add 7 tbsp. of cinnamon and 3 tbsp. of allspice and nutmeg.
3. **Cinnamon:** Add ½ cup of cinnamon.
4. **Raisin:** Add 5 lbs. of raisins (or currants). Dust with part of the flour and add last.
5. **Raisin Spice:** Add spices and raisins as in making Spice Cake and Raisin Cake.
6. **White Cake:** Substitute 1 qt. (40) egg whites for the whole eggs. Hold back part of the milk as less may be needed.

## ECONOMY JELLY ROLL

| | | |
|---|---|---|
| 2⅓ qts. | **Fine Sugar** | 5 lbs., 4 oz. |
| 21 | **Medium-sized Eggs** | 2 lbs., 3 oz. |
| 5 qts. | **Unsifted Pastry Flour** | 6 lbs., 4 oz. |
| 10 tbsp. | **Baking Powder** | 4 oz. |
| 1¾ qts. | **Milk** | 4 lbs., 6 oz. |

**METHOD**

1. Warm the sugar slightly.
2. Beat the eggs until light. Add the sugar gradually and continue beating until the mixture is stiff and lemon-coloured.
3. Sift flour and baking powder together. Fold the flour and the milk alternately into the beaten eggs.
4. Pour the batter to the depth of ¼ inch into 7 baking sheets (approx. 15 inches by 21 inches), which have been lined with greased paper.
5. Bake in a hot oven (400°F.).
6. When the cake is cooked and while still hot, turn it on to a slightly sugared towel or clean white cloth. Trim off any dried edges. Roll in the towel and place on a rack to cool.
7. Unroll and spread with filling. Re-roll.
8. Cut each roll into 15 slices.

**YIELD**

100 servings.

## JELLY ROLL

| | | |
|---|---|---|
| 3 c. | **Sifted Cake Flour** | 9½ oz. |
| 2 c. | **Sifted Potato Flour** | 9 oz. |
| 5 tbsp. | **Baking Powder** | 2 oz. |
| 32 | **Eggs** | 3 lbs., 6 oz. |
| 6 c. | **Fine Sugar** | 2 lbs., 7 oz. |

**METHOD**

Make as Economy Jelly Roll.

**YIELD**

100 servings.

**NOTE**

6 c. Cake Flour may be used instead of the two flours given in the recipe.

## SPONGE CAKE

| | | |
|---|---|---|
| 48 | **Egg Yolks** | 2 lbs. |
| 2½ qts. | **Sugar** | 5 lbs. |
| 1 pt. | **Warm Water** | 1 lb., 4 oz. |
| 1 cup | **Lemon Juice** | |
| | **Rind of 4 Lemons, grated** | |
| 6½ pts. | **Unsifted Pastry Flour** | 4 lbs. |
| 5 tbsp. | **Baking Powder** | 2 oz. |
| 5 tsp. | **Salt** | 1 oz. |
| 48 | **Egg Whites** | 3 lbs., 2 oz. |

**METHOD**

1. Beat the egg yolks, sugar and water on low speed or by hand until thick and lemon-coloured.
2. Add the lemon juice and finely grated rind.
3. Sift the flour, baking powder and salt. Fold into the egg mixture by hand.
4. Fold in the stiffly-beaten egg whites by hand.
5. Pour into cake tins which have been greased on the bottom only. Fill each tin ⅔ full.
6. Bake in a slow oven (300-325°F.) for about 1 hour. Sponge cakes are cooked if they do not retain the impression of the finger when lightly touched.
7. Allow to cool in the tins.
8. Remove from the tins carefully.
9. Serve plain, or split each cake through the centre and use one of the fillings listed on page 31. Use forks for dividing the Sponge Cake or for splitting it in half.

**YIELD**

100 2-oz. servings.

# COMMON FAULTS IN CAKE MAKING

## SINKING IN THE MIDDLE, DURING OR AFTER COOKING

**May be due to:**

1. Too much baking powder.
2. Too much sugar.
3. Too much liquid.
4. Not enough eggs.
5. Insufficient cooking.
6. Opening the oven door before the cake is at least half cooked.
7. Moving the cake before it has set.

**To avoid:**

1. Use a standard recipe.
2. Weigh the ingredients accurately and use exactly the amounts called for in the recipe.
3. Look at the time when the cakes are put in the oven and know how long they will take to cook.
4. Do not open the oven door until at least half the time is up.
5. Do not move the cakes until they have stopped rising and are firm.

## POOR VOLUME

**May be due to:**

1. Ingredients that are too cold.
2. Ingredients that are too warm.
3. Over-mixing.
4. Not enough baking powder.
5. Too slow an oven.

**To avoid:**

1. Have ingredients at 73°-75°F.
2. Follow directions for mixing.
3. Use a standard recipe.
4. Regulate the oven before starting the cake.

## SUGARY CRUST

**May be due to:**

1. Too much sugar.
2. Too slow an oven.

**To avoid:**

1. Weigh or measure accurately.
2. Regulate the oven to the temperature required.

## THICK CRUST

**May be due to:**

1. Too much flour.
2. Not enough liquid.
3. Over-mixing.
4. Too hot an oven.

**To avoid:**

1. Weigh or measure accurately.
2. Follow directions for mixing.
3. Do not put cake in the oven until the temperature is correct.

## CRACKED OR PEAKED SURFACE

**May be due to:**

1. Too much flour.
2. Not enough liquid.
3. Over-mixing the flour.
4. Too hot an oven.

**To avoid:**

1. Use a standard recipe.
2. Weigh or measure accurately.
3. Follow directions for mixing.
4. Regulate the oven. Do not put cakes in until temperature is correct.

## A DRY CAKE

**May be due to:**

1. Too slow an oven.
2. Cooking the cake too long.
3. Not enough liquid.
4. The use of unsuitable fat.

**To avoid:**

1. Regulate the oven before starting to mix.
2. Watch the time required for cooking.
3. Use accurate measurements.
4. Use a good quality of shortening and butter.

## COARSE TEXTURE

**May be due to:**

1. Over-mixing of the flour.
2. Under-creaming the fat and sugar.
3. Too much baking powder.
4. Too slow an oven.

**To avoid:**

1. Follow directions for mixing and creaming.
2. Measure ingredients carefully.
3. Regulate the oven beforehand.

## CLOSE, HEAVY TEXTURE

**May be due to:**

1. Ingredients that are too cold.
2. Too much liquid.
3. Too much flour.
4. Not enough baking powder.
5. Insufficient creaming.
6. Over-mixing of the flour.
7. Too slow an oven.
8. Too hot an oven.

**To avoid:**

1. Have all ingredients at 73°-75°F.
2. Use a standard recipe and weigh accurately.
3. Do not alter the recipe.
4. Observe directions for mixing.
5. Regulate the oven before starting to mix. Do not put the cakes in until the temperature is correct.

## TUNNELS

**May be due to:**

1. Over-mixing of the flour.
2. Ingredients that are too warm.

**To avoid:**

1. Follow directions for mixing.
2. Have all ingredients at 73°-75°F.

## APRICOT FILLING

| | | |
|---|---|---|
| 2 qts. | Dried Apricots | 3 lbs., 6 oz. |
| 2 qts. | Boiling Water | 5 lbs. |
| 1 tbsp. | Grated Lemon Rind | |
| 1¼ pts. | Sugar | 1 lb., 4 oz. |
| ¼ c. | Lemon Juice | 2 oz. |

**METHOD**

1. Wash the apricots and put through a coarse mincer.
2. Add the boiling water and soak for 2 hours.
3. Add the lemon rind and cook below boiling until thick.
4. Add the sugar and lemon juice. Continue cooking until the sugar is dissolved.
5. Cool before using.

**YIELD**

Approx. 10 lbs. of filling.
Sufficient for 2½ layer cakes 15″ x 21″.

## OTHER FILLINGS

Butterscotch (see page 222). Use ¼ recipe.
Chocolate (see page 223). Use ¼ recipe.
Cream (see page 224). Use ¼ recipe.
Date (see page 54).
Jam, Jelly and Ice cream may also be used.

## LEMON FILLING

| | | |
|---|---|---|
| 1 pt. | Cornstarch | 12 oz. |
| 2½ pts. | Sugar | 2 lbs., 8 oz. |
| 2½ qts. | Boiling Water | 6 lbs., 4 oz. |
| ⅓ c. | Grated Lemon Rind | |
| 22 | Egg Yolks | 14 oz. |
| 1 pt. | Lemon Juice | 1 lb., 4 oz. |
| ¼ c. | Butter | 2 oz. |

**METHOD**

1. Combine the cornstarch and sugar. Add the boiling water gradually.
2. Cook until there is no taste of raw starch. Add the lemon rind.
3. Beat the egg yolks slightly, add part of the cornstarch mixture and blend well. Stir this into the cooked cornstarch.
4. Cook until there is no taste of raw egg (3 to 5 minutes). Stir continuously.
5. Remove from the heat, add the lemon juice and butter. Mix well.
6. Cool. Spread between layers of Plain Cake or on Jelly Roll.

**YIELD**

Approx. 1 gal. Filling for 2½ layer cakes 15" x 21".


## WHIPPED CREAM FILLING OR ICING

### A

| | | |
|---|---|---|
| ¾ c. | Cocoa | 2 oz. |
| ¾ c. | Icing Sugar | 3 oz. |
| ¾ tsp. | Salt | |

### B

| | |
|---|---|
| 6 c. | Whipping Cream |

**METHOD**

1. Combine A. Add B. Chill for one hour.
2. Beat until stiff enough to spread.

**YIELD**

Approx. 2½ qts.

## BUTTER ICING

| 1½ c. | Butter or Margarine | 12 oz. |
|---|---|---|
| 2½ qts. | Icing Sugar | 3 lbs., 7 oz. |
| 1½ c. | Milk | 12 oz. |
| 2 tsp. | Vanilla or other flavouring | |

**METHOD**

1. Cream butter until soft.
2. Add sifted icing sugar gradually, work into butter very thoroughly.
3. Add milk, a small amount at a time. Add vanilla.
4. Beat thoroughly.
5. Spread on cold cake.

**VARIATIONS**

**Chocolate:** Add ¾ c. cocoa with the sugar.
**Coffee:** Substitute strong coffee for the milk. Omit vanilla.
**Lemon:** Add grated rind and juice of 4 lemons in place of part of the milk. Omit vanilla.
**Mocha:** Add 6 tbsp. instant coffee to the chocolate icing.
**Orange:** Add juice and grated rind of 3 medium oranges and 1 lemon in place of part of the milk. Omit vanilla.

**NOTE**

For a richer, creamier icing, add 12 egg yolks or 6 eggs and reduce the butter and milk to ¾ cup each.

## QUICK FOAMY FROSTING

| 5 c. | Tart Jelly or Corn Syrup |
|---|---|
| 10 | Egg Whites (at room temperature) |
| | Salt to taste |

**METHOD**

1. Combine the ingredients and beat until the mixture stands in peaks.

**NOTE**

This frosting must be used on the day that it is made.

## ORANGE ICING

| 8 | Egg Whites | |
| 1 ½ qts. | Granulated Sugar | 3 lbs. |
| 1 c. | Orange Juice | 10 oz. |
| 2 tbsp. | Lemon Juice | |
| 4 tsp. | Grated Orange Rind | |

**METHOD**

1. Make as Seven-Minute Icing—adding the orange rind just before spreading on the cake.

**YIELD**

Icing for 100 servings of cake.

## SEVEN-MINUTE ICING

| 8 | Egg Whites, unbeaten | |
| 1 ½ qts. | Granulated Sugar | 3 lbs. |
| ¼ c. | Corn Syrup | |
| 1 c. | Cold Water | 10 oz. |
| 1 tbsp. | Vanilla or Almond Flavouring | |

**METHOD**

1. Combine unbeaten egg whites, sugar, corn syrup and cold water. Beat with a whip until thoroughly mixed.
2. Place over boiling water and continue beating until the mixture stands in peaks.
3. Remove from heat, add flavouring, and continue beating until thick enough to spread.
4. Spread on cake cooled to room temperature.

**YIELD**

Icing for 100 servings of cake.

### BROWN SUGAR ICING

1. Omit corn syrup.
2. Substitute 1 ½ qts. brown sugar.
3. Use vanilla for flavouring.
4. Make as Seven-Minute Icing.

## UNCOOKED MARSHMALLOW ICING

| | |
|---|---|
| **1 pt.** | **Corn Syrup or Honey** |
| **$\frac{1}{16}$ tsp.** | **Cream of Tartar** |
| **12** | **Egg Whites** |

**METHOD**

1. Heat the corn syrup or honey until lukewarm.
2. Add the cream of tartar to the egg whites and beat until stiff but not dry.
3. Add the honey or syrup gradually to the beaten whites and continue to beat until the mixture is stiff enough to spread.
4. If corn syrup is used, add either grated lemon rind or 2 tbsp. of spice to the icing.
5. Spread on cake.

**YIELD**

Icing for 100 orders of cake.

## FRENCH CHOCOLATE ICING

**A**

| | | |
|---|---|---|
| | **Unsweetened Chocolate** | **1 lb., 4 oz.** |
| **$\frac{1}{2}$ c.** | **Butter or Margarine** | **4 oz.** |

**B**

| | | |
|---|---|---|
| **2 qts.** | **Icing Sugar** | **2 lbs., 12 oz.** |
| **1 pt.** | **Milk** | **1 lb., 4 oz.** |
| **10** | **Eggs** | **1 lb.** |

**METHOD**

1. Melt A over hot water (see note below).
2. Combine B and beat until thoroughly blended.
3. Add A slowly, continuing to beat until the icing is thick enough to spread.

**YIELD**

Icing for 100 servings of cake.

**NOTE**

The success of this icing depends upon cooling the chocolate sufficiently. When tested on the wrist, a drop should feel cool.

## BROILED ICING

| | | |
|---|---|---|
| 1 c. | Butter | 8 oz. |
| 4 c. | Brown Sugar | 1 lb., 6 oz. |
| 1½ c. | Cream | 12 oz. |
| 1½ tsp. | Vanilla | |
| ¾ tsp. | Salt | |
| 4 c. | Coconut or Chopped Nuts | |

### METHOD

1. Melt butter and add the other ingredients.
2. Spread on cooked cake while it is still warm.
3. Return to oven and broil until the icing bubbles.

### YIELD

Icing for 100 servings of cake.

## GINGER MERINGUE TOPPING

| | | |
|---|---|---|
| 12 | Egg Whites | 12 oz. |
| ¼ tsp. | Salt | |
| 6 c. | Brown Sugar | 2 lbs., 2 oz. |
| 2 c. | Chopped, Preserved Ginger | 8 oz. |
| 3 c. | Chopped Nuts | 12 oz. |

### METHOD

1. Have the egg whites at room temperature. Add salt and beat until they stand in soft peaks.
2. Use brown sugar that is free of lumps and beat it gradually into the meringue.
3. When stiff enough to hold its shape, fold in the ginger and nuts.
4. Spread on the batter just before putting the cake in the oven and bake with the cake.

### YIELD

Sufficient for 100 servings of cake.

# Cereals

## PORRIDGE

Porridge should have the consistency of soft jelly and should be free of lumps.

### GENERAL RULES FOR MAKING AND SERVING PORRIDGE

1. A steam-jacketed kettle should be used for porridge. If this is not available, use a heavy stock-pot and when the porridge becomes thick, place the stock-pot over another one containing water.
2. Cereals should be added slowly to boiling, salted water.
3. Porridge should not be stirred as stirring makes it sticky.
4. Long cooking improves the flavour.
5. Always serve porridge very hot.

### GENERAL PROPORTIONS FOR MAKING PORRIDGE

| Cereal | Weight | | Measure | Water | Salt |
|---|---|---|---|---|---|
| Rolled Oats (quick) | 5 lbs. | or | 5 qts. | 5 gals. | ½ c. |
| Rolled Wheat | 5 lbs. | or | 5 qts. | 4 gals. | ½ c. |
| Cracked Wheat | 4 lbs. | or | 2½ qts. | 5 gals. | ½ c. |
| Wheatlets or other fine Cereals | 5 lbs. | or | 2⅔ qts. | 5 gals. | ½ c. |

**YIELD**

100 6-oz. servings.

**METHOD**

1. Bring salted water to a vigorous boil.
2. Add cereal slowly so that the water does not stop boiling. To avoid the formation of lumps, the dry cereal may be beaten in with a wire whip.
3. Cook **without stirring**. As the porridge becomes thick, scrape a wooden paddle across the bottom of the pot to prevent scorching.
4. Cook over hot water or in a steam-jacketed kettle until thick. With the proportions given this should take from 30 to 40 minutes. **Do not stir.**
5. Cover and cook for at least one hour.
6. Serve very hot.

## BAKED RICE

| | | |
|---|---|---|
| 1 pt. | Fat or Butter | 1 lb. |
| 1 pt. | Onions, Finely Diced | 12 oz. |
| 2½ qts. | Rice | 6 lbs., 4 oz. |
| 1½ gals. | Meat or Vegetable Stock | 15 lbs. |
| ¼ c. | Salt | 2½ oz. |

**METHOD**

1. Melt the fat, add the onion and cook for 2 minutes.
2. Wash the rice thoroughly in cold water, drain well.
3. Add to the melted fat, stir to coat the rice with the fat.
4. Cook on top of the stove for 5 to 6 minutes.
5. Add boiling stock. Bake in a hot oven until tender (approximately 20 minutes).
6. Serve with stews, creamed fish or eggs, or curry sauce.

**NOTE**

Do not attempt to prepare Baked Rice in a larger batch than the one given above.

**YIELD**

100 3-oz. servings.

## BOILED RICE

| | | |
|---|---|---|
| 4 qts. | Rice | 10 lbs. |
| 8 gals. | Boiling Water | 80 lbs. |
| ½ c. | Salt | 5 oz. |

**METHOD**

1. Wash the rice thoroughly in cold water.
2. Add gradually to the rapidly boiling salted water.
3. Boil vigorously for 20 to 30 minutes, or until the kernels are tender. Test a few kernels by pressing with a fork.
4. Drain well.
4. If the rice is to be used as a vegetable, rinse with boiling water to separate the kernels.
6. Season before serving.

**YIELD**

100 5-oz. servings (approximately 4 gals.).

## BOILED MACARONI, SPAGHETTI, OR NOODLES

| 5 qts. | Macaroni, Spaghetti or | |
| | Noodles | 6 lbs., 4 oz. |
| 1 c. | Salt | 10 oz. |
| 5 gals. | Water | 50 lbs. |

**METHOD**

1. Break into 1-inch pieces, wash in cold water.
2. Add gradually to rapidly boiling salted water. Boil until tender (about 20 minutes).
3. Strain and rinse in hot water.

**YIELD**

3 gals. or 25 lbs. cooked macaroni, spaghetti, or noodles.

# Cookies

## GENERAL DIRECTIONS FOR COOKIES

### METHODS OF MIXING

#### 1. BY MACHINE

Put all the ingredients into the mixing bowl. Mix at medium speed for 2 to 3 minutes.

#### 2. BY HAND

Combine the ingredients as in making cake by hand.

Whichever method is used, the dough must be handled only enough to combine all the ingredients thoroughly.

### BAKING

Cookies should be golden-brown on the top and bottom. Avoid flash heat as this browns the cookies before they are cooked.

## CHOCOLATE CHIP COOKIES

| | | |
|---|---|---|
| 2½ c. | **Butter or Shortening** | 1 lb., 4 oz. |
| 1½ pts. | **White Sugar** | 1 lb., 8 oz. |
| 8 | **Eggs** | 14 oz. |
| 2 qts. | **Unsifted Pastry Flour** | 2 lbs., 8 oz. |
| 5 tsp. | **Salt** | 1 oz. |
| 5 tbsp. | **Baking Powder** | 2 oz. |
| | **Chipped Semi-Sweet Chocolate** | 1 lb., 4 oz. |

#### METHOD

1. Combine all the ingredients but the chocolate, by machine.
2. Add the chipped chocolate by hand. Chill.
3. Roll on a lightly floured board to ⅛" thickness.
4. Cut with a cookie cutter or a knife.
5. Bake in a moderate oven (350°F.) until lightly browned on both top and bottom (10 to 15 minutes).

#### YIELD

200 medium-sized cookies.

## FRUIT COOKIES

A

| 1 qt. | Butter or Shortening | 2 lbs., 8 oz. |
| 2 qts. | White Sugar | 4 lbs. |

B

| 6 | Eggs | 10 oz. |
| | Flavouring | 1 oz. |

C

| 1½ pts. | Milk | 1 lb., 14 oz. |

D

| 5 qts. | Unsifted Pastry Flour | 6 lbs., 4 oz. |
| 10 tbsp. | Baking Powder | 4 oz. |
| 5 tsp. | Salt | 1 oz. |
| 2 qts. | Raisins | 3 lbs., 4 oz. |

**METHOD**

1. See general directions for mixing cookies, page 42.
2. Roll out to ¼-inch thickness and cut with 2¾-inch cutter. Place on greased baking sheets.
3. Bake in a moderate oven (350°F.) 10-15 minutes.

**YIELD**

100 cookies.


## SUGAR COOKIES

| 1 qt. | Butter or Shortening | 2 lbs., 8 oz. |
| 3 pts. | Sugar | 3 lbs. |
| | Flavouring | 1 oz. |
| 1 pt. | Milk | 1 lb., 4 oz. |
| 4½ qts. | Unsifted Pastry Flour | 5 lbs., 10 oz. |
| 1 tbsp. | Salt | |
| 10 tbsp. | Baking Powder | 4 oz. |

**METHOD**

1. See general directions for mixing cookies, page 42.
2. Shape into a roll 1 inch in diameter and as long as the baking pan.
3. Place on greased baking sheets and flatten to ¼-inch thickness with the fingers.
4. Bake in a moderate oven 10-15 minutes. Cut into squares.

**YIELD**

200 cookies.

## BUTTER COOKIES

| 3 c. | Butter or Margarine | 1 lb., 8 oz. |
|------|---------------------|--------------|
| 3 c. | Sugar | 1 lb., 3 oz. |
| 8 | Eggs | 14 oz. |
| ¼ tsp. | Vanilla or other flavouring | |
| 2 qts. | Unsifted Pastry Flour | 2 lbs., 8 oz. |
| ¼ c. | Baking Powder | 1½ oz. |

**METHOD**

1. Combine all the ingredients by machine (page 42) or mix by hand as in making cakes (page 20).
2. Divide into 5 pieces.
3. Roll 1 piece at a time on a lightly floured board to ⅛″ thickness.
4. Cut into shapes.
5. Place on a lightly greased baking sheet and bake in a moderate oven (350°F.) until golden brown on top and bottom (10 to 15 minutes).

**YIELD**

200 small cookies.


## CHOCOLATE COOKIES

**METHOD**

1. Leave out ½ c. flour.
2. Add 5 oz. cocoa to the recipe and sift it with the flour.
3. Finish as butter cookies.


## COCONUT COOKIES

**METHOD**

1. Add ¾ lb. (1 qt.) shredded coconut with the flour.
2. Finish as butter cookies.

## FILBERT WAFERS

| 1½ c. | Butter | 12 oz. |
|---|---|---|
| 1½ c. | Sugar | 10 oz. |
| 1½ c. | Sifted Pastry Flour | 5 oz. |
| 3 | Egg Yolks | |
| 1½ c. | Very Finely Chopped Nuts | 6 oz. |

**METHOD**

1. See general directions for mixing cookies, page 42.
2. Spread in a very thin layer on greased baking sheets.
3. Bake at 350°F. for about 15 to 20 minutes.
4. Cut into bars or squares while hot.

**YIELD**

Approx. 120 bars 1″ x 1½″.


## FILBERT DREAMS

| 2 c. | Butter or Margarine | 1 lb. |
|---|---|---|
| 3 c. | Unsifted Pastry Flour | 12 oz. |
| ½ c. | Sugar | 3 oz. |
| 4 c. | Finely Chopped Filberts | 1 lb. |
| | Icing Sugar | |

**METHOD**

1. See general directions for mixing cookies, page 42.
2. Form the dough into balls of about ¾″ diameter.
3. Roll in fruit sugar.
4. Place on ungreased baking sheets.
5. Bake at 300°F. for 30 to 40 minutes.
6. Place on a rack to cool.

**YIELD**

Approximately 120 cookies.

## MOLASSES ICE-BOX COOKIES

| | | |
|---|---|---|
| 1 pt. | Shortening | 1 lb. |
| 1 qt. | Sugar | 2 lbs. |
| 4 | Eggs | 7 oz. |
| ½ pt. | Molasses | 14 oz. |
| 2 qts. | Unsifted Pastry Flour | 2 lbs., 8 oz. |
| 2 tbsp. | Ground Ginger | |
| 2 tsp. | Baking Soda | |
| 1 tsp. | Salt | |

**METHOD**

1. Combine the ingredients by machine or mix by hand using the cake method (page 20).
2. Shape dough into rolls 3″ x 3″ x 18″ long.
3. Chill in the ice-box.
4. Cut into ⅛″ slices. Place on greased baking sheets.
5. Bake in a moderate oven (350°F.) for 10 minutes.

**NOTE**

1. 4 oz. of dried eggs (1 pt.) and ½ pt. water may be used instead of fresh eggs.
2. Rendered beef or chicken fat may be used in place of shortening.

**YIELD**

200 cookies.

## SHORTBREAD

| 1½ qts. | Butter and Margarine | 3 lbs., 12 oz. |
| 3¾ c. | Brown Sugar | 1 lb., 5 oz. |
| 3 qts. | Unsifted All Purpose Flour | 4 lbs., 5 oz. |

**METHOD**

1. Cream butter and sugar.
2. Add the flour. Blend well together until the dough cracks slightly.
3. Make dough into rolls 1 inch in diameter. Chill thoroughly.
4. Cut into slices ⅓-inch thick. Bake in a slow oven (275°F.) until the shortbread is firm and lightly coloured.

**YIELD**

200 shortbreads.

## DROP COOKIES

Use recipe given for Butter Cookies (page 44). Drop from a teaspoon onto greased baking sheets.

### RAISIN DROP COOKIES

Add 2 lbs. (1¼ qts.) of raisins that have been picked over, washed and dried or well-drained.

### DATE DROP COOKIES

Add 2 lbs. (5¾ c.) chopped pitted dates, ¼ oz. (1½ tsp.) almond extract, and ¼ oz. (1½ tsp.) vanilla to the standard recipe. Omit the vanilla given in the standard recipe.

### COCONUT DROP COOKIES

Add 1 lb. (1¼ qts.) shredded coconut to the standard recipe. If the coconut is dry, soak in milk for one-half hour and drain thoroughly before using.

### MARMALADE DROP COOKIES

Reduce milk slightly (about ¼ cup less) and add 1 c. stiff orange marmalade before adding the flour.

### NUT DROP COOKIES

Add 1 lb. (4 c.) finely chopped nuts with the flour. Thinly shaved bitter chocolate may be sprinkled over each cookie before baking.

## PEANUT COOKIES

| | | |
|---|---|---|
| 1½ pts. | Shortening | 1 lb., 8 oz. |
| 1½ qts. | Sugar | 3 lbs. |
| 24 | Eggs | 2 lbs., 8 oz. |
| ½ pt. | Milk | 10 oz. |
| 3 qts. | Unsifted Pastry Flour | 3 lbs., 12 oz. |
| 10 tbsp. | Baking Powder | 4 oz. |
| 1 tbsp. | Salt | |
| 1 gal. | Peanuts, chopped | 5 lbs., 4 oz. |
| 2 tbsp. | Lemon Juice or | |
| | Grapefruit Juice | 1 oz. |

**METHOD**

1. Combine all ingredients by machine (page 42) or if mixed by hand, use the method given for cakes (page 20), and add the chopped peanuts and lemon juice at the last.
2. Drop from a spoon onto greased and floured baking sheets. Place the cookies 1 to 1½ inch apart.
3. Bake in a hot oven (400°F.) for 10 to 15 minutes.

**YIELD**

200 medium-sized cookies.

## HERMITS

| | | |
|---|---|---|
| 1½ qts. | Shortening | 3 lbs. |
| 4½ pts. | Brown Sugar | 4 lbs. |
| 1 pt. | (12) Eggs | 1 lb., 5 oz. |
| 1 c. | Water | |
| 1¼ tbsp. | Baking Soda | |
| 3½ qts. | Unsifted Pastry Flour | 4 lbs., 6 oz. |
| 1 tbsp. | Salt | |
| 4 tbsp. | Cinnamon | |
| ½ tsp. | Allspice | |
| 1 tsp. | Mace | |
| 4½ pts. | Raisins | 3 lbs., 10 oz. |
| 4½ pts. | Dates | 4 lbs. |
| 1½ pts. | Nuts | 1 lb. |

**METHOD**

1. Combine all the ingredients except the fruit and nuts by machine (page 42) or mix by hand using the cake method. Add fruit and nuts by hand.
2. Drop in teaspoonfuls onto greased baking pan. The cookies should be 1″ apart.
3. Bake in a moderate oven (350°F.) for 12 to 15 minutes.
4. Remove from pan while warm.

**YIELD**

200 medium-sized cookies.

## GINGER SNAPS

| | | |
|---|---|---|
| 1½ c. | Shortening | 10 oz. |
| 2 c. | Sugar | 13 oz. |
| ½ c. | Light Molasses | 5 oz. |
| 2 | Eggs | |
| 3 c. | Unsifted Pastry Flour | 12 oz. |
| 4 tsp. | Baking Soda | |
| 2 tsp. | Cinnamon | |
| 2 tsp. | Cloves | |
| 4 tsp. | Ginger | |

**METHOD**

1. See general method for mixing cookies, page 42.
2. Drop by teaspoonfuls onto a greased baking sheet.
3. Bake at 350°F. for about 20 minutes.
4. Remove at once from baking sheet and place on cake rack.

**YIELD**

Approx. 120 cookies (2").

## NUT CRISPIES

| | | |
|---|---|---|
| 1 c. | Shortening | 6 oz. |
| 1 c. | Margarine | 8 oz. |
| 4 c. | Brown Sugar | 1 lb., 6 oz. |
| 4 | Eggs | 7 oz. |
| 1 qt. | Sifted All Purpose Flour | 1 lb., 4 oz. |
| ½ tsp. | Salt | |
| 1 tsp. | Baking Soda | |
| 2 c. | Chopped Nuts | 8 oz. |

**METHOD**

1. See general method for mixing cookies, page 42.
2. Drop from a teaspoon onto a greased baking sheet.
3. Bake at 350°F. for 12 to 15 minutes.
4. Remove at once from baking sheet and place on cake rack.

**YIELD**

120 medium size cookies.

**NOTE**

This dough can be shaped into rolls 1½ inches in diameter, chilled for several hours and cut into ⅛ inch slices.

## OATMEAL CRISPS

| | | |
|---|---|---|
| 2¼ c. | Butter or Margarine | 1 lb., 2 oz. |
| 1½ c. | Brown Sugar | 8 oz. |
| 1½ c. | White Sugar | 9 oz. |
| 3 | Eggs | |
| 3 c. | Quick Oats | 9 oz. |
| 2 c. | Coconut | 5 oz. |
| 3 c. | Unsifted Pastry Flour | 12 oz. |
| 2½ tsp. | Baking Powder | |
| 1½ tsp. | Baking Soda | |
| 1½ tsp. | Salt | |
| ¾ tsp. | Almond Flavouring | |

**METHOD**
1. See general directions for mixing cookies, page 42.
2. Drop from a spoon onto a greased baking sheet.
3. Press flat if a thin cookie is desired.
4. Bake at 325°F. for approximately 15 minutes.
5. Remove at once from pans.

**YIELD**
Approximately 120 2½″ cookies.

**VARIATION**
Replace 1 c. coconut with chopped nuts.

## BROWNIES

| | | |
|---|---|---|
| 1½ c. | Butter or Margarine | 12 oz. |
| 1 tsp. | Vanilla | |
| 8 c. | Brown Sugar | 2 lbs., 9 oz. |
| 2 c. | Eggs | 1 lb. |
| 8 squares | Unsweetened Chocolate | 8 oz. |
| 4½ c. | Unsifted Pastry Flour | 1 lb., 2 oz. |
| 2 tsp. | Baking Powder | |
| 1 tsp. | Salt | |
| 5 c. | Nuts, Coarsely Chopped | 1 lb., 4 oz. |

**METHOD**
1. Mix by cake method, adding the cooled, melted chocolate to the creamed sugar and egg mixture.
2. Pour into greased cake tins, to the depth of ⅓″.
3. Bake at 325°F. for 30 to 40 minutes.
4. Cool. Cut into squares or bars, and ice if desired.

**YIELD**
Approximately 100 bars.

## FIG BARS

| | | |
|---|---|---|
| 4¼ qts. | Unsifted Bread Flour | 5 lbs., 5 oz. |
| 6 tbsp. | Baking Powder | 2½ oz. |
| 2 tsp. | Salt | |
| 1½ pts. | White Sugar | 1 lb., 8 oz. |
| 1 qt. | Brown Sugar | 1 lb., 12 oz. |
| 2½ pts. | Butter or Shortening | 3 lbs. |
| 1 pt. | Milk | 1 lb., 4 oz. |

**METHOD**

1. Sift the dry ingredients.
2. Rub in the fat as in making pastry.
3. Add just enough milk to make the mixture suitable for rolling.
4. Divide the dough into four pieces.
5. Roll each piece into strips ⅛" thick and 3" wide.
6. Spread fig filling down the centre of the strip, leaving about ¾" uncovered, on each side.
7. Fold the edges towards the centre, so that they meet, and press the edges together.
8. Cut into bars, 3" long.
9. Place on floured cookie sheets, with the pressed edges down.
10. Bake in a hot oven (400°F.) until thoroughly browned on the top and the bottom (12 to 15 minutes).

## FILLING FOR FIG BARS

| | | |
|---|---|---|
| 1 gal. | Chopped Figs | 7 lbs. |
| ½ pt. | Brown Sugar | 7 oz. |
| 2 qts. | Water | 5 lbs. |

**METHOD**

1. Add the sugar and water to the chopped figs.
2. Cook until the figs are tender.
3. Cool before spreading on the cookie dough.

**YIELD**

Approx. 200 bars.

## CHINESE CHEWS

| | | |
|---|---|---|
| 2¼ c. | **Unsifted Pastry Flour** | 9 oz. |
| ¾ tsp. | **Salt** | |
| 2¼ tsp. | **Baking Powder** | |
| 3 c. | **Brown Sugar** | 1 lb. |
| ¾ tsp. | **Nutmeg** | |
| 9 | **Beaten Eggs** | 1 lb. |
| 6 tbsp. | **Melted Butter** | |
| ¾ tsp. | **Vanilla** | |
| 3 c. | **Walnuts, Coarsely Chopped** | 12 oz. |
| 4 c. | **Dates** | 1 lb., 6 oz. |

**METHOD**

1. Mix and sift the dry ingredients.
2. Stir in the remaining ingredients.
3. Pour into greased 9″ x 12″ pans.
4. Bake at 350°F. for 30 minutes.
5. When cool enough to handle, cut each pan into 30 pieces.
6. Roll each piece in fruit sugar if desired.

**YIELD**

120 cookies.

**VARIATIONS**

1. Substitute cherries for part of the dates.
2. Use filberts instead of walnuts.

## DATE SQUARES

| | | |
|---|---|---|
| 5 qts. | Unsifted Pastry Flour | 6 lbs., 4 oz. |
| 1 tbsp. | Salt | |
| 8 tbsp. | Baking Powder | 3 oz. |
| 3⅓ tbsp. | Baking Soda | 1½ oz. |
| 5 qts. | Quick Oats | 5 lbs. |
| 2 qts. | Brown Sugar | 3 lbs., 8 oz. |
| 5 pts. | Butter or Shortening | 5 lbs. |
| | Date Filling | |

**METHOD**

1. Sift the flour, salt, baking powder and baking soda.
2. Add the quick oats and sugar to the other ingredients.
3. Work in the fat.
4. Spread the mixture about ¼″ deep on greased baking pans. Spread with date filling to ½″ depth and cover with the remainder of the mixture.
5. Bake in a moderate oven (350°F.) for 1 hour.
6. Cut into squares. Serve cold.

**YIELD**

100 2½-oz. squares.

## FILLING FOR DATE SQUARES

| | | |
|---|---|---|
| | Dates, A.P. | 15 lbs. |
| ½ pt. | Brown Sugar | 7 oz. |
| 1 gal. | Boiling Water | 10 lbs. |
| 1 c. | Lemon Juice | 8 oz. |

**METHOD**

1. Wash and pit the dates.
2. Add the sugar and boiling water. Cook until thick. Cool.
3. Remove from the heat. Add the lemon juice.

## APRICOT BARS

### A

| | | |
|---|---|---|
| 2⅔ c. | Dried Apricots | 14 oz. |

### B

| | | |
|---|---|---|
| 2 c. | Margarine | 1 lb. |
| 1 c. | Sugar | 6 oz. |
| 4 c. | Sifted Bread Flour | 1 lb. |

### C

| | | |
|---|---|---|
| 1⅓ c. | Sifted Bread Flour | 5 oz. |
| 2 tsp. | Baking Powder | |
| 1 tsp. | Salt | |
| 4 c. | Brown Sugar | 1 lb., 6 oz. |
| 8 | Eggs | 14 oz. |
| 2 tsp. | Almond Flavouring | |
| 2 c. | Chopped Nuts | |

### D

Icing Sugar

**METHOD**

1. Wash apricots. Cover with water and boil for 10 minutes.
2. Drain thoroughly. Dry between towels. Cool. Chop.
3. Cream margarine and sugar in B.
4. Add flour. Mix until crumbly.
5. Spread evenly on the bottom of cake pans. Bake in a moderate oven (350°F.) until lightly browned (25 to 30 minutes).
6. Sift flour, baking powder and salt in C.
7. Beat eggs, add sugar and mix well.
8. Combine 6 and 7.
9. Add apricots and nuts.
10. Spread over the baked cookie dough (B).
11. Return to oven and bake at 350°F. for approximately 30 minutes.
12. When cooked, cool, cut into bars ¾" x 2½".
13. Roll in icing sugar if desired.

**YIELD**

Approximately 120 bars.

## 1. LEMON NUT SQUARES

### A

**Prepare cookie dough as in Apricot Bars (B).**

### B

| | | |
|---|---|---|
| 8 | **Eggs** | 14 oz. |
| 6 c. | **Brown Sugar** | 2 lbs., 2 oz. |
| ½ c. | **Sifted Pastry Flour** | 1½ oz. |
| 2 tsp. | **Baking Powder** | |
| 1 tsp. | **Salt** | |
| 2 c. | **Coconut** | 5 oz. |
| 4 c. | **Chopped Nuts** | 1 lb. |
| 1 tbsp. | **Vanilla** | |

### C

| | | |
|---|---|---|
| 7 c. | **Icing Sugar** | 2 lb. |
| | **Lemon Juice** | |

**METHOD**

1. Beat the eggs, add the sugar.
2. Sift flour, baking powder and salt.
3. Combine all the ingredients.
4. Spread on the baked cookie dough.
5. Bake at 350°F. for approximately 25 minutes.
6. When cool, spread with icing made by thinning icing sugar (C) with lemon juice.
7. Cut into 1½″ squares.

**YIELD**

Approximately 120 squares.

## 2. ROMAN BARS

### A

**Prepare cookie dough as in Apricot Bars (B).**

### B

| | | |
|---|---|---|
| 8 | **Egg Whites** | 8 oz. |
| 1 qt. | **Brown Sugar** | 1 lb., 12 oz. |
| 2 tsp. | **Baking Powder** | |
| ½ c. | **Sifted Pastry Flour** | 1½ oz. |
| 2 c. | **Coconut, Cherries or Chopped Dried. Apricots or Dates or a combination of these** | |
| 4 c. | **Nuts, chopped or whole** | 1 lb. |

**METHOD**

1. Beat egg whites until stiff.
2. Sift the sugar, baking powder and flour. Fold into the beaten whites.
3. Fold in the fruit and nuts.
4. Spread on the baked cookie dough.
5. Bake at 325°F. for ½ hr. or until light brown in colour.
6. Cut while warm.

**YIELD**

Approximately 120 bars.

## DATE-NUT DIAGONALS

| | | |
|---|---|---|
| 1 c. | **Shortening** | 6 oz. |
| 2 c. | **Sugar** | 13 oz. |
| 1 tsp. | **Vanilla** | |
| 4 | **Eggs** | 10 oz. |
| 3½ c. | **Unsifted All Purpose Flour** | 1 lb. |
| 4 tsp. | **Baking Powder** | |
| 1 tsp. | **Salt** | |
| 1 tsp. | **Cinnamon** | |
| 1 tsp. | **Cloves** | |
| 1 tsp. | **Nutmeg** | |
| 2 c. | **Chopped Dates** | 11 oz. |
| 1 c. | **Chopped Nuts** | 4 oz. |

**METHOD**

1. See general method for mixing cookies (page 42).
2. Chill.
3. On baking sheets shape into strips 2½ inches wide, ½ inch thick and as long as the sheet permits. The strips should be 4 inches apart.
4. Bake at 375°F. for 20 to 25 minutes.
5. While warm, cut diagonally into bars.
6. Place the bars on cake racks and sprinkle with icing sugar.

**YIELD**

120 bars.

## TUTTI-FRUTTI BARS

| | | |
|---|---|---|
| 8 | Eggs | 14 oz. |
| 1 tsp. | Vanilla | |
| 4 c. | Sugar | 1 lb., 10 oz. |
| 3 c. | Unsifted Pastry Flour | 12 oz. |
| 4 tsp. | Baking Powder | |
| 3 c. | Raisins, Chopped | 1 lb. |
| 2 c. | Candied Peel | 10 oz. |
| 1 c. | Nuts | 4 oz. |

**METHOD**
1. Beat eggs until thick and light. Add vanilla.
2. Add sugar gradually, beating until thoroughly combined.
3. Stir in the sifted dry ingredients.
4. Fold in fruit and nuts.
5. Spread in cake pans which have been lined with waxed paper.
6. Bake at 350°F. for approximately 40 minutes.
7. Cool. Cut into bars $\frac{3}{4}$" x $2\frac{1}{2}$".

**YIELD**
120 bars.

## CORNFLAKE MACAROONS

| | | |
|---|---|---|
| 2 c. | Brown Sugar | 11 oz. |
| 2 | Egg Yolks, Beaten | |
| 2 c. | Cornflakes | |
| 3 c. | Chopped Nuts | 12 oz. |
| 1½ c. | Glacéed Cherries | 9 oz. |
| 4 c. | Coconut | 10 oz. |
| 4 | Egg Whites | |

**METHOD**
1. Mix the sugar and beaten egg yolks.
2. Add all the other ingredients except the egg whites.
3. Beat the egg whites until stiff.
4. Fold into the fruit mixture.
5. Drop by teaspoonfuls onto a greased baking sheet—about 2" apart.
6. Bake at 325°F. for approximately 12 minutes.
7. Remove from baking sheets immediately.

**YIELD**
100 cookies.

**VARIATION**
Use 1 c. whole almonds unblanched and 1 c. of cut dates instead of the chopped nuts and cherries.

## COCONUT MERINGUES

| | | |
|---|---|---|
| 10 | **Egg Whites (at room** | |
| | **temperature)** | 10 oz. |
| 1 pt. | **Fine White Sugar** | 1 lb. |
| 1 qt. | **Moist Shredded Coconut** | 12 oz. |
| 2 tsp. | **Vanilla** | |

1. Beat the egg whites until they begin to stiffen.
2. Add the sugar gradually and continue to beat until the mixture will hold its shape.
3. Fold in the coconut and flavouring.
4. Drop from a teaspoon onto buttered baking sheets.
5. Bake at 250°F. for 20 to 30 minutes or until they feel firm.
6. Remove from baking sheets at once and cool on cake racks.

120 meringues—1 $\frac{1}{2}$" in size.

## DATE AND NUT MERINGUES

Replace coconut by

| | | |
|---|---|---|
| 1 pt. | **Chopped Dates** | 14 oz. |
| 4 c. | **Coarsely Chopped or** | |
| | **Whole Nuts** | 1 lb. |

## FRUIT MERINGUES

Replace coconut with a combination of chopped glacéed fruits, candied ginger, dried apricots and nuts.

## NUT MERINGUES

Replace coconut with

| | | |
|---|---|---|
| 1 qt. | **Finely Chopped Nuts** | 1 lb., 5 oz. |

These may be dropped from a teaspoon or shaped into fingers 2$\frac{1}{2}$" x $\frac{1}{2}$" from a pastry tube.

## SCRUMMIES

### A

| 4 | Eggs | |
|---|------|---|
| 3½ c. | Chopped Dates | 1 lb., 4 oz. |
| 2 c. | Sugar | 13 oz. |
| 1 c. | Chopped Nuts | 4 oz. |

### B

| 4 c. | Rice Crispies |
|------|---------------|

### C

Coconut

**METHOD**

1. Combine A and cook in a frying pan, over a moderate heat, stirring constantly, until the mixture comes away from the sides.
2. Add B.
3. Cool. Form into ¾" balls and roll in coconut.

**YIELD**

Approx. 120 balls.

**VARIATION**

Mould each ball around a miniature marshmallow.

## COOKIE TROUBLES

### DRYNESS OR HARDNESS

**Cause:**

1. Too slow an oven.
2. Too much flour.
3. Too little fat.
4. Too little sugar.
5. Over-baking.

**Cure:**

1. Regulate the oven.
2. Use a standard recipe.
3. Weigh carefully.
4. Measure carefully.
5. Time the baking accurately.

### TOUGHNESS

**Cause:**

1. Over-mixing.
2. Use of bread flour.
3. Not enough fat.
4. Not enough sugar.
5. Too many eggs.

**Cure:**

1. Reduce mixing time.
2. Reduce the amount of bread flour when it is substituted for pastry flour.
3. Use a standard recipe.
4. Weigh carefully.
5. Measure carefully.

### TOO MUCH SPREAD

**Cause:**

1. Insufficient mixing.
2. Too much sugar.
3. Too much fat.
4. Too much liquid.
5. Too much soda.

**Cure:**

1. Follow directions in recipe.
2. Use a standard recipe.
3. Weigh carefully.
4. Measure carefully.
5. Time the baking accurately.

### NOT ENOUGH SPREAD

**Cause:**

1. Over-mixing.
2. Not enough sugar.
3. Not enough fat.
4. Not enough liquid.
5. Too much flour.

**Cure:**

1. Reduce mixing time.
2. Use a standard recipe.
3. Weigh carefully.
4. Measure carefully.
5. Time the baking accurately.

# Desserts

## BAKED CUSTARD

| | | |
|---|---|---|
| 3 gals. | Hot Milk | 30 lbs. |
| 5 doz. | Eggs | 6 lbs., 4 oz. |
| 1½ qts. | Sugar | 3 lbs. |
| 1 tbsp. | Salt | |
| 2 tbsp. | Vanilla Extract | |
| | or | |
| ½ tbsp. | Cinnamon or Nutmeg | |
| | or | |
| 1 tbsp. | Almond Extract | |

**METHOD**

1. Heat the milk over hot water.
2. Beat the eggs sufficiently to mix them.
3. Add sugar, salt and flavouring.
4. Add part of the hot milk to the egg and sugar, stirring as you add.
5. Return this mixture to the hot milk and combine thoroughly.
6. Pour into baking pans or custard cups.
7. Place these in pans of hot water.
8. Bake in a moderate oven until a knife thrust into the centre comes out clean.
9. Remove immediately from the hot water and cool as quickly as possible.
10. Serve plain, or with whipped cream, fruit sauce, butterscotch or chocolate sauce.

**YIELD**

100 6-oz. servings.

## BREAD PUDDING

|            | Stale Bread or Cake | 5 lbs.        |
|------------|---------------------|---------------|
| 2 gals.    | Hot Milk            | 20 lbs.       |
| 1½ pts.    | Eggs                | 2 lbs.        |
| ¾ qt.      | Sugar               | 1 lb., 8 oz.  |
| 5 tsp.     | Salt                | 1 oz.         |
| 3 tbsp.    | Vanilla             |               |
| 1 pt.      | Butter              | 1 lb., 4 oz.  |

**METHOD**

1. Crumb, slice, dice or break the bread into pieces.
2. Combine the remaining ingredients as for baked custard, adding the butter last.
3. Pour over the bread mixture and leave for ½ hour. If broken bread is used, beat with a wire whip after it has stood. Pour into greased pans.
4. Bake in slow oven (300°F.) until a knife thrust into the centre comes out clean (about 1 hour).
5. Serve hot with milk or cream.

**YIELD**

100 4-oz. servings.

**VARIATIONS**

1. 2½ quarts raisins (4 lbs.) may be added to the recipe.
2. Drop spoonfuls of jam on the pudding just before baking it. Use about 2 lbs. of jam.

## CHOCOLATE BREAD PUDDING

| | | |
|---|---|---|
| 1¼ gals. | Stale Bread or Cake | 5 lbs. |
| 2 gals. | Hot Milk | 20 lbs. |
| 16 | Eggs | 1 lb., 12 oz. |
| 1½ qts. | Sugar | 3 lbs. |
| 5 tsp. | Salt | 1 oz. |
| 1 pt. | Cocoa | 8 oz. |
| 3 tbsp. | Vanilla | |
| 1 pt. | Butter | 1 lb., 4 oz. |

**METHOD**

1. Use the method for plain bread pudding. Combine the cocoa with the sugar before adding to the other ingredients.
2. Serve hot with milk or cream or cold with hard sauce.

**YIELD**

100 4-oz. servings.


## LEMON PUDDING

| | | |
|---|---|---|
| 1 pt. | Butter | 1 lb., 4 oz. |
| 4 qts. | Sugar | 8 lbs. |
| 46 | Eggs | 5 lbs. |
| 1 qt. | Unsifted Pastry Flour | 1 lb., 4 oz. |
| 5½ qts. | Milk | 13 lbs., 12 oz. |
| 24 | Lemons (juice and rind) | |

**METHOD**

1. Cream butter.
2. Add sugar gradually, cream well.
3. Add beaten egg yolks, beat thoroughly.
4. Add flour and milk.
5. Add lemon juice and rind.
6. Fold in beaten egg whites.
7. Pour into baking dishes. Cook in a pan of water in a moderate oven (350°F.) until a knife thrust into the spongy top comes out clean.

**YIELD**

100 4-oz. servings.

## BAKED LEMON PUDDING

### A

| 40 | Egg Yolks | 1 lb., 9 oz. |

### B

| 5 c. | Lemon Juice | 2 lbs., 8 oz. |
| ½ c. | Grated Lemon Rind | |

### C

| 1 pt. | Sifted Pastry Flour | 8 oz. |
| 2½ qts. | Sugar | 5 lbs. |

### D

| 1 gal. | Hot Milk | 10 lbs. |

### E

| 40 | Egg Whites | 2 lbs., 10 oz. |
| 5 tbsp. | Salt | |

**METHOD**

1. Beat A until light.
2. Add B and mix.
3. Combine C thoroughly; add gradually to the above.
4. Stir D in slowly.
5. Beat E until stiff and fold into the other ingredients.
6. Pour into greased baking dishes and place these in pans of warm water. The water should come at least half-way up the pudding dish.
7. Oven-poach in a 350°F. oven for about one hour.
8. Serve warm or chilled—with cream.

**YIELD**

100 3-oz. servings.

## BLANCMANGE

| | | |
|---|---|---|
| 3½ gals. | Hot Milk (dried or fresh only) | 35 lbs. |
| 5 tsp. | Salt | 1 oz. |
| 2 qts. | Cold Milk | 5 lbs. |
| 1½ qts. | Cornstarch | 2 lbs., 4 oz. |
| | or | |
| 3 qts. | Unsifted Pastry Flour | 3 lbs., 12 oz. |
| 2¼ pts. | Sugar | 2 lbs., 4 oz. |
| 4 tbsp. | Vanilla | 2 oz. |

**METHOD**

1. Heat the milk in a double boiler or steam kettle.
2. Combine the salt and cornstarch. Add the cold milk and mix to a thin paste.
3. Stir this gradually into the hot milk. Continue stirring until the pudding thickens. Cover.
4. Cook until there is no taste of raw starch. Stir occasionally.
5. Add the sugar.
6. Remove from heat. Add vanilla. Cool before serving. If possible cover tightly with waxed paper to prevent a skin from forming.
7. Serve with milk, fruit, jam, butterscotch or custard sauce.

**YIELD**

100 7-oz. servings.

## CUSTARD CORNSTARCH PUDDING

Reduce the cornstarch to 1 quart (1½ lbs.) or reduce flour to 2 quarts (2½ lbs.).

**METHOD**

1. Follow the method given for blancmange.
2. Add 2½ pts. eggs. Beat the eggs slightly.
3. When the cornstarch is cooked, add some of the hot mixture to the beaten eggs, stirring as you add. Return this to the original mixture and continue cooking until there is no taste of raw egg (about 5 minutes).
4. Remove from heat. Cool.
5. This may be served with fruit or sauce as suggested for blancmange.

**YIELD**

100 7-oz. servings.

## BUTTERSCOTCH PUDDING

| | | |
|---|---|---|
| 1¾ qts. | Brown Sugar | 3 lbs. |
| 1 qt. | Butter | 2 lbs., 8 oz. |
| 1¾ pts. | Cornstarch | 1 lb., 5 oz. |
| 5 tsp. | Salt | 1 oz. |
| 3½ gals. | Hot Milk | 35 lbs. |
| 1 qt. | (25) Eggs | 2 lbs., 10 oz. |
| 2 tbsp. | Vanilla | |

#### METHOD

1. Cook the brown sugar and butter in a steam-jacketed kettle or over a low heat until it becomes golden-brown in colour. Stir constantly.
2. Add the cornstarch and salt. Mix thoroughly.
3. Add the hot milk slowly—stir continually until the mixture thickens.
4. Cover, cook until there is no taste of raw starch (25 to 30 minutes). Stir occasionally.
5. Add some of the hot pudding to the beaten eggs, mix well and then stir back into the cooked mixture.
6. Cook for 3 to 5 minutes stirring gently.
7. Remove from the heat, add the vanilla. Cover tightly with waxed paper and cool before serving.
8. Serve plain or with milk.

#### NOTE

1. The eggs may be omitted and the cornstarch increased to 1 lb. 12 oz. (approx. 1 qt.).
2. 12 oz. dehydrated eggs (1½ pts.) mixed with 1½ pts. cold water may be substituted for fresh eggs.

#### YIELD

100 6-oz. servings.

## CARAMEL PUDDING

| | | |
|---|---|---|
| 3 gals. | Hot Milk | 30 lbs. |
| 5 tsp. | Salt | 1 oz. |
| 1½ qts. | Cornstarch | 2 lbs., 4 oz. |
| | or | |
| 3 qts. | Unsifted Pastry Flour | 3 lbs., 12 oz. |
| 2 qts. | Cold Milk | 5 lbs. |
| 4½ qts. | White Sugar | 9 lbs. |
| 2 qts. | Boiling Water | 5 lbs. |
| 4 tbsp. | Vanilla | 2 oz. |

**METHOD**

1. Heat the milk in a double boiler or steam kettle.
2. Combine the salt, cornstarch or flour and the cold milk.
3. Stir gradually into the hot milk, continue stirring until it thickens. Cover.
4. Caramelize the sugar; add the boiling water gradually. Boil 10 minutes.
5. Add to the cornstarch mixture.
6. Continue cooking until there is no flavour of raw starch. Stir occasionally.
7. Remove from heat. Add vanilla. Cool.
8. Serve plain or with milk or cream.

**YIELD**

100 7-oz. servings.

## CHOCOLATE PUDDING
**(COCOA)**

| | | |
|---|---|---|
| 3½ gals. | Hot Milk | 35 lbs. |
| 3 tbsp. | Salt | 2 oz. |
| 1½ qts. | Cocoa | 1 lb., 8 oz. |
| 1¼ qts. | Cornstarch | 1 lb., 14 oz. |
| 2 qts. | Cold Milk | 5 lbs. |
| 4½ pts. | White Sugar | 4 lbs., 8 oz. |
| 3 tbsp. | Vanilla | |

**METHOD**

1. Heat the milk in a double boiler or steam kettle.
2. Combine the salt, cocoa and cornstarch. Add the cold milk and mix to a thin paste.
3. Stir this gradually into the hot milk. Continue stirring until the pudding thickens. Cover.
4. Cook until there is no taste of raw starch. Stir occasionally.
5. Add the sugar and mix well.
6. Remove from the heat. Cool slightly, add the vanilla. Cover tightly with waxed paper and cool before serving.
7. Serve with milk or cream.

**NOTE**

When chocolate is used, melt the chocolate over hot water, stir into the pudding when the latter begins to thicken.

**YIELD**

100 7-oz. servings.

### Chocolate Soufflé

Stir 32 stiffly beaten egg whites into the pudding just before removing from the heat.

## LEMON SNOW

### A

| 2½ gals. | Water | 25 lbs. |
| 3 qts. | Sugar | 6 lbs. |
| ½ c. | Lemon Rind | 2 oz. |

### B

| ½ gal. | Cold Water | 5 lbs. |
| 1¼ qts. | Cornstarch | 2 lbs. |

### C

| 1 qt. | Lemon Juice | 2 lbs., 8 oz. |

### D

| 1 qt. | (40) Egg Whites | 2 lbs., 10 oz. |

**METHOD**

1. Bring ingredients in A to the boil.
2. Mix ingredients in B together and add gradually to A, stirring constantly. Cook until there is no taste of raw starch.
3. Remove from the heat and add C. Pour into pans and allow to set until fairly firm.
4. Beat D until stiff but not dry. Add the cornstarch mixture and continue to beat until quite stiff.
5. Serve with custard sauce.

**YIELD**

100 3-oz. servings.

## RICE PUDDING
(WITHOUT EGGS)

|              |           |              |
|--------------|-----------|--------------|
| 1½ qts.      | Raw Rice  | 3 lbs., 12 oz. |
| 3 gals.      | Hot Milk  | 30 lbs.      |
| 5 tsp.       | Salt      | 1 oz.        |
| 2½ pts.      | Sugar     | 2 lbs., 8 oz. |
| ¾ tbsp.      | Nutmeg    |              |
| 1 pt.        | Butter    | 1 lb., 4 oz. |

**METHOD**

1. Pick over the rice and wash it in warm water. Drain.
2. Add the rice to the hot milk and salt. Cook slowly in a steam-jacketed kettle or over hot water until the rice is almost tender.
3. Add the sugar, nutmeg and butter.
4. Continue cooking until the rice has absorbed most of the milk and is tender.
5. This pudding should be creamy and not stiff. It may be necessary to add more hot milk. When doing so, mix it in very gently—do not stir.
6. Serve hot with cream, milk, jam sauce or corn syrup.

**YIELD**

100 4-oz. servings.


## RAISIN RICE PUDDING

Add 2½ qts. of washed raisins (4 lbs.) with the sugar.


## BAKED RICE PUDDING

**METHOD**

1. After adding the sugar, nutmeg and butter, pour into greased baking tins and finish cooking in a slow oven (300°F.).
2. More hot milk will probably be needed—mix in with a fork.

## BAVARIAN RICE

### A

| 1½ qts. | Raw Rice | 3 lbs., 12 oz. |
| 7½ qts. | Hot Milk | 18 lbs., 12 oz. |
| 5 tsp. | Salt | 1 oz. |

### B

| 1 qt. | Sugar | 2 lbs. |

### C

| 3 qts. | Crushed Pineapple | |
| 1 qt. | Marshmallows, cut | 1 lb. |
| 2 c. | Maraschino Cherries (chopped) | 12 oz. |

### D

| 3 qts. | Whipping Cream | 7 lbs., 8 oz. |

**METHOD**

1. Cook A as directed on page 73, until the rice is tender and the milk is absorbed.
2. Add B and chill.
3. Drain pineapple and cherries thoroughly, chill.
4. Whip the cream.
5. Shortly before serving, fold C and D into A.

**YIELD**

100 4-oz. servings.

**VARIATIONS**

1. Add 1 c. finely chopped, preserved ginger.
2. Add 1 lb. blanched, slivered almonds, lightly browned.
3. Replace cherries with well-drained, cooked apricots, cut into pieces.
4. Use fresh raspberries or diced raw peaches in place of the fruit given in the recipe.

## BAKED RICE CUSTARD

| | | |
|---|---|---|
| 2⅔ pts. | Raw Rice | 3 lbs., 4 oz. |
| 4 gals. | Hot Milk | 40 lbs. |
| 1 pt. | Sugar | 1 lb. |
| 1 qt. | (25) Eggs | 2 lbs., 10 oz. |
| ⅓ c. | Salt | 3 oz. |
| 2 tbsp. | Vanilla | |
| | or | |
| 1 tbsp. | Almond Flavouring | |

#### METHOD

1. Pick over the rice and wash it in warm water.
2. Add to the hot milk and cook slowly in a steam-jacketed kettle or over hot water until the rice is almost tender. Turn off the steam or remove from the heat.
3. Beat the eggs only sufficiently to mix, add the sugar, salt, and then a small quantity of the hot rice and milk.
4. Stir this mixture slowly into the pudding.
5. Pour immediately into greased baking pans.
6. Bake in a slow oven (300°F.) until a knife thrust into the centre comes out free of custard.
7. Serve hot or cold with milk or cream.

#### YIELD

100 6-oz. servings.

#### VARIATION

Add 2½ qts. washed raisins (4 lbs.) just before adding the eggs.

## TAPIOCA CREAM
**(GRANULATED TAPIOCA)**

| | | |
|---|---|---|
| 2 gals. | Hot Milk | 20 lbs. |
| ¾ pt. | (24) Egg Yolks | 1 lb. |
| ½ gal. | Cold Milk | 5 lbs. |
| 1 qt. | Granulated Tapioca | 1 lb., 10 oz. |
| 1½ qts. | Sugar | 3 lbs. |
| 5 tsp. | Salt | 1 oz. |
| 24 | Beaten Egg Whites | |
| 1 tbsp. | Almond Flavouring | |
| | or | |
| 2 tbsp. | Vanilla Flavouring | |

**METHOD**

1. Heat the milk in a steam-jacketed kettle or over hot water.
2. Beat the egg yolks slightly and mix with the cold milk.
3. Stir the tapioca, sugar, salt and the egg and milk mixture into the hot milk.
4. Cook, stirring constantly, until there is no taste of raw egg and the tapioca is clear (3 to 5 minutes).
5. Remove at once from the heat, fold in the beaten whites, add the flavouring.
6. Serve warm with milk and sugar or chill and serve with canned fruit or jam.

**NOTE**

1½ pts. dried eggs (12 oz.) mixed with 1½ pts. cold water may be used in place of fresh eggs. Add to the milk and cook as above.

## FRUIT TAPIOCA CREAM

2 qts. sliced bananas or
2 qts. canned peaches, sliced and drained or
2 qts. cooked dried apricots drained
may be folded into the cooled tapioca cream. Chill. Serve with a sauce made from the fruit juice.

## COCONUT TAPIOCA CREAM

Fold 1 qt. moist shredded coconut into the cool tapioca cream.

# FRUIT TAPIOCA
**(GRANULATED TAPIOCA)**

| | | |
|---|---|---|
| 1½ pts. | **Granulated Tapioca** | 1 lb., 3 oz. |
| 1½ gals. | **Boiling Water** | 15 lbs. |
| ½ gal. | **Raw Sliced Fresh Fruit** | |
| | or | |
| ½ gal. | **Raw Soaked Dried Fruit** | 5 lbs. |
| 1 qt. | **Sugar** | 2 lbs. |
| ½ pt. | **Lemon Juice** | 10 oz. |
| ½ pt. | **Butter** | 10 oz. |

**METHOD**

1. Cook the tapioca and boiling water in a steam-jacketed kettle until it is transparent (3 to 5 minutes). Have the steam pressure as low as possible.
2. Place the fruit in greased baking pans. Sprinkle with sugar and lemon juice.
3. Pour the cooked tapioca over it, dot with butter, cover and bake in a slow oven (300°F.) until the fruit is tender.
4. Serve warm with sugar and milk.

**YIELD**

100 4-oz. servings.

**VARIATION**

Use 1 # 10 tin canned fruit such as cherries or pineapple. Drain and use the juice as part of the liquid in which the tapioca is cooked.

# BUTTERSCOTCH APPLE TAPIOCA

**METHOD**

Follow the method given for Fruit Tapioca but make the following changes in the ingredients:

1. Use ¾ gal. (3 lbs. 12 oz.) of thinly sliced raw apple in place of the fruit given in the recipe.
2. Use 1¼ qts. (2 lbs. 3 oz.) brown sugar in place of the white sugar.
3. Add 7 tbsp. cinnamon.

## APPLE BETTY

|            | Apples, A.P.              | 30 lbs.        |
|------------|---------------------------|----------------|
| 1½ qts.    | Sugar                     | 3 lbs.         |
| 4 tbsp.    | Cinnamon                  | 1 oz.          |
| ⅓ c.       | Salt                      | 3 oz.          |
| 1 c.       | Lemon Juice               | 8 oz.          |
| 6 qts.     | Crumbs (bread or cake)    | 6 lbs.         |
| 1 pt.      | Butter                    | 1 lb., 4 oz.   |

**METHOD**

1. Wash, pare and cut apples into thin slices.
2. Combine sugar and flavourings with the apples.
3. Melt butter, add crumbs, mix together thoroughly.
4. Fill greased shallow baking pans with alternate layers of apples and crumbs. Finish with crumbs on top.
5. Bake in a moderate oven (375°F.) until apples are tender.

**YIELD**

100 4-oz. servings.


## BAKED APPLE PUDDING

|           | Fresh Apples, Sliced   | 20 lbs.  |
|-----------|------------------------|----------|
| 4 gals.   | White Sugar            | 1 lb.    |
| 1 pt.     | Cinnamon               |          |
| 3 tbsp.   | Salt                   | 2½ oz.   |
| 4 tbsp.   | ½ Tea Biscuit Recipe   |          |

**METHOD**

1. Mix sugar, cinnamon and salt together. Add to the sliced apples.
2. Place mixture in shallow baking pans.
3. Cover with the tea biscuit dough rolled to ¼-inch thickness and bake in a moderate oven (350°F.) for about 45 minutes.
4. Serve hot with butterscotch, nutmeg, lemon sauce or milk.

**YIELD**

100 3-oz. servings.

## APPLE PUDDING

### A

| 2 doz. | Slightly Beaten Eggs | 2 lbs., 9 oz. |
| 2½ qts. | Sugar | 5 lbs. |
| ¼ c. | Vanilla | |

### B

| 2½ qts. | Sifted Pastry Flour | 2 lbs., 8 oz. |
| 1 c. | Baking Powder | 6 oz. |
| 2 tbsp. | Salt | |

### C

| 1 qt. | Chopped Walnuts | 1 lbs., 5 oz. |
| 5 qts. | Diced Raw Apple | 6 lbs., 4 oz. |

**METHOD**

1. Blend A.
2. Sift B and add to A.
3. Fold in C.
4. Pour into greased pudding pans to a depth of about 2″.
5. Bake at 350°F. for approximately 45 minutes.
6. Serve warm with cream or Lemon or Orange Sauce.

**YIELD**

100 3-oz. servings.

## APPLE CRISP

| | | |
|---|---|---|
| 1¾ qts. | Brown Sugar | 3 lbs. |
| 5 tbsp. | Cinnamon | 1 oz. |
| ⅓ c. | Salt | 3 oz. |
| 3 qts. | Unsifted Pastry Flour | 3 lbs., 12 oz. |
| 1 qt. | Butter or Margarine | 2 lbs., 8 oz. |
| | Apples, A.P. | 30 lbs. |
| 1½ pts. | White Sugar | 1 lb., 8 oz. |
| 1½ pts. | Water | 1 lb., 4 oz. |
| ½ c. | Lemon or Grapefruit Juice | 4 oz. |

**METHOD**

1. Mix the brown sugar, cinnamon, flour and salt.
2. Rub in the fat as in making pastry.
3. Wash, quarter, core and slice apples.
4. Spread the sliced apples in greased enamel or aluminum baking pans. Sprinkle with white sugar.
5. Add the water and fruit juice.
6. Spread the flour mixture over the apples.
7. Bake in a moderate oven (350°F.) until the apples are tender and the crust is crisp.
8. Serve hot or cold with lemon sauce or with milk.

**YIELD**

100 4-oz. servings.

## APPLE ROLLED OATS CRISP

| | | |
|---|---|---|
| 1¾ qts. | Brown Sugar | 3 lbs. |
| 5 tbsp. | Cinnamon | 1 oz. |
| ⅓ c. | Salt | 3 oz. |
| 5½ pts. | Unsifted Pastry Flour | 3 lbs., 8 oz. |
| 3 qts. | Rolled Oats | 3 lbs. |
| 2 qts. | Butter or Margarine | 5 lbs. |
| | Apples, A.P. | 30 lbs. |
| 1½ pts. | White Sugar | 1 lb., 8 oz. |
| ¾ pt. | Lemon or Grapefruit Juice | 15 oz. |

**METHOD**

1. Combine the dry ingredients as in making Apple Crisp. Add the rolled oats with the flour.
2. Spread ⅓ of mixture on the bottom of greased baking pans.
3. Put the raw apples, white sugar and fruit juice on top.
4. Cover with the remainder of the dry mixture.
5. Bake as Apple Crisp.
6. Serve plain, with cream or with lemon sauce.

**YIELD**

100 6-oz. servings.

## DUTCH APPLE CAKE

**BISCUIT DOUGH**

**A**

| | | |
|---|---|---|
| 6½ qts. | **Unsifted Pastry Flour** | 8 lbs. |
| 1¼ c. | **Baking Powder** | 8 oz. |
| 3 tbsp. | **Salt** | 2 oz. |
| 1 pt. | **Fat** | 1 lb. |

**B**

| | | |
|---|---|---|
| 1 pt. | **Sugar** | 1 lb. |

**C**

| | | |
|---|---|---|
| 12 | **Eggs** | 1 lb., 4 oz. |
| 1½ qts. | **Milk** | 3 lbs., 12 oz. |

**APPLES**

| | | |
|---|---|---|
| | **Fresh Apples** | 20 lbs. |
| | or | |
| 2 # 10 tins | **Solid Pack Apples** | 13 lbs. |

**SUGAR AND SPICE MIX**

| | | |
|---|---|---|
| 1 pt. | **Sugar** | 1 lb. |
| 1½ tsp. | **Cinnamon** | |
| 1 tsp. | **Mace or Nutmeg** | |

**BUTTER**

| | | |
|---|---|---|
| 1 c. | **Butter** | 8 oz. |

**METHOD**

1. Combine A as in making Tea Biscuit dough (page 340).
2. Add B and mix in lightly.
3. Mix ingredients in C and combine with the dry ingredients as in making Tea Biscuits.
4. Place the dough on greased baking sheets, roll or press out to ¾-inch thickness.
5. Prepare raw apples, cutting them into eights, lengthwise. If the skins are tender, they may be left on. When canned apples are used, cut in lengthwise pieces, similar in size to the raw.
6. Press the thin edge of the pieces of apple into the dough.
7. Combine the sugar and spice and sprinkle over the apples and dough.
8. Melt the butter and pour over the top.
9. Bake in a hot oven (400°-425°F.) for approximately 20 to 25 minutes.
10. Serve hot with butterscotch or lemon sauce or fresh milk.

**YIELD**

100 4-oz. servings.

## FRUIT SHORTCAKE

**A**

| 6½ qts. | Unsifted Pastry Flour | 8 lbs. |
|---|---|---|
| 1 c. | Baking Powder | 6 oz. |
| 1 qt. | Shortening | 2 lbs. |
| 1 pt. | Butter | 1 lb., 4 oz. |
| ½ pt. | Sugar | 8 oz. |
| 3 tbsp. | Salt | 2 oz. |
| 1½ qts. | Milk | 3 lbs., 12 oz. |

| | Melted Butter | |
| 4 | # 10 tins Sweetened Fruit | 26 lbs., 8 oz. |
| | or | |
| | Fresh Fruit | 25 lbs. |

**METHOD**

1. Combine A as in making Tea Biscuits (page 340).
2. Roll the dough ¼" thick and cut into 2" biscuits.
3. Place half the biscuits on greased bun pans or baking sheets. Brush the top surface of the biscuits with the melted butter.
4. Place the remaining biscuits on top.
5. Bake in a hot oven (425°F.) for 12 to 15 minutes.
6. When cooked, split open (do not cut). Pile the crushed or sliced sweetened fruit between the halves and on top.
7. Serve hot with whipped cream.

**YIELD**

100 shortcakes.

## GENERAL DIRECTIONS FOR STEAMED PUDDINGS

Steamed puddings should be very light, tender and rather delicate in texture.

### Solid, heavy puddings may be due to:

(1) Too stiff a mixture—it should be about as thin as cake batter.
(2) Insufficient leavening.
(3) Having too great a depth of batter in the container.
(4) Opening the steamer before the pudding is cooked.

#### CONTAINERS

Steamed puddings will be lighter and will be more easily cooked if small tins such as empty tomato cans (No. 2½), honey pails or bread tins are used.
The tins should be thoroughly greased and should be from ½ to ⅔ full. If they do not have close-fitting lids, tie waxed paper or greased brown paper tightly over the top.

#### COOKING

(1) In a steamer:
   Place the tins of pudding in the steamers and steam for 1½ to 2 hours or longer. The time required for cooking will depend on the depth of the pudding. Do not open the steamer door until the period of cooking is almost completed.
(2) If no steamer is available:
   (a) Cook the tins of pudding in pots of simmering water. The water must reach almost to the top of the tins and it must be kept at simmering point. The pot must be closely covered and the lid must not be lifted until the puddings have cooked for at least 2 hours.
   (b) Bake the puddings in a moderate oven (350°).
(3) Use the tests given for cakes (page 18) to find out whether the puddings are cooked.

#### STORING

(1) Steamed puddings may be left in their containers for 2 or 3 days and then reheated. The lids or papers should be removed to allow the steam to escape. Cover the puddings lightly, when they are cool.
(2) For longer storage, remove from the tins when cool and wrap each pudding in waxed paper. Store in a dry, cool place.

#### REHEATING

Reheat in the containers. Cover with waxed or greased brown paper and steam for 1 to 1½ hours.

#### SERVING

Always serve steamed puddings very hot, with a sauce.

## MARMALADE PUDDING

### A

| | | |
|---|---|---|
| 3¼ qts. | Unsifted Pastry Flour | 4 lbs. |
| 1 gal. | Dried Bread Crumbs | 4 lbs. |
| 2 qts. | Sugar | 4 lbs. |
| 5 tsp. | Salt | 1 oz. |
| 6 tbsp. | Baking Soda | 2½ oz. |
| | | |
| ½ gal. | Suet | 2 lbs., 8 oz. |
| ½ gal. | Water | 5 lbs. |
| 1½ qts. | Marmalade | 4 lbs., 11 oz. |

**METHOD**

1. Read general direction for steamed puddings (page 84).
2. Mix and sift ingredients in A.
3. Add finely chopped suet.
4. Add water and marmalade and mix until smooth.
5. Finish as Steamed Fruit Pudding (page 86). Serve hot with butterscotch sauce.

**NOTE**

If the bread crumbs are very dry, more water may be needed to make the consistency that of a cake batter.

**YIELD**

100 3½-oz. servings.

## STEAMED FRUIT PUDDING

### A

| | | |
|---|---|---|
| 4 qts. | Unsifted Pastry Flour | 5 lbs. |
| 5 tbsp. | Baking Powder | 2 oz. |
| 4 tsp. | Baking Soda | ½ oz. |
| 2 tbsp. | Cinnamon | |
| 1 tbsp. | Cloves | |
| 1 tbsp. | Nutmeg | |
| 5 tsp. | Salt | 1 oz. |
| 1½ pts. | Sugar | 1 lb., 8 oz. |

### B

| | | |
|---|---|---|
| 1 qt. | Finely Chopped Suet | 1 lb., 4 oz. |

### C

| | | |
|---|---|---|
| 2 qts. | Raisins | 3 lbs., 4 oz. |
| 1¾ qts. | Peel | 2 lbs., 8 oz. |
| 1 pt. | (12) Eggs, slightly beaten | 1 lb., 5 oz. |

### D

| | | |
|---|---|---|
| 1½ qts. | Molasses | 5 lbs., 4 oz. |
| 1 qt. | Water | 2 lbs., 8 oz. |

**METHOD**

1. Read the general directions for steamed puddings (page 84).
2. Mix and sift A.
3. Add B and blend well.
4. Add C and mix until the fruit is well coated with flour.
5. Pour D into the dry ingredients and mix only enough to moisten the flour.
6. Pour into greased tins. Cover.
7. Steam.
8. Serve hot with butterscotch sauce.

**NOTE**

1. 1 lb. shortening may be used in place of the suet in the recipe.
2. When peel is not available, replace it with the same weight of raisins.

**YIELD**

100 3½-oz. servings.

### STEAMED APPLE OR APRICOT PUDDING

Omit the raisins and peel from the recipe on page 86 and add 5½ lbs. of washed, drained, raw dried apricots or dried apples, cut into pieces.

### STEAMED DATE OR FIG PUDDING

Omit the raisins and peel and add 6 lbs. dried figs or dates which have been washed and cut into pieces.

### STEAMED GINGER PUDDING

Omit the spices from the recipe and add ⅓ cup (1 oz.) ground ginger.

## CARROT PUDDING

|  | **A** |  |
|---|---|---|
| 1½ qts. | **Unsifted Pastry Flour** | 2 lbs. |
| 3 tbsp. | **Baking Soda** | 1½ oz. |
| 1 gal. | **Brown Sugar** | 7 lbs. |
| 5 qts. | **Dry Bread Crumbs** | 5 lbs. |
| 6 tbsp. | **Salt** | 4 oz. |
| 6 tbsp. | **Cinnamon** | 1 oz. |
| 2 tsp. | **Ginger** |  |
| 2½ tbsp. | **Allspice** |  |
|  | **B** |  |
| 1 gal. | **Raisins** | 6 lbs., 8 oz. |
| ½ gal. | **Currants** | 3 lbs., 4 oz. |
| ½ gal. | **Finely Chopped Peel** | 3 lbs., 4 oz. |
| 3 qts. | **Suet (finely chopped)** | 3 lbs., 12 oz. |
|  | **C** |  |
| 1 gal. | **Minced Raw Carrots** | 8 lbs. |
| 1 gal. | **Minced Raw Potatoes** | 8 lbs. |
| 1 pt. | **Sour Milk** | 1 lb., 4 oz. |

**METHOD**
1. Read general directions for steamed puddings (page 84).
2. Mix and sift ingredients in A.
3. Add B.
4. Add C and combine well.
5. Finish as Steamed Fruit Pudding, page 86. Serve with lemon or butterscotch sauce.

**YIELD**
100 4-oz. servings.

## COTTAGE PUDDING

### A

| 1 qt. | Margarine or Butter | 2 lbs., 8 oz. |
| 2½ qts. | Sugar | 5 lbs. |

### B

| 1½ pts. | Eggs | 2 lbs. |

### C

| 1¾ qts. | Milk | 4 lbs., 6 oz. |
| ¼ c. | Vanilla | 2 oz. |

### D

| 5½ qts. | Unsifted Pastry Flour | 7 lbs. |
| 1 c. | Baking Powder | 6 oz. |
| 3 tbsp. | Salt | 2 oz. |

**METHOD**

Make according to general cake method, page 20.
Serve hot with butterscotch, lemon or jam sauce.

**YIELD**

100 3-oz. servings.

## CHOCOLATE COTTAGE PUDDING

Add 1 lb. 4 oz. chocolate to recipe. Reduce flour to 5 quarts (6 lbs. 6 oz.).

## APPLE COTTAGE PUDDING

Pour batter over 15 lbs. apple-pie filling.

## RASPBERRY COTTAGE PUDDING

Pour batter over 10 lbs. raspberry jam.

## FRUIT UPSIDE-DOWN CAKE

**Unsweetened Cooked Fruit—see Chart**
| | | |
|---|---|---|
| **1 qt.** | **Brown Sugar** | **1 lb., 12 oz.** |
| **1 pt.** | **Corn Syrup** | **2 lbs.** |

**Cottage Pudding Batter (page 88)**

**METHOD**

1. Drain the fruit and save the juice.
2. Grease the baking pans heavily with butter or shortening.
3. Mix the brown sugar and corn syrup together and spread on bottom of the pans. Put fruit on top.
4. Pour cottage pudding batter over the fruit and bake as cottage pudding.
5. Make a sauce from the fruit juice according to recipe (page 111).
6. Serve the pudding hot with the fruit on top and pour the sauce over it.

**YIELD**

100 5-oz. servings.

| Fruit | Amount | Preparation |
|---|---|---|
| 1. Apricots (dried) | 5½ lbs. | Wash, soak, cook. |
| 2. Peaches (canned) | 18 # 2 Cans | |
| 3. Peaches (dried) | 5½ lbs. | Wash, soak, cook. |
| 4. Pineapple (sliced) | 14 # 2 Cans | |
| 5. Prunes (dried) | 8 lbs. | Wash, soak, cook, pit. |
| 6. ⎧ Apples (raw) | 9 lbs. | Wash, core, slice ¼-⅓" thick. |
| ⎩ Raisins | 3 lbs. | Pick over, wash, drain. |
| 7. ⎧ Apricots (cooked) | 4 lbs. | |
| ⎨ Prunes (cooked) | 5 lbs. | Pit. |
| ⎩ Raisins | 3 lbs. | Pick over, wash, drain. |

## BAKED CHOCOLATE PUDDING

### A

| 1½ c. | Butter or Margarine | 12 oz. |
| 1½ qts. | Sugar | 3 lbs. |
| ¾ c. | Cocoa | 2 oz. |

### B

| 2½ qts. | Sifted Pastry Flour | 2 lbs., 8 oz. |
| ½ c. | Baking Powder | 3 oz. |
| 1 tbsp. | Salt | |

### C

| 6 c. | Milk | 3 lbs. |
| 4 tbsp. | Vanilla | |

### D

| 1 qt. | Chopped Nuts | 1 lb., 4 oz. |

### E

| 3½ qts. | Brown Sugar | 6 lbs. |
| 3 c. | Cocoa | 9 oz. |
| 2½ qts. | Boiling Water | 6 lbs., 4 oz. |

**METHOD**

1. Combine A, B, C, D as in mixing cake.
2. Spread the batter in greased baking pans to the depth of about 1".
3. Mix ingredients in E and toss over the batter.
4. Bake at 350°F. for about 45 minutes.
5. Cut and serve while warm, either plain or with whipped cream or ice cream.

**YIELD**

100 3-oz. servings.

## BAKED DATE PUDDING

### A

| 4 c. | Shortening | 1 lb., 10 oz. |
|---|---|---|
| 2 qts. | Sugar | 4 lbs. |
| 32 | Eggs | 3 lbs., 6 oz. |
| | | |
| 9½ qts. | Fresh Bread Crumbs | 6 lbs. |
| 6½ qts. | Chopped Dates | 11 lbs., 6 oz. |
| 6 c. | Milk | 3 lbs. |

### B

| 4 c. | Sifted Pastry Flour | 11 oz. |
|---|---|---|
| 3 tbsp. | Salt | 2 oz. |
| ⅔ c. | Baking Powder | 4 oz. |
| 2 tsp. | Baking Soda | |
| 2 tsp. | Ground Cinnamon | |
| ⅓ c. | Ground Ginger | |

**METHOD**

1. Cream A until light.
2. Add half the bread crumbs and the dates.
3. Add the remaining bread crumbs alternately with the milk, about one-third of each at a time. Mix well after each addition.
4. Sift B once and then sift it into the date mixture. Beat for one minute.
5. Pour into greased cake pans. Bake at 325°F. for about one hour.
6. Serve hot with Butterscotch or Lemon Sauce.

**YIELD**

100 4½-oz. servings.


## BAKED APPLES

1. Select 100 medium-sized apples, suitable for baking and free from bruises.
2. Wash, core, score and place in baking dishes.
3. Fill each centre with sugar, about 1 tbsp. to an apple.
4. Pour boiling water around apples, allowing 3 quarts to 100 apples.
5. Bake in a moderate oven until tender—35 to 45 minutes. Baste frequently.
6. Lift into serving dishes. Pour the syrup over the fruit.

**YIELD**

100 servings.

## APPLE SAUCE

| 1¼ bus. | Apples, A.P. | 50 lbs. |
| 1 qt. | Sugar | 2 lbs. |
| 3 qts. | Boiling Water | 7 lbs., 8 oz. |

**METHOD**

1. Wash the apples. Cut in quarters, core and peel, removing all bruised parts. Place in a brine made of ½ tbsp. salt to 1 gallon cold water.
2. Lift the apples from the brine, rinse in cold water.
3. Slice thin if there is time, otherwise cook the quarters.
4. Add the boiling water, cover and cook quickly until tender. If the apples are dry, add more water. Stir frequently.
5. When cooked, add the sugar. If the apples are very tart, more sugar may be required.

**NOTE**

1. When possible, cook the apple sauce in two lots in order to prevent dis-colouration.
2. If the skin of the apple is very tender, apple sauce, pie fillings and puddings may be made by slicing the apples thinly and leaving skins on.

**YIELD**

100 6-oz. servings.


## APPLE SAUCE
**(CANNED APPLES)**

| 3 # 10 tins | Canned Apples | 20 lbs. |
| 1 qt. | Boiling Water | 2 lbs., 8 oz. |
| 1 qt. | White Sugar | 2 lbs. |
| 1 tbsp. | Whole Cloves | |

**METHOD**

1. Drain apples. Save juice. Put apples on a board and chop with a knife.
2. Add boiling water to sugar and cloves and apple-juice. Heat to dissolve the sugar.
3. Add chopped apples and cook until all the apple is soft.
4. Chill and serve.

**YIELD**

100 3½-oz. servings.

## STEWED FRESH FRUIT

**Fresh Raw Fruit, A.P., 30-40 lbs.**
**2½ gals.  Syrup**

**METHOD**

1. Prepare a syrup, suitable for the fruit which is to be cooked.
2. Wash and prepare fruit for cooking—it may be left whole or cut into halves or quarters.
3. Add the raw fruit to the boiling syrup.
4. Cook gently until the fruit is tender. Turn occasionally.

**YIELD**

100 5-oz. servings.


### SYRUP FOR STEWED FRUIT

To make 1 gallon of syrup:
1. For sweet fruits—3 lbs. sugar to 3 qts. boiling water.
2. For sour fruits—5 lbs. sugar to 2½ qts. boiling water.

**METHOD**

1. Add the boiling water to the sugar. Stir until dissolved.
2. Boil for 3 minutes.


## STEWED RHUBARB

| 5 gals. | Diced Rhubarb | 25 lbs. |
|---------|---------------|---------|
| 4 qts.  | Sugar         | 8 lbs.  |
| 1 qt.   | Water         | 2 lbs., 8 oz. |

**METHOD**

1. Wash rhubarb. Peel if the skin is very tough. Cut into 1-inch pieces.
2. Put in a stock pot, add sugar and water. Mix well; cover. Let stand 20 minutes.
3. Cook slowly until tender.

**NOTE**

1. Rhubarb may be cooked in a covered dish in a moderate oven.
2. If orange rind is available, add 1 cup grated rind with the sugar.

**YIELD**

100 5-oz. servings.

## DRIED AND EVAPORATED FRUITS

All dried and evaporated fruit must be picked over and thoroughly washed before it is used.

Soaking in water is necessary in order to produce cooked fruit that has a good colour, flavour and texture. The length of time required for soaking varies and depends chiefly upon the dryness of the fruit.

### PROPORTIONS AND AVERAGE TIME REQUIRED FOR SOAKING FRUIT FOR 100 ORDERS

| Fruit | APPLES | APRICOTS | PRUNES OR FIGS | PEACHES |
|---|---|---|---|---|
| Weight | 5 lbs. | 9 lbs. | 9 lbs. | 10 lbs. |
| Water | 2½ gals. | 6 gals. | 4½ gals. | 4 gals. |
| Time | 18 hrs. | 4-5 hrs. | 4-5 hrs. | 12 hrs. |
| Sugar | 1½ lbs. | 2 lbs. | 1½ lbs. | 2 lbs. |

#### METHOD OF COOKING

1. Pick over and wash the fruit thoroughly.
2. Add the cold water and soak for the required length of time.
3. Cook in the water in which the fruit was soaked.
4. Cook below boiling until tender.
5. Add sugar, stir until dissolved. Remove from heat.
6. Cool before serving.

#### PREPARATION OF RAISINS AND CURRANTS

1. Pick over and wash very thoroughly by placing the fruit in a colander and running warm water through it until all the sand is removed.
2. Drain well and, if possible, dry between towels. If the raisins and currants are dry, place them in a colander, cover and steam them until softened. Do not soak them in water unless it can be used with the fruit as in making raisin filling.

## APRICOT JELLY

### A

| | | |
|---|---|---|
| 3½ qts. | Dried Apricots | 6 lbs. |
| 2 gals. | Water | 20 lbs. |

### B

| | | |
|---|---|---|
| ⅔ pt. | Gelatine | 8 oz. |
| 1 qt. | Cold Water | 2 lbs., 8 oz. |

### C

| | | |
|---|---|---|
| 3 qts. | Sugar | 6 lbs. |
| 5 tsp. | Salt | 1 oz. |

### D

| | | |
|---|---|---|
| 1 pt. | Lemon Juice | 1 lb., 4 oz. |

**METHOD**

1. Soak A overnight. Cook until apricots are tender. Strain off the juice. (If there is not 1½ gallons, add water.)
2. Soak B for 5 minutes.
3. Add B and C to hot apricot juice. Heat until both are dissolved. Cool slightly.
4. Add D and pour into moistened pans to set.
5. When partially set, add apricots, whole or diced. Chill until firm.
6. Serve with custard sauce or cream.

**YIELD**

100 5-oz. servings.

## PRUNE JELLY

Substitute 1 gal. dried prunes (8 lbs.) for the apricots in the Apricot Jelly recipe.

## LEMON JELLY

**A**

| ⅔ pt. | Gelatine | 8 oz. |
|---|---|---|
| 1 qt. | Cold Water | 2 lbs., 8 oz. |

**B**

| 4 qts. | Granulated Sugar | 8 lbs. |
|---|---|---|
| 5 tsp. | Salt | 1 oz. |
| 2½ gals. | Boiling Water | 25 lbs. |
| 1 pt. | Lemon Rind | 8 oz. |

**C**

| 1 qt. | Lemon Juice | 2 lbs., 8 oz. |
|---|---|---|

**METHOD**

1. Soak A for 5 minutes.
2. Combine ingredients in B and boil until the sugar is dissolved.
3. Add A and stir to dissolve gelatine.
4. Add C and strain into moistened pans to set.
5. Serve with custard sauce or with fruit or cream.

**NOTE**

1. This jelly makes an excellent base for the addition of many fruits.
2. When partially set, the jelly may be whipped until foamy, chilled, and served with custard sauce.

**YIELD**

100 5-oz. servings.

## SNOW PUDDING

1. Make Lemon Jelly as directed above. When the jelly begins to set, add 50 (1¼ qts.) unbeaten egg whites and beat until the mixture begins to stiffen.
2. Pour into moistened serving dishes or moulds.
3. Serve with custard sauce.

## LEMON CREAM

1. Make as Snow Pudding, using 25 (3 c.) unbeaten egg whites.
2. When sufficiently beaten, fold in 2 qts. of cream, whipped.
3. Pour into serving dishes or moulds as above. Garnish with cherries, mint leaves or raw fruit.

## MIXED FRUIT JELLY

### A

| ⅔ pt. | Gelatine | 8 oz. |
|---|---|---|
| 1 qt. | Cold Water | 2 lbs., 8 oz. |

### B

| 3 qts. | Sugar | 6 lbs. |
|---|---|---|
| 5 tsp. | Salt | 1 oz. |

### C

| 2 gals. | Fruit Juice | 20 lbs. |
|---|---|---|
| 1 pt. | Lemon Juice | 1 lb., 4 oz. |

### D

| 1 gal. | Mixed Fruits | 8 lbs. |
|---|---|---|

**METHOD**

1. Soak A for 5 minutes and then put over low heat to dissolve gelatine.
2. Add B to A and continue heating until sugar is dissolved. Cool slightly.
3. Add C and pour into moistened pans to set.
4. When partially set, add D. Chill until firm.
5. Serve with custard sauce or cream.

**YIELD**

100 5-oz. servings.

## PRUNE WHIP

### A

| 3 qts. | Prunes | 5 lbs., 8 oz. |
| 2 gals. | Water | 20 lbs. |

### B

| ⅔ pt. | Gelatine | 8 oz. |
| 1½ pts. | Cold Water | 1 lb., 14 oz. |

### C

| 2 qts. | Sugar | 4 lbs. |

### D

| ½ pt. | Lemon Juice | 10 oz. |
| | Grated Rind of 5 Lemons | |

### E

| 1 qt. | (40) Egg Whites | |

**METHOD**

1. Soak A. Cook until tender. Remove prunes from juice, pit and cut in pieces or purée. Measure prune juice and make up to 7 quarts with boiling water.
2. Soak B for 5 minutes.
3. Add B and C to the hot prune juice. Stir until dissolved.
4. Add D.
5. Cool until partially set. Beat until foamy.
6. Beat E until stiff but not dry. Add the gelatine mixture and continue to beat until quite stiff. Fold in the prunes.
7. Serve cold with custard sauce.

**NOTE**

1 quart cornstarch (1½ lbs.) may be substituted for gelatine. Mix the cornstarch with cold water to make a paste. Pour gradually into hot prune juice, stirring constantly, and cook until there is no taste of raw starch. Finish as above.

**YIELD**

100 3-oz. servings.

## APRICOT WHIP

Substitute 2 qts. dried apricots (4 lbs.) for the prunes in the above recipe.

## ORANGE CREAM

### A

| | | |
|---|---|---|
| ½ pt. | Orange Rind (thinly pared) | |
| 1 gal. | Milk | 10 lbs. |

### B

| | | |
|---|---|---|
| 1 c. & 2 tbsp. | Gelatine | 5½ oz. |
| 1 pt. | Milk | 1 lb., 4 oz. |

### C

| | | |
|---|---|---|
| 3½ pts. | Sugar | 3 lbs., 8 oz. |
| 45 | Egg Yolks | |

### D

| | | |
|---|---|---|
| 3 pts. | Orange Juice | 3 lbs., 12 oz. |
| 1 c. | Lemon Juice | 8 oz. |

### E

| | | |
|---|---|---|
| 45 | Egg Whites | |

**METHOD**

1. Heat A.
2. Combine B and let stand for 10 minutes.
3. Combine C. Add a small quantity of A and mix well. Stir this mixture back into A.
4. Cook over a low heat, stirring gently until there is no taste of raw egg.
5. Remove at once from the heat and strain over the moistened gelatine. Mix thoroughly. Cool.
6. Add D.
7. When partially set, carefully fold in the stiffly beaten egg whites.
8. Chill. Serve with orange sections or other fresh fruit.

**NOTE**

Diluted orange concentrate may be used instead of fresh orange juice.

**YIELD**

100 3-oz. servings.

## LEMON FLUFF

| | | |
|---|---|---|
| 7 | 15 oz. tins Evaporated Milk | 6 lbs., 9 oz. |
| 6 c. | Lemon Jelly Powder | 2 lbs., 11 oz. |
| 5 qts. | Hot Water | 12 lbs., 8 oz. |
| 3 qts. | Sugar | 6 lbs. |
| 4 c. | Fresh Lemon Juice | 2 lbs. |
| 3 qts. | Vanilla or Graham Wafer Crumbs | 3 lbs., 12 oz. |

**METHOD**

1. Chill tins of evaporated milk until icy cold.
2. Dissolve jelly powder in the hot water; then add the sugar and stir until it dissolves.
3. Chill the gelatine mixture until it is partly set; then whip until fluffy and add the lemon juice.
4. Whip the cold milk until stiff and fold into the lemon jelly.
5. Line the bottom of pans with half the crumbs. Pour the dessert over them and sprinkle the remainder on top.
6. Chill until firm. Cut into pieces and top with a cherry.

**YIELD**

100 5-oz. servings.

**VARIATIONS**

Any of the red coloured jelly powders may be substituted for the lemon in the above recipe. This makes an attractive dessert if it is moulded in angel cake pans, the sides of which have been lined with thin chocolate wafers. Use the graham crumbs as above.

## FRUIT MALLO

### A

| 6 qts. | Marshmallows | 4 lbs., 8 oz. |
| 1¼ c. | Lemon Juice | 10 oz. |

### B

| 2 qts. | Fruit and Juice (rasp-<br>berries, strawberries<br>or canned pineapple) | 7 lbs., 8 oz. |

### C

| 1½ qts. | Whipping Cream | 3 lbs., 12 oz. |

**METHOD**

1. Place A over a low heat and stir frequently until marshmallows are melted.
2. Heat juice of the fruit slightly.
3. Combine A and B. Cool, until partially set.
4. Beat C. Fold into A and B.
5. Chill and serve as dessert **or** freeze for 2 to 3 hours.

**YIELD**

100 2½-oz. servings.

**NOTES**

1. If made into ice cream, the fruit should be very finely chopped or put through a sieve.
2. More lemon juice may be needed if the fruit or juice is very sweet.

## STRAWBERRY CREAM

### A

| 2¼ pts. | Strawberry Jelly Powder | 3 lbs. |
| 3 qts. | Boiling Water | 7 lbs., 8 oz. |

### B

| 2 gals. | Ice Cream (Strawberry) |

### C

| 1 gal. | Fresh or Frozen (drained) Strawberries |
| | Lemon Juice |

**METHOD**

1. Combine A and stir until dissolved.
2. Stir in B.
3. Fold in C.
4. Add lemon juice to taste.
5. Chill.

**YIELD**

100 servings.

**NOTES**

1. If frozen strawberries are used, the juice from them should be substituted for part of the water.
2. Other fruits may be used in the same way, by substituting the corresponding jelly powder.
3. Should pineapple be used, it **must** be cooked pineapple.

## CREAM PUFFS

### A

| 1½ qts. | Boiling Water | 3 lbs., 12 oz. |
| 1½ pts. | Margarine or Butter | 1 lb., 14 oz. |

### B

| 1½ qts. | Sifted All Purpose Flour | 1 lb., 14 oz. |
| 2½ tsp. | Salt | |

### C

| 30 | Eggs | 3 lbs., 2 oz. |

**METHOD**

1. Combine A in a saucepan and boil until the fat is melted.
2. Add B all at once and stir continually over the heat until smooth. Continue cooking and stirring until the batter leaves the sides of the pan. Remove from the heat at once. Do not over-cook.
3. Cool slightly, add unbeaten eggs one at a time. Beat until smooth after each egg is added. Continue beating until the batter becomes shiny.
4. Drop by the tablespoonful, 2″ apart, onto a slightly greased baking sheet.
5. Bake at 425°F. for 15 minutes. Lower heat to 375°F. and continue cooking for about 30 minutes more. When cooked, they will feel very light and will be light brown in colour.
6. Cool on cake racks. When cool, cut a gash in the side of each puff.
7. Just before serving, fill with sweetened, flavoured whipped cream, cream filling or Ice Cream. When Ice Cream is used, a sauce such as Butterscotch or Chocolate may be poured over the top of the puff.

**YIELD**

100 fairly large puffs.

## CHOCOLATE ÉCLAIRS

1. Follow the recipe for Cream Puffs.
2. Shape on greased baking sheets into strips 3″ long and 1″ wide. Have them 2″ apart.
3. Bake as Cream Puffs. Cool.
4. Fill with sweetened, flavoured whipped cream or a cream filling.
5. Frost with chocolate glaze.

## CHOCOLATE GLAZE FOR ÉCLAIRS

| | | |
|---|---|---|
| 2 c. | Hot Water | 1 lb. |
| 1 c. | Butter or Margarine | 8 oz. |
| | Unsweetened Chocolate (Melted) | 1 lb. |
| 4 tsp. | Vanilla | |
| 3 qts., 1 c. | Icing Sugar | 4 lbs., 6 oz. |

**METHOD**

1. Combine the ingredients and beat until thick enough to spread.
2. Dip the top of each éclair in the glaze, or spoon a small quantity over each.

**YIELD**

100 Éclairs.

## BOUCHÉES

1. Prepare one quarter of the recipe for Cream Puffs.
2. Drop by rounded half teaspoonfuls (about the size of a quarter) on to a lightly greased baking sheet.
3. Bake at 425°F. for 10 minutes, lower heat to 375°F. and bake about 15 minutes longer.
4. When cooked, make a cut in the side of each.
5. Fill as for éclairs.

**NOTE**

These may also be filled with chicken or tuna salad and used on sandwich plates.

**YIELD**

Approximately 125 Bouchées.

## MERINGUE SHELLS

| 1½ qts. | Egg Whites | 4 lbs. |
| 2½ tsp. | Cream of Tartar | |
| 3 qts. | Fine Sugar | 6 lbs. |

**METHOD**
1. Grease or oil baking sheets well.
2. Have the egg whites at room temperature, add the cream of tartar.
3. Beat until the whites stand in soft, moist peaks.
4. Add the sugar very slowly, continuing to beat until the meringue will hold its shape.
5. The shells may be dropped from a tablespoon or put through a pastry tube. Shape into nests about 2½" in diameter and 1½" high.
6. Bake at 250°F. for approximately 1 to 1¼ hours. The meringues are sufficiently cooked when they feel firm and slightly crisp.
7. Just before serving fill with ice cream, water ice, fruit or a combination of these. Garnish with whipped cream.

**YIELD**
100 shells.

**VARIATIONS**

## MERINGUE TARTS
1. Prepare meringue as for shells.
2. Cover baking sheets with unglazed brown paper.
3. Shape the meringue into 8 to 9" rounds ¼" thick. Build up the edge to about 1".
4. Bake as directed for shells.
5. When cooked, remove from paper and place on serving plates.
6. Shortly before serving fill with:
   Cooked or raw fruit; ice cream or water ice; cream or lemon filling.
7. Garnish with whipped cream.

**YIELD**
100 servings.

## MERINGUE GLACÉE
1. Prepare meringue as for shells.
2. Shape into mounds about 1½" in diameter.
3. Bake as directed for shells.
4. When cooked, but still warm, push in the flat side with the back of a teaspoon.
5. Just before serving, fill the cavities with ice cream and place two filled meringues together.
6. Garnish with whipped cream.

**YIELD**
100 servings.

# Dessert Sauces

## APRICOT SAUCE

| 3 qts. | Dried Apricots | 5 lbs. |
| 5 qts. | Cold Water | 12 lbs., 8 oz. |
| 2½ pts. | White Sugar | 2 lbs., 8 oz. |

**METHOD I**

1. Wash apricots thoroughly.
2. Soak in the cold water for 4 to 5 hours, according to the dryness.
3. Bring to the boil in the water in which they were soaked. Reduce the heat and simmer until tender.
4. Add sugar and cook until it is dissolved.
5. Purée through a fine sieve.
6. Cook for 10 minutes.
7. Serve hot or cold on Cottage Pudding, Blancmange, Bread Pudding, Custard or Ice Cream.

**YIELD**

100 2½-oz. servings.

**METHOD II**

1. Cook the fruit as above.
2. When the sugar has dissolved, drain and measure the syrup. Add water if required, to make one gallon.
3. Blend 4 oz. cornstarch with a small quantity of cold water. Add gradually to the boiling syrup, stirring as you add. Boil until there is no taste of raw cornstarch.
4. Chop the cooked apricots with a knife and add to the thickened syrup.

**YIELD**

100 2½-oz. servings.

## BUTTERSCOTCH SAUCE

| | | |
|---|---|---|
| 2 qts. | Brown Sugar | 3 lbs., 8 oz. |
| 1 pt. | Butter | 1 lb., 4 oz. |
| 1½ c. | Cornstarch | 7 oz. |
| | or | |
| 3 c. | Unsifted Pastry Flour | 12 oz. |
| 5 tsp. | Salt | 1 oz. |
| 1½ gals. | Boiling Water | 15 lbs. |
| 2 tbsp. | Vanilla | |

**METHOD**

1. Melt butter, add sugar and cook over a low heat until it becomes golden brown in colour. Stir constantly.
2. Remove from heat, add cornstarch or flour and salt gradually, mixing well after each addition.
3. Add boiling water slowly, stirring as you add. Boil until there is no taste of raw starch.
4. Remove from heat, add vanilla.

**YIELD**

100 2½-oz. servings.


## CHOCOLATE SAUCE

| | | |
|---|---|---|
| | Bitter Chocolate | 3 lbs. |
| 4 qts. | Brown Sugar | 7 lbs. |
| 1 gal. | Corn Syrup | 13 lbs. |
| 2 tsp. | Salt | |
| 2½ qts. | Water | 6 lbs., 4 oz. |
| 2 tbsp. | Vanilla | |

**METHOD**

1. Melt the chocolate slowly.
2. Boil sugar, syrup, salt and water for 5 minutes.
3. Add gradually to melted chocolate and continue cooking until of desired consistency.
4. Add vanilla.

**YIELD**

2 gals.

## CUSTARD SAUCE
**(USING CORNSTARCH)**

| | | |
|---|---|---|
| 1¾ gals. | **Milk** | 17 lbs., 8 oz. |
| ½ pt. | **Cornstarch** | 6 oz. |
| 1 tbsp. | **Salt** | |
| 1 qt. | **Cold Milk** | 2 lbs., 8 oz. |
| 16 | **Eggs** | 1 lb., 12 oz. |
| 1 qt. | **Sugar** | 2 lbs. |
| 2 tbsp. | **Vanilla** | |

**METHOD**

1. Heat the milk in a double boiler or steam kettle.
2. Mix the cornstarch, salt and cold milk to a thin paste. Add the paste gradually to the hot milk, stirring as you add.
3. Cook until the mixture thickens slightly and there is no taste of raw starch. Stir constantly.
4. Beat the eggs slightly, add the sugar and then part of the thickened milk, stirring as you add. Return to the original mixture and continue cooking until there is no taste of raw egg (about 5 minutes).
5. Remove from the heat and add the vanilla.
6. Strain at once into cold containers and stir for several minutes to cool quickly.
7. Cover and chill.
8. Serve as a sauce for fruit or jelly.

**YIELD**

100 3½-oz. servings.


## LEMON CUSTARD SAUCE

Heat 8 tbsp. thinly shaved lemon rind with the milk. Omit the vanilla.

## CUSTARD SAUCE

| 2 gals. | Milk | 20 lbs. |
| 2 qts. | Eggs | 5 lbs. |
| 1 qt. | Sugar | 2 lbs. |
| 1 tbsp. | Salt | |
| 1 tbsp. | Vanilla Extract | |
| | or | |
| 1 tsp. | Almond Extract | |

**METHOD**
1. Combine ingredients as in making baked custard.
2. Cook over hot water, or in a steam kettle, stirring slowly and continuously until the sauce is thick enough to coat a metal spoon.
3. Strain at once into a cold container, add the flavouring, and stir for several minutes to cool quickly.
4. Cover and chill.
5. Serve as a sauce for fruit or jelly.

**NOTE**
If the custard curdles, beat with a wire whip until smooth.

**YIELD**
100 3½-oz. servings.


## MIXED FRUIT SAUCE

| 1 gal. | Fruit Syrup | 10 lbs. |
| 1 c. | Cornstarch | 5 oz. |
| ½ pt. | Cold Water | 10 oz. |
| | Grated Rind of 3 Lemons | |
| ½ c. | Lemon Juice | 4 oz. |
| 1 qt. | Diced Fruit | 2 lbs. |

**METHOD**
1. Heat the fruit syrup.
2. Blend the cornstarch with the cold water and stir into the hot syrup. Stir until the mixture thickens. Cook until there is no taste of raw starch.
3. Add the grated lemon rind.
4. Cool, add the lemon juice and diced fruit.

**YIELD**
100 2-oz. servings.

## HARD SAUCE

| 1 qt. | Butter | 2 lbs., 8 oz. |
|---|---|---|
| 2½ qts. | Icing Sugar | 3 lbs., 7 oz. |
| | or | |
| 2½ qts. | Brown Sugar | 4 lbs., 6 oz. |
| 2 tbsp. | Lemon Juice | |
| | or | |
| 3 tbsp. | Vanilla Extract | |

**METHOD**

1. Cream the butter until very soft.
2. Sift the sugar and add it gradually to the butter until the two are well combined.
3. Add the flavouring and blend thoroughly.
4. Pack into shallow pans and chill, then slice or press through a pastry tube.
5. Serve on steamed puddings, Apple Pie, Mince Pie.

**YIELD**

100 servings.

## JAM SAUCE

| 1 qt. | White Sugar | 2 lbs. |
|---|---|---|
| 1½ c. | Cornstarch | 7 oz. |
| | or | |
| 3 c. | Unsifted Pastry Flour | 12 oz. |
| 5 qts. | Boiling Water | 12 lbs., 8 oz. |
| 1 qt. | Jam | 3 lbs. |
| ½ pt. | Lemon or Grapefruit Juice | 10 oz. |

**METHOD**

1. Mix the sugar and cornstarch
2. Add the boiling water gradually, stir constantly until the mixture boils. Cook until there is no taste of raw starch. Add the jam, mix well.
3. Remove from the heat and add the lemon juice.

**NOTE**

A few drops of colouring may be required to improve the colour.

**YIELD**

100 2½-oz. servings.

## MARSHMALLOW SAUCE

| | | |
|---|---|---|
| 2¼ qts. | Sugar | 4 lbs., 8 oz. |
| 1¼ pts. | Water | 1 lb., 9 oz. |
| 15 | Egg Whites | 1 lb. |
| 1 tsp. | Cream of Tartar | |
| 3 tbsp. | Vanilla | |
| ¾ pt. | Milk | 15 oz. |

**METHOD**

1. Boil sugar and water for 2 minutes.
2. Put egg whites and cream of tartar in mixer and turn on high speed. Beat until stiff but not dry.
3. Add the hot syrup very slowly to the beaten egg whites and beat for 10 minutes.
4. Add vanilla and milk. Keep warm but not hot.
5. Serve on Chocolate Pudding.

**YIELD**

100 servings.


## MINT MARSHMALLOW SAUCE

Omit vanilla and substitute about 1 tsp. peppermint flavouring.

## LEMON SAUCE

| | | |
|---|---|---|
| 1½ qts. | White Sugar | 3 lbs. |
| 1½ c. | Cornstarch | 7 oz. |
| | or | |
| 3 c. | Unsifted Pastry Flour | 12 oz. |
| 1½ gals. | Boiling Water | 15 lbs. |
| 1 pt. | Butter | 1 lb., 4 oz. |
| ½ pt. | Lemon Juice | 10 oz. |
| 2 tbsp. | Lemon Rind (grated) | |

**METHOD**

1. Combine sugar, cornstarch or flour.
2. Add boiling water gradually. Stir as you add and continue stirring until the mixture boils.
3. Cook until there is no taste of raw starch. Add butter.
4. Remove from heat, add lemon juice and rind.

**YIELD**

100 2½-oz. servings.

## MOCK MAPLE SYRUP

| | |
|---|---|
| 1 gal. | Water |
| 2 gals. | Brown Sugar |
| 1 tsp. | Maplex |
| 1 qt. | Maple Syrup |

**METHOD**

1. Boil water and brown sugar together for 2 minutes.
2. Add the Maplex and maple syrup.
3. Serve hot with pancakes or with Rice Pudding.

**YIELD**

100 4-oz. servings.


## ORANGE SAUCE

| | | |
|---|---|---|
| 1½ qts. | White Sugar | 3 lbs. |
| 1½ c. | Cornstarch | 7 oz. |
| 1 tsp. | Salt | |
| 1 tsp. | Cinnamon | |
| 1 gal. | Boiling Water | 10 lbs. |
| 1 pt. | Butter | 1 lb., 4 oz. |
| ⅔ c. | Orange Rind, grated | 3 oz. |
| 2½ pts. | Orange Juice | 3 lbs., 2 oz. |
| ½ c. | Lemon or Grapefruit Juice | 4 oz. |

**METHOD**

1. Mix sugar, cornstarch, salt and cinnamon. Add enough boiling water to make a thin paste and then pour slowly into the remaining water, stirring as you add.
2. Continue to stir until the mixture boils.
3. Cook until the sauce is clear and there is no taste of raw starch.
4. Remove from heat, add butter, orange rind and fruit juices.
5. Serve hot on Bread, Rice Custard, Cottage Puddings, or on Apple Crisp or steamed puddings.

**YIELD**

100 2½-oz. servings.

## FOAMY ORANGE SAUCE
(USING MERINGUE POWDER)

| | | |
|---|---|---|
| 1 qt. | Sugar | 2 lbs. |
| ¾ pt. | Boiling Water | 15 oz. |
| | Powdered Meringue | 5 oz. |
| 1 c. | Cold Water | 8 oz. |
| 12 | Oranges (juice and grated rind) | |

METHOD

1. Add the boiling water to the sugar and boil for 3 minutes. Remove from the heat.
2. Whip the meringue powder and cold water.
3. Pour the syrup slowly over the beaten meringue, beating as you add.
4. Add the orange juice and grated orange rind.
5. Beat until smooth and stiff.

YIELD

100 servings.

## VANILLA SAUCE

| | A | |
|---|---|---|
| 1½ qts. | Sugar | 3 lbs. |
| 1½ c. | Cornstarch | 7 oz. |
| 5 tsp. | Salt | 1 oz. |
| | B | |
| 1½ gals. | Boiling Water | 15 lbs. |
| | C | |
| 1 pt. | Butter | 1 lb., 4 oz. |
| 6 tbsp. | Vanilla | 3 oz. |

METHOD

1. Combine sugar, cornstarch and salt.
2. Add boiling water gradually, stirring as you add, and boil until there is no taste of raw starch.
3. Remove from heat, add butter and vanilla.

YIELD

100 2½-oz. servings.

## NUTMEG SAUCE

Add 3 tbsp. nutmeg and reduce vanilla to 2 tbsp.

**Eggs**

## SOFT COOKED OR "BOILED" EGGS

**METHOD**

1. In order to cook eggs evenly and prevent them from becoming rubbery, it is advisable to cook them below the boiling point of water, using about 4 gallons water for 100 eggs.
2. If the eggs are to be evenly done, they should be cooked in lots of 25.
3. Place the eggs in the boiling water. Leave over the direct heat until the water begins to boil again. Cover and place the pot at the back of the stove where it will keep hot without boiling.
4. Cooking time:

| | |
|---|---|
| Soft | 4 minutes |
| Firm | 5 minutes |
| Very Firm | 6 minutes |
| Hard Cooked | ½ hour |

## FRIED EGGS

**METHOD**

1. Heat about ⅛" of fat in a shallow pan but do not let it smoke.
2. Break each egg into a saucer and slip into the hot fat.
3. Cook slowly, basting the eggs with the hot fat until the white is firm and a film forms on the yolk. If cooked at too high a temperature or for too long a time, the eggs will become shrivelled and rubbery.
4. Drain well and serve.

## POACHED EGGS

**METHOD**

1. Boil water in a shallow pan. Remove to a cooler part of the stove, where the water will simmer but not boil.
2. Slip in each egg carefully. There should be enough water to cover the eggs.
3. When the white is firm and a film forms over the yolk, lift carefully from the water, drain well and serve at once.

## SCRAMBLED EGGS

| | | |
|---|---|---|
| 1½ gals. | Cracked Eggs | 15 lbs. |
| 1 qt. | Water | 2 lbs., 8 oz. |
| ⅓ c. | Salt | 3 oz. |
| 1 tbsp. | Pepper | |

**METHOD**

1. Beat the eggs slightly. Add water and seasonings.
2. The eggs may be cooked slowly over a low heat or in a water bath.
3. As the egg cooks on the bottom, lift carefully with a spoon and allow the un-cooked egg to run under. Do not stir.
4. Remove from pan and serve at once. Keep warm over water which is hot but not boiling.

**YIELD**

100 4-oz. orders.


### EGGS SCRAMBLED WITH BACON

1. Dice 5 lbs. raw bacon and cook until crisp and brown. Drain well.
2. Add to the egg mixture before cooking.
3. Finish as Scrambled Eggs.


### EGGS SCRAMBLED WITH SAUSAGE OR PREPARED MEATS

1. Dice 5 lbs. cooked sausage or prepared meat.
2. Add to the egg mixture before cooking.
3. Finish as Scrambled Eggs.


### SCRAMBLED EGGS AND CHEESE

1. Add 3 lbs. grated cheese to the egg mixture and finish as Scrambled Eggs.

## FRENCH TOAST

| 100 slices | Stale Bread | 6 lbs., 4 oz. |
| 32 | Eggs | 3 lbs., 6 oz. |
| 3 qts. | Milk | 7 lbs., 8 oz. |
| 1 tsp. | Salt | |

**METHOD**

1. Beat eggs sufficiently to mix them.
2. Add milk and salt.
3. Melt bacon fat in a heavy pan. Have it hot but do not allow it to smoke.
4. Cut bread into slices of medium thickness and dip in the milk and egg. Moisten both sides well.
5. Fry in bacon fat over a medium heat.

**NOTE**

French Toast should be a golden brown in colour and should not be greasy. It must be served very hot, and should be prepared just before it is to be used. Serve with corn syrup, maple syrup, jam or bacon.

**YIELD**

100 slices.

## OMELETS

An omelet should be light, moist, and golden brown on the under surface.
Omelets have to be made in small quantities and served immediately. For this
reason they are unsuitable for large numbers.
When served to more than 4 to 6 people, omelets have to be cooked in relays.

## PLAIN OMELET

**FOR 25**

| | | |
|---|---|---|
| 1 qt. | Fresh Eggs | 2 lbs., 10 oz. |
| ¾ pt. | Water | 15 oz. |
| 1 tbsp. | Salt | |
| ½ tsp. | Pepper | |
| ½ c. | Butter or Bacon Fat | 4 oz. |

**METHOD**

1. Beat the eggs sufficiently to mix them.
2. Add the water and seasonings.
3. Heat a heavy omelet pan, add 1 oz. of fat. When melted, spread it evenly over the surface of the pan.
4. Pour in about ¼ of the egg mixture—it should not be more than ¼" deep in the pan.
5. Cook over a low heat. As the egg cooks lift it up from the bottom of the pan with a palette knife. **Do not stir.**
6. When almost cooked, increase the heat for about ½ minute.
7. Remove from heat, fold in half, turn on to a hot plate and serve at once. Tomato, Spanish or Barbecue Sauce may be served with it.
8. Repeat until all the egg mixture has been cooked.

**YIELD**

25 servings of approx. 3½-oz.

## BACON OMELET

### 1 lb. Bacon
### Omelet Mixture

**METHOD**

1. Dice the raw bacon and cook in the omelet pan until crisp. Cook the amount required for each omelet as required.
2. Pour the omelet mixture over the hot bacon fat and bacon.
3. Finish as Plain Omelet.

**NOTE**

The bacon may be cooked, lifted from the pan and spread over the cooked omelet before it is folded.

## CHEESE OMELET

### ¾ pt. Grated Cheese (6 oz.)
### Omelet Mixture

**METHOD**

Sprinkle the grated cheese on each omelet before folding, allowing 1 tbsp. to each serving.

## JELLY OMELET

### 1½ c. Jelly or Jam
### Omelet Mixture (omit Pepper)

**METHOD**

1. Prepare Plain Omelet.
2. When cooked, spread with jelly or jam and fold.
3. Serve immediately.

## HAM OMELET

### 1 lb. Ham
### Omelet Mixture

**METHOD**

**Cooked Ham:**
1. Trim all fat from the ham.
2. Dice the meat.
3. Add to the omelet mixture.
4. Finish as Plain Omelet.

**Raw Ham:**
Make as Bacon Omelet.

## SPANISH OMELET

**1 pt. Spanish Sauce (page 289)**
**Omelet Mixture (page 121)**

**METHOD**

1. Make Plain Omelets.
2. Spread the Spanish Sauce over each omelet before folding.

## PLAIN OMELET

**(DEHYDRATED EGGS)**

**FOR 24**

| | | |
|---|---|---|
| 1½ qts. | Dried Egg Powder | 1 lb., 8 oz. |
| 1 qt. | Cold Water | 2 lbs., 8 oz. |
| 1½ qts. | Milk | 3 lbs., 12 oz. |
| 2 tbsp. | Salt | |
| 1 tsp. | Pepper | |
| | Bacon Fat | |

**METHOD**

1. Mix the egg powder with the cold water.
2. Add the milk and seasonings.
3. Melt the fat in a heavy pan. There should be about $\frac{1}{4}''$ in the pan.
4. Pour in 1½ pts. of the egg mixture ($\frac{1}{4}$ of the total amount).
5. Finish as Plain Omelet made with fresh eggs. Serve immediately.
6. Repeat until all the mixture is used.

**NOTE**

1. Variations of omelet, suggested under omelet made with fresh eggs, may be used with dehydrated eggs.
2. 1½ qts. Cream Sauce may be substituted for 1½ qts. of milk.

**YIELD**

24 servings.

# PROPORTIONS FOR RECONSTITUTING DRIED EGGS

| Equivalent number of fresh eggs | Amount of egg powder to use | | Amount of water to use | Yield of reconstituted eggs | | |
| --- | --- | --- | --- | --- | --- | --- |
| | **Weight** lbs. / oz. | **Measure** (approx.) | | **Weight** lbs. / oz. | | **Measure** (approx.) |
| 12 Eggs | 6 | ¾ pt. | ¾ pt. | 1 | 5 | 1 pt. |
| 16 Eggs | 8 | 1 pt. | 1 pt. | 1 | 12 | 1¼ pts. |
| 24 Eggs | 12 | 1½ pts. | 1½ pts. | 2 | 10 | 2¼ pts. |
| 32 Eggs | 1 | 2 pts. | 1 qt. | 3 | 8 | 2¾ pts. |
| 40 Eggs | 1    4 | 2½ pts. | 2½ pts. | 4 | 6 | 3½ pts. |
| 56 Eggs | 1    12 | 3½ pts. | 3½ pts. | 6 | 2 | 5 pts. |
| 64 Eggs | 2 | 4 pts. | 2 qts. | 7 | | 5½ pts. |

## TO RECONSTITUTE DRIED EGGS

1. Weigh the dried egg powder.
2. Measure the cold water.
3. Sift the egg powder over the water and stir or whip until smooth.
4. Strain before using.
5. Use within 15 minutes of mixing.

# Fish

## BAKED FISH WITH DRESSING

|            | Dressed Fish, A.P. | 50 lbs.  |
|            | or                 |          |
|            | Fillets of Fish    | 30 lbs.  |
|            | Dressing           | 10 lbs.  |
| 3 tbsp.    | Salt               | 2 oz.    |
| ½ tbsp.    | Pepper             |          |

**METHOD**

1. Bone the fish.
2. Spread half the fish in greased baking pans. When boned fish is used, place skin side down.
3. Cover with dressing ¾ to 1 inch in depth.
4. Place the remaining fish on top (have skin side up).
5. Season with salt and pepper, brush with melted fat.
6. Bake in a hot oven (450°F.) for 20 to 25 minutes.
7. If the surface looks dry, brush with melted fat once during the cooking time.
8. Cut into portions and serve with Barbecue, Tomato, Quick Chili, Mushroom, Vegetable or Tartare sauce.

**NOTE**

1. The fish may be spread in greased baking pans and covered with ½″ of dressing and then baked. Brush the top of the dressing with melted fat and cover the pan for the first 15 minutes of baking to prevent the crumbs from burning. Remove lid and brown.
2. Cut into portions and serve with sauces as above.

**YIELD**

100 4½-oz. servings.

## FISH DRESSING

| | | |
|---|---|---|
| 1 qt. | Finely Chopped or Grated Onions | 1 lb., 8 oz. |
| 1½ pts. | Melted Fat or Butter | 1 lb., 14 oz. |
| 3 gals. | Fresh Bread Crumbs | 7 lbs., 8 oz. |
| ½ c. | Salt | 5 oz. |
| 1 tsp. | Pepper | |
| 3 tbsp. | Savoury, Sage, Thyme or Oregano or a combination of these herbs | |

**METHOD**

1. Cook the onions in the melted fat until tender but not browned.
2. Combine the crumbs and seasonings.
3. Add to melted fat and onions.

**YIELD**

10 lbs. dressing.

**VARIATIONS**

One or more of the following may be added:
1 pt. of chopped parsley.
½ gal. of chopped celery (2 lbs. 8 oz.).
½ pt. lemon juice.
1 qt. chopped green pepper or 1 pt. of chopped pimiento.
1 qt. sweet or mustard pickles drained and chopped.

## SAUTÉD FILLETS OR STEAKS

|            | Fillets of Fish or Fish         |              |
|------------|---------------------------------|--------------|
|            | Steaks                          | 30 lbs.      |
| 2½ pts.    | Unsifted Pastry Flour           | 1 lb., 8 oz. |
| 6 tbsp.    | Salt                            | 4 oz.        |
| 1 tbsp.    | Pepper                          |              |
|            | Egg Wash (page 142)             |              |
| 3 qts.     | Sifted Dry Bread Crumbs         | 3 lbs.       |

**METHOD**

1. Cut fresh or frozen fillets into 5 oz. servings.
2. Dry the surface of the fish with a clean cloth.
3. Mix the seasonings with the flour.
4. Dip each piece in the seasoned flour, then in the egg wash and then in bread crumbs.
5. Heat heavy pans and add melted fat to the depth of $\frac{1}{8}$". The pans should be as hot as it is possible to have them without causing the fat to smoke.
6. Put in the fillets, brown on one side, turn and brown on the other.
7. Lower the heat and finish cooking.
   Fresh or thawed fish will require 15 minutes per inch of thickness.
   Frozen fish will require 20 minutes per inch of thickness.
8. Lift from the pan, drain and keep warm while serving. Serve at once with lemon points or Browned Butter Sauce.

**NOTE**

Fresh fish may be sautéd after it has been coated with the seasoned flour only. This is not as satisfactory when used on frozen fish owing to its tendency to fall apart.

**YIELD**

100 5-oz. servings.

## BAKED FILLETS OR STEAKS

**(BREADED)**

**METHOD**

1. Bread fillets or steaks as directed for sautéing.
2. Brown lightly on both sides in a hot pan containing ⅛″ fat.
3. Transfer to baking pans. Stand the pieces of fish on edge or place in single layers in the pans. Do not pile.
4. Finish cooking in a hot oven (450°F.).
   Fresh or thawed fish—15 minutes per inch of thickness.
   Frozen fish         —20 minutes per inch of thickness.
5. When the fish is cooked, remove at once from the hot oven and keep warm while serving.
6. Serve with lemon points or Tomato or Barbecue Sauce or any of the sauces listed for fish.

## BAKED FILLETS OR STEAKS

|         | Fillets of Fish            | 30 lbs.      |
|---------|----------------------------|--------------|
| 6 tbsp. | Salt                       | 4 oz.        |
| 1 tbsp. | Pepper                     |              |
| ½ pt.   | Lemon Juice                | 10 oz.       |
|         | or                         |              |
| 1 pt.   | French Dressing            | 20 oz.       |
|         | or                         |              |
| 1 qt.   | Finely Chopped Braised     |              |
|         | Onions                     | 1 lb., 8 oz. |
| 2 qts.  | Fine Buttered Crumbs       |              |

**METHOD**

1. Spread the fish fillets in greased baking pans.
2. Season with salt and pepper.
3. Sprinkle with lemon juice, French dressing or braised onions.
4. Cover lightly with buttered crumbs.
5. Bake in a hot oven (450°F.) until the fish is cooked and the crumbs brown.
   Fresh or thawed fish—15 minutes per inch of thickness.
   Frozen fish         —20 minutes per inch of thickness.
6. Serve with Tomato Sauce or variations of a brown butter sauce.

**YIELD**

100 5-oz. servings.

## FISH FRIED IN BATTER

| | | |
|---|---|---|
| 1 gal. | Flour | 5 lbs. |
| ⅓ c. | Salt | 3 oz. |
| 16 | Eggs | 1 lb., 11 oz. |
| 1 gal. | Milk | 10 lbs. |
| ½ pt. | Shortening (melted) | 8 oz. |
| | Fillets of Fish | 30 lbs. |

**METHOD**

1. Cut fillets into 5-oz. servings.
2. Sift the flour and salt.
3. Beat the eggs slightly, add the milk and melted shortening.
4. Pour the eggs and milk into the flour, mix until smooth and then beat thoroughly.
5. Dip the fish fillets into the batter.
6. Fry in deep fat at a temperature of 370°-375°F. for 4 to 6 minutes, until well browned.
7. Lift out, drain well and serve immediately with Tomato, Barbecue, Tartare or Quick Chili Sauce.

**NOTE**

1. Thaw and dry frozen fish before dipping in batter.
2. If the fish is not thoroughly cooked by the time it is brown—stand the fillets on edge in a roasting pan and finish cooking in a hot oven.
3. Fried fish will become soft if allowed to stand in the steam table for more than a few minutes. Pans of fish, ready for serving, should be kept in the oven. The fish should be arranged in a single layer or should stand on edge.

## DEEP FRIED FILLETS OR STEAKS

**METHOD**

1. Use only fresh or completely thawed frozen fish.
2. Prepare the fish as directed under sautéing.
3. Fry in deep fat (350°F.) until golden brown on both sides.
4. Lift from fat, drain, stand on edge in baking pans and cook in a hot oven (450°F.) for 5 to 7 minutes.
5. Remove from the oven and serve with Tartare Sauce.

**YIELD**

100 5-oz. servings.

## FISH LOAF

|          | Cooked Fish       | 20 lbs.         |
|----------|-------------------|-----------------|
| 40       | Eggs              | 4 lbs., 3 oz.   |
| 2 gals.  | Thick Cream Sauce | 20 lbs.         |
| 5 qts.   | Fresh Bread Crumbs | 3 lbs., 4 oz.  |
|          | or                |                 |
| 3 qts.   | Dry Bread Crumbs  | 3 lbs.          |
| 1 qt.    | Butter            | 2 lbs., 8 oz.   |
| ½ c.     | Salt              | 5 oz.           |
| 2 tbsp.  | Pepper            |                 |

**METHOD**

1. Flake the fish after removing bones and skin. When canned salmon is used, drain off the liquid, remove skin, crush bones and use them.
2. Beat eggs.
3. Combine all the ingredients.
4. Pack into greased tins. Bake in a moderate oven (350°F.) for one hour.
5. Serve hot with Egg or Yellow Béchamel Sauce or serve cold with salad.

**YIELD**

100 6-oz. servings.

**VARIATION**

Add 2½ quarts grated cheese (2½ lbs.) to the Cream Sauce.

## FISH CAKES

| | | |
|---|---|---|
| 1½ gals. | Cooked Flaked Fish | 15 lbs. |
| 3 gals. | Mashed Potatoes | 30 lbs. |
| 1½ c. | Cooked Diced Onions | 1 lb. |
| 2 tbsp. | Pepper | |
| ½ c. | Salt | 5 oz. |
| | Egg Wash (page 142) | |
| 3 qts. | Sifted Dry Bread Crumbs | 3 lbs. |
| 2½ pts. | Unsifted Pastry Flour | 1 lb., 8 oz. |

**METHOD**

1. Combine the first five ingredients.
2. Mould into 6 oz. cakes.
3. Dip in flour, egg wash and crumbs.
4. Fry in deep fat (375°F.).

or

5. Coat with flour and sauté in a small amount of fat either on top of the stove or in the oven.
6. Serve with Tomato, Barbecue, Quick Chili, or Tartare Sauce.

**YIELD**

100 6-oz. cakes.

## SCALLOPED FISH

| | | |
|---|---|---|
| 2½ gals. | Cooked Fish or Canned Salmon | 20 lbs. |
| 2 gals. | Medium Cream Sauce | 20 lbs. |
| ⅓ c. | Salt | 3 oz. |
| 4 tsp. | Pepper | 1 oz. |
| 3 qts. | Buttered Bread Crumbs | 3 lbs., 6 oz. |

**METHOD**

1. Prepare Cream Sauce.
2. Prepare buttered crumbs.
3. Remove skin and bones, and then break the fish into pieces. If canned salmon is used, crush the bones and add to the fish.
4. Fill greased baking tins with alternate layers of fish and sauce.
5. Cover with buttered crumbs.
6. Bake in a moderate oven (350°F.) until the fish is thoroughly heated and the crumbs are brown, about 35 minutes.

**YIELD**

100 6½-oz. servings.

## SCALLOPED FISH, POTATOES AND EGGS

1. Reduce fish to 10 lbs. Add 7 lbs. diced cooked potatoes and 4 dozen hard-cooked eggs, cut in quarters.
2. In place of the Cream Sauce, a creamed canned soup such as mushroom, celery, chicken or tomato may be used. It will require approximately 2½ #10 tins of soup diluted with 2½ qts. of milk for all soups except tomato. Use 3 #10 tins of tomato and do not dilute.

## CREAMED SALMON, PEAS AND HARD COOKED EGGS

### A

| | | |
|---|---|---|
| | Whole Fresh Salmon | 20 lbs. |

### B

| | | |
|---|---|---|
| 4 pts. | Shortening or Butter | 4 lbs. |
| 3 qts. | Unsifted Pastry Flour | 4 lbs. |
| 9 tbsp. | Salt | 6 oz. |
| | Cayenne | |

### C

| | | |
|---|---|---|
| 1 | Diced Green Pepper | |
| 2½ gals. | Milk | 25 lbs. |
| 2 gals. | Fish Stock | 20 lbs. |

### D

| | | |
|---|---|---|
| 6 doz. | Hard Cooked Eggs | 10 lbs., 8 oz. |
| 8 #2 tins | Peas and Juice | 9 lbs., 8 oz. |
| 4 1-lb. tins | Salmon and Juice | 4 lbs. |
| 3 | Lemons (juice) | |

**METHOD**

1. Boil salmon with celery and bay leaf. Save the stock (2 gals.).
2. Remove skin and bone, separate salmon into large flakes.
3. Make a roux from B.
4. Add C to make a sauce.
5. Add D and the flaked salmon. Reheat.

**YIELD**

8 gallons (100 12-oz. servings).

## LOBSTER NEWBURG

| | | |
|---|---|---|
| ¾ c. | Butter | 6 oz. |
| 1½ c. | Unsifted Flour | 6 oz. |
| 2 qts. | Milk | 2 lbs., 8 oz. |
| ⅔ c. | Butter | 5 oz. |
| | Lobster Meat | 2 lbs., 8 oz. |
| 1 tsp. | Paprika | |
| 1 pt. | Cream | 1 lb., 4 oz. |
| 6 | Egg Yolks | |
| 5 tsp. | Salt | 1 oz. |
| 1 tsp. | Pepper | |
| ⅓ c. | Sherry | 3 oz. |

**METHOD**

1. Melt the butter (6 oz.), add the flour and cook for 10 minutes.
2. Add the milk gradually, stir until free from lumps and cook for 10 minutes.
3. Melt the butter (5 oz.) and add the lobster. Fry for 5 minutes.
4. Add the paprika and cook for 2 minutes longer.
5. Add the cream and simmer for 10 minutes.
6. Combine with the first mixture.
7. Stir a small amount of the hot sauce into the beaten yolks and then add this mixture to the lobster. Add the seasonings.
8. Cook over a low heat for 3 to 5 minutes. Keep very hot until ready to serve.
9. Add the sherry just before serving.

**YIELD**

3 qts. 25 servings.

## SEA FOOD NEWBURG

In place of the lobster substitute an equal weight of one of, or a combination of, cooked shrimps, scallops, crab meat.

## BAKED FILLETS VINAIGRETTE

|  |  |  |
|---|---|---|
|  | **Frozen or Fresh Fish Fillets** | **30 lbs.** |
| **4 qts.** | **Fresh Bread Crumbs** | **2 lbs., 8 oz.** |
| **1 c.** | **Worcestershire Sauce** | **8 oz.** |
| **1 c.** | **Lemon Juice** | **8 oz.** |
| **1 c.** | **Vinegar** | **8 oz.** |
| **1½ qts.** | **Melted Butter or** | |
| | **Margarine** | **3 lbs., 12 oz.** |
| **5 tbsp.** | **Prepared Mustard** | **1 oz.** |
| **5 tbsp.** | **Salt** | **3½ oz.** |
| **2 tsp.** | **Pepper** | |

**METHOD**

1. Cover the bottom of baking pans with bread crumbs.
2. Lay the fillets on top.
3. Mix the remaining ingredients and pour over the fish.
4. Sprinkle with paprika.
5. Bake in a hot oven (450°F.) allowing about
   15 minutes for each inch thickness of fresh fish,
   20 minutes for each inch thickness of frozen fish.

**YIELD**

100 5-oz. servings.


## SALT FISH

Salt fish must be freshened before it is used.

### TO FRESHEN SALT FISH

1. Break the fish into pieces or shred. Do not use a steel knife or fork for this purpose.
2. Wash to remove the salt from the surface.
3. Cover with cold water, heat to boiling. Pour off the water.
4. Repeat No. 3 until the water is only slightly salty.

## SALT COD HASH

|  | Flaked Salt Cod | 25 lbs. |
| 3½ gals. | Cooked Diced Potatoes | 25 lbs. |
| 2 tbsp. | Fat |  |
| 1 c. | Raw Chopped Onions | 6 oz. |

**METHOD**

1. Freshen the salt cod according to the directions given above.
2. Cook the onions in fat until tender.
3. Combine all the ingredients.
4. Put the hash in heavy pans which have been greased, and brown on top of the stove or in a slow oven (300°F.).

**YIELD**

100 8-oz. servings.

## CODFISH CAKES

|  | Salt Codfish | 12 lbs., 8 oz. |
| 4¼ gals. | Raw Diced Potatoes | 25 lbs., 8 oz. |
| 1 pt. | Butter | 1 lb., 4 oz. |
| 20 | Eggs | 2 lbs. |
| 2 tbsp. | Salt |  |
| 1 tbsp. | Pepper |  |

**METHOD**

1. Shred the codfish. Freshen according to the method, page 136.
2. Simmer the fish and the potatoes until tender but not overdone.
3. Remove from the fire and drain thoroughly, shaking over the heat to make mealy and dry. Mash well.
4. Add butter, beaten eggs and seasonings. Mix thoroughly.
5. Form into 2½-oz. cakes 2 hours before frying, so that the cakes will be dry on the outside. This will prevent them from soaking up the grease and from falling apart.
6. Fry to a golden brown in deep fat (Temp. 360°F.) or sauté in a small quantity of fat on top of the stove.

**YIELD**

100 servings of two cakes each.

## SMOKED FISH

## BOILED SMOKED FILLETS

### Smoked Fillets     30 lbs.

**METHOD**

1. Cut the fillets into 5-oz. servings and put in baking pans.
2. Cover with boiling water and cook in a hot oven.
3. Drain the fish well.
4. Serve with a cream or egg sauce.

**YIELD**

100 4-oz. servings.

## CREAMED SMOKED FILLETS

|          | **Smoked Fillets** | **30 lbs.** |
|----------|--------------------|-------------|
| **2 gals.** | **Cream Sauce** | **20 lbs.** |

**METHOD**

1. Boil the whole fillets on top of the stove or in the oven.
2. Remove the bones and break into pieces.
3. Add the Cream Sauce and reheat.

**YIELD**

100 7-oz. servings.

**VARIATIONS**

1. Cover with buttered crumbs and bake in the oven.
2. Add 1 pint finely chopped parsley to the cream sauce.
3. Serve on baked or steamed rice.
4. Add 1 cup finely chopped green pepper.

### SCALLOPED FINNAN HADDIE AND POTATO

Reduce the quantity of fish to 20 lbs. and add 10 lbs. sliced cooked potatoes and ½ cup chopped, cooked onion. Arrange fish, potatoes and onions in alternate layers in a greased baking dish. Add cream sauce, cover with buttered crumbs and bake in a moderate oven until thoroughly heated and the crumbs are brown.

# Frying

## GENERAL DIRECTIONS FOR DEEP-FAT FRYING

### CHOICE OF FAT

When the ordinary commercial fats are not available and the choice is limited to animal fats, use one of the following:

1. Rendered Beef Suet.
2. Rendered Beef Suet—2 parts.
   Rendered Pork or Bacon Fat—1 part.

### PREPARATION OF FAT FOR USE

The fat must be melted and strained in order to separate it from the connective tissue which surrounds it. This process is called rendering.

#### TO RENDER FAT

1. Chop the fat and remove as much of the connective tissue as possible or put through a grinder.
2. Add a small quantity of water (1 quart to 10 lbs. fat) and bring to a boil.
3. Boil over a low heat until the fat is melted.
4. Strain through a cloth or fine sieve.
5. Stir the fat occasionally as it cools.

### TO REMOVE DISAGREEABLE FLAVOURS FROM FAT

Slightly burned fat, bacon dripping and other fats having an objectionable flavour may be improved by boiling in water.

#### METHOD

1. Allow the rendered fat to harden.
2. Scrape all sediment from the bottom of the cake of fat.
3. Place the fat in a pot and add boiling water.
4. Boil 5 to 10 minutes.
5. Cool.
6. Remove the cake of fat from the surface of the water.
7. Melt this fat and boil until bubbling ceases. This will remove all water. Fat containing water spoils quickly.

## TEMPERATURE OF FAT

1. Fat used for frying must be heated to the exact temperature required for cooking the food.
2. The fat must be held at that temperature throughout the period of cooking.
3. If the temperature is too high, the food will burn and will have a disagreeable flavour, due to the fact that the fat has been allowed to "smoke." If the temperature of the fat is too low, the food becomes greasy.

#### HOW TO TEST THE TEMPERATURE OF THE FAT

1. For Raw Food—A cube of fresh bread, crusts removed, should turn golden brown when cooked in the fat for 60 seconds. Temperature on thermometer 360°-365°F.
2. For Cooked Foods—A cube of fresh bread, crusts removed, should turn golden brown when cooked in the fat for 40 seconds. Temperature on thermometer 375°-380°F.

## METHOD FOR DEEP-FAT FRYING

1. Have the frying kettle half-full of melted fat.
2. Test the temperature of the fat.
3. Have the food at room temperature, if this can be done without danger of spoilage.
4. Lower the food into the kettle. Be sure that all the food is covered by the fat. Do not put in large quantities of food at a time as this lowers the temperature of the fat.
5. When the food is a delicate brown, remove from the fat and drain on racks or crumpled brown paper. Keep the food hot until ready to serve.
6. Test the temperature of the fat before putting in the next lot of food.
When large quantities of food are being fried, they may be browned in the fat and then placed in pans in the oven to finish cooking.

## CARE OF FAT AFTER USING

1. Cool the fat slightly and gradually sprinkle in a small quantity of water, about 1 cup per gallon, or cook 1 cup of raw potato slices in the fat. Either method will remove foreign flavours.
2. Strain through a cloth.
3. Store in covered containers in a cool, dark place.

## TO BREAD FOODS FOR DEEP-FAT FRYING

1. Coat with flour.
2. Dip in egg wash.
3. Roll in finely sifted bread crumbs.

## EGG WASH

| 12 | Eggs |
|------|--------|
| 1 gal. | Milk |
| ½ c. | Salt |
| 2 tbsp. | Pepper |

METHOD

1. Beat the eggs.
2. Add the other ingredients.

## DOUGHNUTS

**A**

| ¼ pt. | Butter or Shortening | 4 oz. |
|--------|----------------------|-------|
| 1½ pts. | Sugar | 1 lb., 8 oz. |

**B**

| 8 | Eggs | 14 oz. |
|---|------|--------|

**C**

| 1 pt. | Milk | 1 lb., 4 oz. |
|-------|------|--------------|

**D**

| 3½ qts. | Unsifted Pastry Flour | 4 lbs., 6 oz. |
|---------|----------------------|---------------|
| 10 tbsp. | Baking Powder | 4 oz. |
| 5 tsp. | Salt | 1 oz. |
| 4 tbsp. | Mace | |

METHOD

1. Make according to the general method for cakes, page 20.
2. Turn out onto a floured board, roll to ½-inch thickness and cut with a doughnut cutter.
3. Fry in deep fat at 360°-370°F. according to the general directions, page 141.

YIELD

100 medium-sized doughnuts.

## FRENCH FRIED POTATOES

### 50 lbs. Potatoes, A.P.

**METHOD**

1. Wash and pare the potatoes. Cut into lengthwise fingers about ½-inch in width.
2. Chill by standing in cold water.
3. Dry between cloths.
4. Cook in deep fat at temperature (350°F.) for 7-8 minutes.
5. Lift from fat, drain.

**NOTE**

When preparing large quantities, fry the potatoes for 5 minutes at 350°F. Drain. As required for serving, fry for 2 minutes longer at the same temperature.

**YIELD**

100 5-oz. servings.

## FRENCH FRIED ONION RINGS

**METHOD**

1. Cut large onions into slices about ⅛" thick. Separate into rings.
2. Dip in milk and then in flour.
3. Fry in deep fat at 325°F. until golden brown. Drain.
4. Serve with steaks or curried meat.

**NOTE**

A lower temperature is used for frying onion rings than for other foods in order to prevent them from shrivelling before they are cooked.

## FRITTER BATTER

| 3½ qts. | Unsifted Pastry Flour | 4 lbs., 6 oz. |
| 10 tbsp. | Baking Powder | 4 oz. |
| 4 tsp. | Salt | |
| 1½ pts. | Sugar | 1 lb., 8 oz. |
| ¼ pt. | Shortening | 4 oz. |
| 16 | Eggs | 1 lb., 12 oz. |
| 1 qt. | Milk | 2 lbs., 8 oz. |

**METHOD**

1. Combine ingredients as in making muffins, but beat until smooth.

**NOTE**

Fritters should be crisp. If allowed to stand in the steamtable or the oven, they soon become limp. For this reason, fritters should be cooked in relays and served at once.

## APPLE FRITTERS

**Fritter Batter**
**30 Medium-Sized Apples**
**Deep Fat**

**METHOD**

1. Mix the batter.
2. Test the fat. It should be 365°F. (see tests page 141).
3. Wash, quarter, core and pare the apples. Chop fine.
4. Stir the apples into the batter.
5. Drop from an ice cream scoop (#16) into the deep fat. Cook for 5 to 6 minutes turning frequently.
6. Drain on absorbent paper for 1 or 2 minutes. Sprinkle with sugar immediately or serve with Lemon Sauce or Corn Syrup.

**YIELD**

200 medium-sized fritters.

**VARIATION**

1. Wash and core the apples. Cut into ¼" slices.
2. Sprinkle with lemon juice and fine sugar. Let stand for 15 minutes. Drain.
3. Dip each slice in batter and fry as above. The temperature of the fat should be about 370°F.

## BANANA FRITTERS

**Fritter Batter**
**Bananas 16 to 20 lbs.**
**1 qt. Unsifted Pastry Flour**
**Deep Fat**

**METHOD**

1. Prepare the fritter batter.
2. Heat the fat to 370°F.
3, Peel the bananas. Cut diagonally into halves, or thirds according to the size.
4. Roll each piece in flour and then coat with the batter.
5. Fry in the hot fat until thoroughly browned and cooked. Turn frequently in order to brown evenly.
6. Drain on absorbent paper and serve immediately.

**YIELD**

200 medium-sized fritters.

## CORN FRITTERS

| 1 gal. | Unsifted Pastry Flour | 5 lbs. |
|--------|----------------------|--------|
| 8 tbsp. | Baking Powder | 3 oz. |
| 3 tbsp. | Salt | 2 oz. |
| ¼ c. | Sugar | 2 oz. |
| 8 #2 Cans | Corn (Cream Style) | 10 lbs. |
| 24 | Beaten Egg Yolks | |
| 24 | Beaten Egg Whites | |
| ½ c. | Butter (melted) | 4 oz. |

**METHOD**

1. Sift the dry ingredients.
2. Add the corn and beaten egg yolks. Mix well.
3. Fold in the beaten whites.
4. Drop from an ice cream scoop into hot fat (360°F.).
5. Turn several times to brown evenly. Cook 4-6 minutes.
6. Drain well and serve with corn or maple syrup.

**YIELD**

200 medium-sized fritters.

## CORN AND HAM FRITTERS

1. Use only 4 #2 cans of corn.
2. Add 4 lbs. (2 qts.) finely chopped lean ham.
3. Finish and cook as above.

# Meat

## TERMS USED IN COOKING MEAT

1. **Roasting:** Cooking tender meat uncovered in an oven without the addition of liquid.
2. **Braising:** Browning in the oven or on top of the stove.
3. **Pot Roasting:** Cooking braised meat in an oven or on top of the stove in a closely covered container, with the addition of a small quantity of liquid. This method is used for less tender cuts of meat.
4. **Simmering:** Cooking tough meat on top of the stove in a large volume of water.
5. **Stewing:** Cooking less tender meat, cut into pieces, by the method used in pot roasting.
6. **Pan Broiling:** Cooking tender meat in a shallow pan on top of the stove. The surface of the pan is rubbed with fat just to prevent the meat from sticking, but the cooking is done without the addition of further fat.
7. **Sautéing:** Cooking tender meat in a shallow pan on top of the stove. A small quantity of fat is melted in the pan before the meat is added.
8. **Deep Fat Frying:** Cooking food by immersing it in hot fat.


## HOW TO USE THE MEAT CHARTS

1. Each of the following Charts of Beef, Lamb, Pork and Veal gives the approximate yield of meat, bone and fat from a side of meat. The weights given are averages from a large number of carcasses of comparable size.
2. Each diagram is marked into wholesale cuts.
3. The total weight of each cut is given and the amount of meat, fat and bone which constitutes that total weight.
    M. represents tender and less tender meat.
    S. represents toughest meat, suitable for simmering, stewing, mincing only.
    F. represents Fat.
    B. represents Bone.
    T. represents Tenderloin.
    K. represents Kidney.
    R. represents Rind.
    SP. represents Spareribs.
4. For the sake of brevity, weights are printed thus:
        8.10 stands for 8 lbs. 10 oz.

## USES FOR CUTS OF BEEF

Hip            Rump roast, pot roasts, swiss steaks.
Butt           Steaks, roasts.
Loin           Roasts, T-bone or porterhouse steaks.
Tenderloin     Steaks, roasts.
Ribs           Roast.
Chuck          Pot roast, swiss steaks.
Short ribs
Plate
Brisket
Neck           Stew, meat pie, meat loaf, hamburg steak.
Shank
Trimmings
Kidney         Braised or in stew.
Bones          Soup or gravy stock.
Fat            Render for cooking purposes.

# SIDE OF STEER 333 lbs.

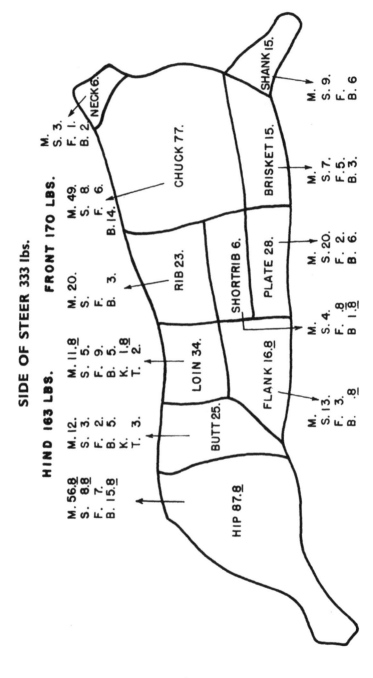

HIND 163 LBS.

FRONT 170 LBS.

NECK 6.
M.
S. 3.
F. I.
B. 2

CHUCK 77.

M. 49.
S. 8.
F. 6.
B.14.

SHANK 15.
M.
S. 9.
F. .
B. 6

BRISKET 15.
M.
S. 7.
F. 5.
B. 3.

RIB 23.
M. 20.
S. .
F. .
B. 3.

SHORTRIB 6.

PLATE 28.
M.
S.20.
F. 2.
B. 6.

LOIN 34.
M. 11.8
S. 5.
F. 9.
B. 5.
K. 1.8
T. 2.

FLANK 16.8
M.
S. 4.
F. .8
B 1.8

BUTT 25.
M. 12.
S. 3.
F. 2.
B. 5.
K. .
T. 3.

M.
S. 13.
F. 3.
B. .8

HIP 87.8
M. 56.8
S. 8.8
F. 7.
B. 15.8

150

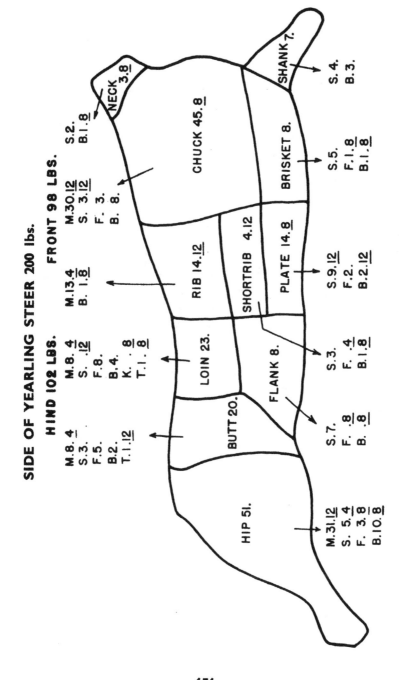

SIDE OF YEARLING STEER 200 lbs.

HIND 102 LBS.          FRONT 98 LBS.

M.8. 4          M.8. 4          M.30.12          S.2.
S.3.            S.   12         S.  3.12         B.1. 8
F.5.            F.8.            F. 3.
B.2.            B.4.            B. 8.
T.1.12          K.   8
                T.1. 8

M.13.4          NECK
B.  1. 8        3.8

                CHUCK 45. 8          SHANK 7.

RIB 14.12

LOIN 23.

BUTT 20.        SHORTRIB  4.12      BRISKET 8.          S. 4.
                                                        B. 3.

                PLATE 14. 8

HIP 51.         FLANK 8.            S.5.
                                    F.1. 8
M.31.12                             B.1. 8
S.  5. 4        S.3.
F.  3.8         F.  4               S.9.12
B.10. 8         B.1. 8              F.2.
                                    B.2.12
S.7.
F.   8
B.   8

151

# SIDE OF COW 210 lbs.

**HIND 110 LBS.**  **FRONT 100 LBS.**

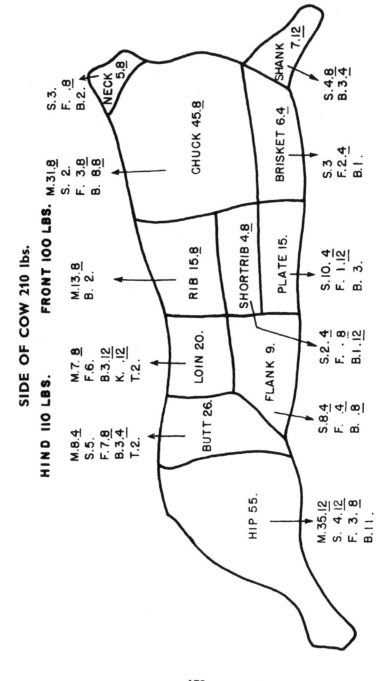

**HIND 110 LBS.**

BUTT 26.

M.8.4
S.5.
F.7.8
B.3.4
T.2.

LOIN 20.

M.7.8
F.6.
B.3.12
K. .12
T.2.

**FRONT 100 LBS.** M.31.8

S. 2.
F. 3.8
B. 8.8

CHUCK 45.8

NECK
5.8

S.3.
F. .8
B.2.

SHANK
7.12

S.4.8
B.3.4

BRISKET 6.4

S.3
F.2.4
B.I.

RIB 15.8

M.13.8
B. 2.

SHORTRIB 4.8

PLATE 15.

S.10. 4
F. 1.12
B. 3.

FLANK 9.

S.2. 4
F. .8
B.I.12

S.8.4
F. 4
B. .8

HIP 55.

M.35.12
S. 4.12
F. 3.8
B.II.

152

## USES FOR CUTS OF VEAL

Legs     Roasts or cutlets.
Loins     Roasts or chops.
Fronts     Roasts, cutlets or shoulder chops.
Neck ⎞
Shanks ⎬ Stew, jellied, veal loaf.
Flanks ⎠
Bone     Soup stock.

SIDE OF VEAL 55 lbs.

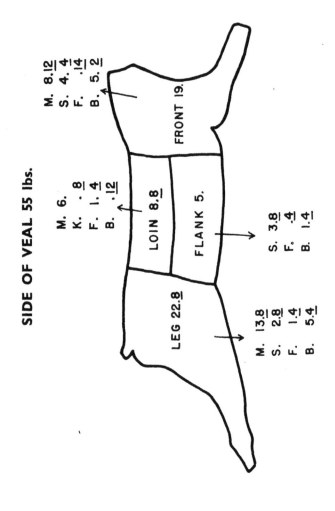

M. 8.12
S. 4. 4
F. . 14
B. 5. 2

FRONT 19.

M. 6.
K. . 8
F. 1. 4
B. . 12

LOIN 8.8

FLANK 5.

S. 3.8
F. . 4
B. 1. 4

LEG 22.8

M. 13.8
S. 2.8
F. 1. 4
B. 5. 4

154

## USES FOR CUTS OF LAMB OR MUTTON

Legs            Roasts, simmered meat.
Loins           Roasts, chops.
Shoulders       Roasts, simmered meat.
Flank or Trim   Irish stew, lamb pie.
Bone            Stock for mutton or Scotch broth.
Fat             Render for cooking purposes.

## SIDE OF YEARLING LAMB 27 lbs.

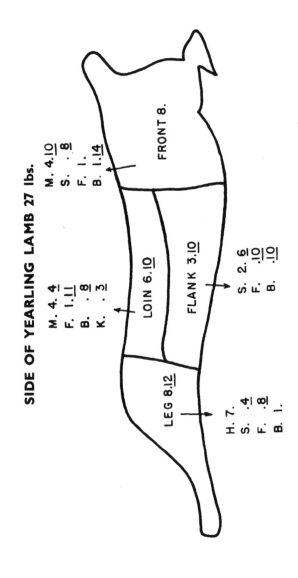

M. 4.10
S.   .8
F.  1.
B.  1.14

FRONT 8.

M. 4. 4
F.  1.11
B.   .8
K.   .3

LOIN 6.10

FLANK 3.10

S. 2. 6
F.   .10
B.   .10

LEG 8.12

H. 7.
S.  .4
F.  .8
B.  1.

## USES FOR CUTS OF HOG

| | |
|---|---|
| Legs | Roasts. |
| Loins | Roasts or chops. |
| Shoulders | Roasts. |
| Tenderloin | Roasts or steaks. |
| Belly | Pork pies, sausages, in baked beans. |
| Spareribs | Roasts or simmered ribs. |
| Feet and Hocks | Jellied, simmered or pickled meat. |
| Fat | Render for cooking purposes. |

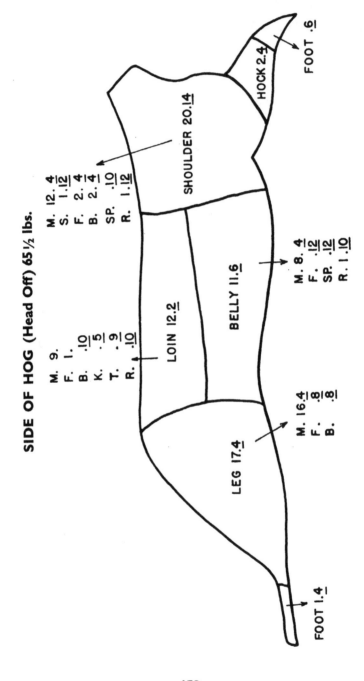

SIDE OF HOG (Head Off) 65½ lbs.

SHOULDER 20.14

M. 12. 4
S. 1.12
F. 2. 4
B. 2. 4
SP. .10
R. 1.12

HOCK 2.4

FOOT .6

LOIN 12.2

M. 9.
F. 1.
B. .10
K. .5
T. .9
R. .10

BELLY 11.6

M. 8. 4
F. .12
SP. .12
R. 1.10

LEG 17.4

M. 16.4
F. .8
B. .8

FOOT 1.4

158

## TIME-TABLE FOR COOKING STEWS AND POT ROASTS

| Meat | Size of Piece | Temp. | Approx. Length of Time |
|---|---|---|---|
| **BEEF** | | | |
| Pot Roast | 7 to 8 lbs. | 325 | 30 min. per inch after browning. |
| Swiss Steak | ¼″ to ¾″ thick | 325 | 1½ to 2 hours after browning. |
| Stewed Steak | ½″ to ¾″ thick | 325 or simmering | 2 to 3 hours after browning. |
| Stew | ½″ to 1″ cubes | 325 or simmering | 2 to 3 hours after browning. |
| **VEAL** | | | |
| Cutlets | ½″ to ¾″ thick | 325 | 45 to 60 min. after browning. |
| Stew | 1½″ to 2″ pieces | 325 | 1 hour after browning. |
| **LAMB** | | | |
| Braised | Servings | 325 | 1 to 1½ hours after browning. |
| Stew | 1″ cubes | 325 | 1 to 1½ hours after browning. |
| Irish Stew | 1″ cubes | simmer | 2 hours. |
| **MUTTON** | | | |
| Braised | Servings | 325 | 2 to 2 hours after browning. |
| **PORK** | | | |
| Chops and Steak | ½″ to ¾″ thick | 325 | 45 to 60 min. |

## STEWS AND MEAT PIES

The method for making stew is the same for all meats. Very lean meat is cut into cubes or into servings and is then browned. The one exception to this is fricassee which should be light in colour and for this reason is made without braising the meat.

Variations can be introduced into stews by the addition of vegetables, the use of tomato juice for part of the liquid and the use of different seasonings.

Meat pies, which are to be served hot, are stews which are covered with pastry or biscuit dough and baked in a hot oven until the crust is cooked through and brown. Any stew can be made into a pie in this way.

### GENERAL METHOD FOR MAKING STEWS

1. Cut the meat into cubes.
2. Place in greased baking pans; brush with fat.
3. Braise for 1 hour in a moderate oven (350°F.) or brown on top of the stove, stirring constantly.
4. Add finely chopped raw onions and cook with the meat for 10 minutes.
5. Lift the meat and onions from the pan, leaving the renderings.
6. Measure the renderings.
7. Add the flour and seasonings, blend well. Cook for one or two minutes.
8. Add the hot liquid slowly, stirring as you add. Boil for two or three minutes.
9. Pour over the meat and onions.
10. Cover closely. Simmer in a slow oven (300°-325°F.), on top of the stove or in a steam-jacketed kettle until the meat is tender.

## BEEF STEW

|              | Lean Boneless Stewing |              |
|--------------|-----------------------|--------------|
|              | Beef                  | 35 lbs.      |
| 1 gal.       | Raw Diced Onions      | 6 lbs.       |

## GRAVY FOR STEW

| 1½ pts.  | Renderings from Pan   | 1 lb., 8 oz.  |
|----------|-----------------------|---------------|
| 1½ qts.  | Unsifted Pastry Flour | 1 lb., 14 oz. |
| 3 gals.  | Boiling Water         | 30 lbs.       |
| ½ c.     | Salt                  | 5 oz.         |
| 2 tsp.   | Pepper                |               |

**METHOD**

1. Cut the beef into 1″ cubes.
2. Make according to the general method for stews (page 160).

**YIELD**

100 8-oz. servings.

## BEEF AND VEGETABLE STEW

Variations of beef stew may be made by substituting 10 lbs. of raw vegetables or 5 lbs. of cooked vegetables for 5 lbs. of meat. Add raw vegetables when the gravy is added to the meat. Add cooked vegetables 10 minutes before the meat is tender. The following vegetables make suitable additions to stew—

|           |            |         |
|-----------|------------|---------|
| Carrots   | Turnips    | Celery  |
| Potatoes  | Green Peas |         |

## BEEF AND KIDNEY STEW

Reduce meat to 22 lbs. and add 8 lbs. of diced kidneys.
Preparation of Kidneys for Stew:
1. Trim and dice kidneys.
2. Simmer for 1 hour in water. Drain and add to the stew with the gravy.

## BEEF AND KIDNEY PIE

**Beef and Kidney Stew—Recipe, page 161.**
**Pastry or Biscuit Dough—½ Standard Recipe.**

**METHOD**

1. Prepare beef and kidney stew in shallow baking pans.
2. Cover with pastry crust or biscuit dough rolled to ¼-inch thickness, making several slits in the dough.
3. Bake in a hot oven 425°F. until the crust is cooked. Cut into portions and serve.

**YIELD**

100 9-oz. servings.


## MEAT PIE

|  |  |  |
|---|---|---|
| 1 gal. | **Recipe for Stew** | |
| | **Raw Diced Potatoes** | 6 lbs. |
| | **½ Standard Recipe for** | |
| |   **Biscuit Dough (page 340)** | |
| |   **or** | |
| | **½ Standard Recipe for Pie** | |
| |   **Dough (page 216)** | |

**METHOD**

1. Make a stew.
2. When the meat is almost tender, add the diced raw potatoes. Continue cooking until both are tender.
3. Pour into baking pans. Cool slightly.
4. Cover with biscuit dough rolled ¼" thick or pie dough rolled ⅛" thick. Make several slits in the dough.
5. Bake in a hot oven (425°F.) until the crust is cooked through and browned.
6. Cut into portions and serve.

**YIELD**

100 9-oz. servings.

## DUTCH BEEF STEW

| | | |
|---|---|---|
| ½ pt. | **Beef Fat or Drippings** | 8 oz. |
| 1 qt. | **Finely Chopped Onions** | 1 lb., 8 oz. |
| | **Minced Beef** | 30 lbs. |
| ⅓ c. | **Salt** | 3 oz. |
| 1 tsp. | **Pepper** | |
| 1 pt. | **Unsifted Pastry Flour** | 10 oz. |
| 3 qts. | **Stock or Tomato Juice** | 7 lbs., 8 oz. |

**METHOD**

1. Cook the onions in the fat until clear. Lift out, drain and save the fat.
2. Braise the beef either in the oven (350°F.) or on top of the stove. It must be stirred frequently with a fork in order to keep the particles of meat separated.
3. When the meat is well browned, drain off the fat.
4. Make a brown gravy, using the fat in which the onions were cooked and fat drained from the meat.
5. Add the onions and gravy to the meat. Cover the pan.
6. Simmer or bake in a slow oven (325°F.) until the meat is tender.
7. Serve very hot on toast, or mashed potatoes.

**YIELD**

100 4- to 4½-oz. servings.

## SWISS STEAK

| 100 | 6 oz. Steaks from Hip or Chuck of Beef | 38 lbs. |
|---|---|---|
| 2 qts. | Unsifted Pastry Flour | 2 lbs., 8 oz. |
| 1 qt. | Fat | 2 lbs. |
| 2 qts. | Diced Onions | 3 lbs. |
| 6 qts. | Gravy | 15 lbs. |
| ½ c. | Salt | 5 oz. |
| 2 tbsp. | Pepper | |

**METHOD**

1. The steaks should be cut ½-inch thick.
2. Dip each piece in the flour and sauté in the fat until brown on both sides. Place in a roasting pan so that the steaks overlap.
3. Sprinkle finely diced onions over the meat, add gravy and seasonings.
4. Cover the pan and bake in a slow oven (325°F.) until the meat is tender (approx. 1½ to 2 hours).

**YIELD**

100 4-oz. servings.

## SPANISH STEAK

Reduce gravy to 4 quarts and add 2 quarts tomato sauce or canned tomatoes.

## SWISS STEAK WITH BROILED MUSHROOMS

Select 200 large mushroom caps and wash.
Sauté in butter until golden brown.
Serve whole on top of the Swiss Steak.

## BRAISED LAMB OR MUTTON

|  |  |  |
|---|---|---|
|  | Stewing Lamb or Mutton | 50 lbs. |
| ¾ c. | Salt | 7 oz. |

**METHOD**

1. Trim meat of excess fat and cut into 5-oz. portions.
2. Braise in a moderate oven (350°F.) for 1 hour. Pour off the melted fat and add the salt.
3. Add boiling water to a depth of about ¼ inch. Cover and continue cooking until the meat is tender.

Serve with baked rice and curry sauce or brown gravy made from the liquid in the pan.

**YIELD**

100 3-oz. servings.

## LAMB STEW

|  |  |  |
|---|---|---|
|  | Lean, Boneless Lamb | 35 lbs. |
| 2 qts. | Chopped Onions | 3 lbs. |
| 1½ qts. | Unsifted Pastry Flour | 1 lb., 14 oz. |
| 3 gals. | Lamb Stock or Water | 30 lbs. |
| 3½ qts. | Diced Celery | 4 lbs., 8 oz. |
| 3 qts. | Diced Carrots | 4 lbs., 8 oz. |
| ½ c. | Salt | 5 oz. |
| 2 tsp. | Pepper |  |

**METHOD**

1. Follow the general directions for making stew but do not cook the onions in the fat until the meat has been lifted out and the fat measured (leave only 1½ pts.).
2. Add the chopped celery and carrots about 1 hour before the meat is tender.

**YIELD**

100 7-oz. servings.

## IRISH STEW

|  | Lean Stewing Lamb or |  |
|---|---|---|
|  | Mutton | 28 lbs. |
| 2½ gals. | Hot Water | 25 lbs. |
| 3½ qts. | Diced Onions | 5 lbs., 4 oz. |
| 3½ qts. | Diced Carrots | 5 lbs., 4 oz. |
| 3½ qts. | Diced Potatoes | 5 lbs., 4 oz. |
| 2 qts. | Unsifted Pastry Flour | 2 lbs., 8 oz. |
| 3 qts. | Cold Water | 7 lbs., 8 oz. |
| ¾ c. | Salt | 7 oz. |
| 2 #2 tins | Peas | 2 lbs., 8 oz. |

**METHOD**

1. Cut meat into 1-inch pieces.
2. Add boiling water and simmer until the meat is almost tender.
3. Add diced raw vegetables and continue cooking until the meat and vegetables are done.
4. Mix flour and cold water. Strain. Add gradually to stew, stirring constantly. Cook until there is no taste of raw starch.
5. Add the salt and green peas.

**NOTE**

By increasing the potatoes to 12 lbs. and omitting the flour and cold water, Irish stew may be served as a main dish without side vegetables.

**YIELD**

100 8-oz. servings.

## CURRIED LAMB

| | | |
|---|---|---|
| | Boneless Lamb | 30 lbs. |
| | Twice Recipe for Curry Sauce (page 285) | |
| 1 pt. | Raisins | 13 oz. |
| 1 gal. | Diced Celery | 5 lbs. |
| 2 qts. | Diced Carrots | 3 lbs. |
| 1 #10 tin | Green Peas (drained) | 4 lbs. |

**METHOD**

1. Cut the lamb into 1″ dice and braise as in making stew.
2. When brown, lift from the fat, drain well, and add to the curry sauce.
3. Add the raisins.
4. Cover closely and simmer for 1 hour.
5. Add the diced celery and carrots. Simmer until the meat and vegetables are almost tender.
6. Add the drained peas and cook 10 minutes longer.
7. Serve on steamed or boiled rice with fried onion rings.

**YIELD**

100 5-oz. servings.

**NOTE**

Beef or veal may be substituted for lamb.

## VEAL STEW

|              | Boneless Veal                      | 30 lbs.        |
|--------------|------------------------------------|----------------|
| 1½ pts.      | Fat                                | 1 lb., 8 oz.   |
| 1½ qts.      | Unsifted Pastry Flour              | 1 lb., 14 oz.  |
| ½ c.         | Salt                               | 5 oz.          |
| 1 tbsp.      | Pepper                             |                |
| 2 gals.      | Water or Stock                     | 20 lbs.        |
| 1½ gals.     | Raw Onions, quartered              |                |
|              |   and blanched                     | 9 lbs.         |
| 1½ gals.     | Diced Celery                       | 7 lbs., 8 oz.  |
| 1½ #10 tins  | Tomatoes                           | 9 lbs., 8 oz.  |
| 2 #10 tins   | Green Beans or                     |                |
|              | Green Peas (drained)               | 8 lbs.         |

**METHOD**

1. Cut the meat into 1½″ to 2″ dice.
2. Follow the general directions for making stew (page 160) but do not cook the onions in the fat.
3. Add the blanched onions and the celery 1 hour before the end of the cooking period. Keep the stew closely covered.
4. Add the tomatoes and drained green beans or peas 15 minutes before the end of the cooking period.
5. Serve very hot with potatoes. No other vegetable is required.

**NOTE**

To blanch onions, place in a large quantity of boiling water, cover the pan, remove from heat and leave for 5 minutes. Drain well.

**YIELD**

100 10-oz. servings.

**VARIATION**

Beef may be substituted for veal to make beef stew.

## POT ROASTS OF BEEF

Pot roasting is used for the less tender cuts of meat, such as the rump, chuck and round.

### Boneless Meat, 35 lbs.

**METHOD I**

1. Cut the meat into 7- to 8-lb. pieces, roll and tie.
2. Grease and salt the meat.
3. Braise for 1 hour in the oven at 350°F.
4. Make a brown gravy from the glaze in the pans, according to recipe, page 161. A few carrots and onions added to the gravy will improve the flavour.
5. Place the roasts in a pot. Add the gravy and cover tightly.
6. Simmer until tender on top of the stove or in a slow oven (325°F.). Approximate time allowance for simmering: 30-35 minutes per inch thickness of roast.

**METHOD II**

1. Prepare the roasts and braise as in Method I.
2. Add a small quantity of water, about $\frac{1}{4}$ inch to each pan. Cover closely.
3. Simmer on top of the stove or in the oven at 325°F. until tender.
4. Diced vegetables may be added 1 hour before the roast is completely cooked.
5. Serve the roast with gravy made from the liquid in the pan. If necessary, add brown gravy stock to make 1½ gallons of gravy.

**YIELD**

100 4-oz. servings.

## VARIATIONS FOR POT ROAST GRAVY

1. Add vegetables as in recipe for Vegetable Gravy, page 286.
2. Use canned tomatoes as part of the liquid in the gravy.
3. Add sliced sautéd mushrooms to the gravy before serving.
4. Sauté 1 pint finely chopped green pepper to the gravy before serving.

## MOCK DUCK

| | |
|---|---:|
| **Boneless Chucks or Hips of Beef** | **30 lbs.** |
| **Dressing** | **12 lbs.** |

**METHOD**

1. Cut lean beef in ½-inch slices—about 12 inches by 10 inches in size.
2. Spread with dressing, roll and tie. Or use thicker pieces of meat, slit them lengthwise, and insert the dressing in the pocket so formed. Tie with string. Brush with grease and salt.
3. Braise for 1 hour at 350°F. Baste frequently.
4. Add hot water to the depth of ¼ inch in the roast pan. Cover and continue cooking until the meat is tender (approx. 1 hour).
5. Prepare gravy from the liquid in the pan.

**YIELD**

100 3-oz. servings.

## DRESSING FOR MOCK DUCK

| | | |
|---|---|---|
| 3½ gals. | **Fresh Bread** | 8 lbs., 12 oz. |
| 1½ pts. | **Margarine** | 1 lb., 14 oz. |
| 3 pts. | **Raw Diced Onions** | 2 lbs., 4 oz. |
| 1 tbsp. | **Pepper** | |
| ¼ c. | **Salt** | |
| ¾ c. | **Savoury, Thyme, Basil** | 1¼ oz. |

**METHOD**

1. Crumb the bread or cut into fine cubes after removing the crusts. Add seasonings.
2. Melt butter, add finely diced onion and cook thoroughly.
3. Combine crumbs, fat and onion.
   (If stale bread is used, add 1 quart of milk or stock.)

**NOTE**

This is a standard dressing suitable for beef, lamb or veal.

## BRAISED HEART WITH DRESSING

| | Beef or Veal Hearts | 31 lbs. |
|---|---|---|
| 1 pt. | Fat | 1 lb. |
| 1 qt. | Raw Chopped Onions | 1 lb., 8 oz. |
| 1 qt. | Raw Diced Celery | 1 lb., 4 oz. |
| ½ pt. | Sage, Thyme, Savoury | |
| 3 gals. | Fresh Bread Crumbs | 7 lbs., 8 oz. |
| 3 tbsp. | Salt | 2 oz. |
| 1 tbsp. | Pepper | |

**METHOD**

1. Wash the hearts thoroughly in warm water.
2. Remove all valves and blood-vessels.
3. Trim off fat.
4. Wash and drain.
5. Melt the fat and cook onions and celery until the onions are clear.
6. Mix the seasonings and bread crumbs and add to the fat and vegetables.
7. Fill the hearts and sew or skewer the openings if necessary.
8. Place the hearts in a greased baking pan, brush with fat and braise in the oven (350°F.) for 1 hour. Turn at least once.
9. Add a small quantity of water. Cover closely and either simmer or cook in a slow oven (325°F.) until tender (3 to 4 hours).
10. Make gravy, using the stock in the pan.
11. Cut the cooked hearts across the grain in ⅓" to ½" slices.
12. Serve very hot with gravy.

**NOTE**

Large beef hearts may have to be covered with water in order to make them tender.

**YIELD**

100 4½-oz. servings.

## BRAISED SPARERIBS

|         | Spareribs                    | 40 lbs. |
|---------|------------------------------|---------|
| ½ c.    | Salt                         | 5 oz.   |
| 2 tsp.  | Pepper                       |         |
|         | Water or Stock               |         |
|         | Pork Dressing (page 181)     |         |

**METHOD**

1. Cut the spareribs into 100 servings, weighing about 6 oz. each.
2. Place in roasting pans—they should not be stacked. Brush with fat.
3. Bake in a moderate oven (375°F.) until brown.
4. Add seasonings and just enough water to cover the bottom of the pan. Cover closely.
5. Bake in a slow oven (325°F.) until the meat will slip from the ribs (1½-2 hours).
6. Serve very hot with Pork Dressing.

**YIELD**

100 approx. 6-oz. servings.

## SPARERIBS WITH BARBECUE SAUCE

**METHOD**

1. Cook as in preparing Braised Spareribs.
2. Pour 1½ gals. of Barbecue Sauce over the browned meat in place of the water.
3. Bake until the meat will slip from the bones.
4. Serve very hot, without dressing.

**YIELD**

100 approx. 6-oz. servings.

## SWEET SOUR SPARERIBS

|         | Spareribs                    | 20 lbs.         |
| ------- | ---------------------------- | --------------- |
|         | Spareribs                    | 20 lbs.         |
| 1 c.    | Honey                        | 10 oz.          |
| 4 c.    | Brown Sugar                  | 1 lb., 6 oz.    |
| ½ c.    | Celery Seed                  |                 |
| ½ c.    | Chili Powder                 |                 |
| 8 cloves| Garlic                       |                 |
| 1 c.    | Freshly Grated Horse-radish  | 6 oz.           |
| 1 c.    | Red Currant Jelly            | 8 oz.           |
| ⅓ c.    | Salt                         | 3 oz.           |
| 1 gal.  | Tomato Juice                 | 10 lbs.         |
| 3 qts.  | Stock                        | 7 lbs., 8 oz.   |
| 1 qt.   | Vinegar                      | 2 lbs., 8 oz.   |

**METHOD**

1. Cut meat into pieces 3″ x 4″. Place in roast pans, meat side up and brown in the oven at 400°F. Drain off the fat.
2. Mix the remaining ingredients and pour over the meat.
3. Bake at 325°F. until the meat is tender and thoroughly cooked. Baste every half hour.
4. Serve two pieces per person.

**NOTE**

If fresh horseradish is not available use ¾ oz. of the dried or 6 oz. of the bottled.

**YIELD**

100 servings.

## TIME-TABLE FOR SIMMERED MEAT

| Meat | Average weight | Minutes per lb. |
|---|---|---|
| **BEEF** | | |
| Brisket, Plate or Flank | 7 to 8 lbs. | 35 to 45 |
| Rolled | 4 to 6 lbs. | 40 to 50 |
| Corned | 7 to 8 lbs. | 35 to 45 |
| | 4 to 6 lbs. | 40 to 50 |
| **MUTTON** | | |
| Boned and Rolled | 7 to 8 lbs. | 35 to 45 |
| **PORK** | | |
| Sweet Pickled | 10 to 12 lbs. | 40 to 45 |
| | 8 to 10 lbs. | 45 to 50 |
| **HAM**—Smoked, Bone in | | |
| Large | 12 to 16 lbs. | 15 to 20 |
| Small | 10 to 12 lbs. | 20 to 25 |
| Half | 8 to 10 lbs. | 25 to 30 |
| Picnic | 4 to 8 lbs. | 35 to 45 |
| **HAM**—Boneless | | |
| Cottage Roll | 4 to 7 lbs. | 45 |
| Large | 12 to 16 lbs. | 15 |
| Small | 10 to 12 lbs. | 20 |
| Half | 6 to 8 lbs. | 25 |
| **TONGUE** | | |
| Fresh | 3½ to 4 lbs. | 50 to 60 |
| Pickled | 3½ to 4 lbs. | 50 to 60 |

## SIMMERED FRESH MEAT

|          | Boneless Meat    | 38 lbs. |
|----------|------------------|---------|
| 2 qts.   | Raw Carrots      | 3 lbs.  |
| 2 qts.   | Raw Onions       | 3 lbs.  |
| ¼ c.     | Salt             | 2 oz.   |
| 5 gals.  | Boiling Water    | 50 lbs. |

**METHOD**

1. Cut the meat into 7- to 8-lb. pieces, roll and tie.
2. Place in stock pot. Add vegetables, seasoning and boiling water. The meat must be completely covered with water throughout the cooking period.
3. Simmer for 2 to 3 hours, or until tender. Do not boil. Skim frequently.
4. Serve cold or serve hot with vegetable sauce.

**NOTE**

Left-over stock may be used for soup.

**YIELD**

100 4-oz. servings.

## VEGETABLE SAUCE FOR SIMMERED BEEF OR MUTTON

|          | Beef Fat or Shortening    | 8 oz.   |
|----------|---------------------------|---------|
| ½ pt.    | Beef Fat or Shortening    | 8 oz.   |
| 1 pt.    | Unsifted Pastry Flour     | 10 oz.  |
| 1 gal.   | Stock from Boiled Meat    | 10 lbs. |
| ½ gal.   | Diced Cooked Vegetables   | 4 lbs.  |
| 5 tsp.   | Salt                      | 1 oz.   |

**METHOD**

1. Blend fat and flour. Cook 4 to 5 minutes, stirring constantly.
2. Add hot stock gradually. Stir until smooth. Cook until there is no taste of raw starch. Strain.
3. Add cooked vegetables (carrots, onions, celery, peas) and salt.

**YIELD**

100 2½-oz. servings.

**VARIATION**

Add 1½ cups horseradish, grated.

## PICKLED BEEF OR PORK

| | | |
|---|---|---|
| 5 gals. | Water | 50 lbs. |
| 2 qts. | Salt | 6 lbs., 4 oz. |
| | Saltpetre | 2½ oz. |
| | Mixed Spice, Whole | 1 lb. |
| 2½ pts. | Brown Sugar | 2 lbs., 3 oz. |
| | Beef or Pork | 50-100 lbs. |

**METHOD**

1. Heat 1 gallon of water and add the salt, saltpetre, spice tied in a bag, and the sugar. Stir until the salt is dissolved.
2. Add to the balance of the water. Chill.
3. Keep in a covered tub that has no metal fittings.
4. Cut the meat into pieces of uniform size (5 to 8 lbs.). Place in the brine, leave for 2 to 3 weeks in a refrigerator. Put a loosefitting cover on the meat and weigh it down so that the meat will be entirely submerged.

**NOTE**

1. To shorten the time required for pickling to 5 to 6 days, increase the salt to 10 lbs.
2. The flavour of the meat will be improved by adding to the brine 1 lb. each of raw sliced carrot, onion and celery.
3. Use only fresh meat. For suitable cuts see Beef and Pork Charts.

## SIMMERED PICKLED MEAT

**1. Corned Beef.**
**2. Pickled Pork.**

**METHOD**

1. Wash the meat before cooking.
2. Use the method and quantity given for simmered fresh meat, page 175.
3. When the pickled meat is half cooked, taste the water. If the water is very salty, pour it off and finish cooking the meat in fresh boiling water.

## SIMMERED TONGUE

### Pickled Beef Tongue, 50 lbs.

**METHOD**

1. Wash the tongues in warm water.
2. Cook according to the general method for pickled meat until the tongue is tender (3 to 4 hours).
3. Remove from water. Plunge into cold water. Skin and cut away the roots.
4. Return to cooking water and reheat. Carve across the grain into $\frac{1}{2}$" slices.
5. Serve hot with Raisin Sauce, Horseradish Sauce or mustard.

**NOTE**

If tongues are to be served cold, allow them to cool in the water in which they were cooked. When cool, remove from the liquid, skin and trim.

For jellied tongue, add gelatine to the water in which they were cooked, tasting water beforehand to be sure that it is not too salty.

**YIELD**

100 4- to 5-oz. servings.

## SIMMERED SMOKED HAM

### Smoked Ham (Boneless), 25 lbs. A.P.

**METHOD**

1. Follow the method used for simmering fresh meat. Consult chart (page 174) for time required.
2. Remove ham from the liquid and take off the skin. Save the ham stock for split pea or bean soup.
3. If ham is very fat, trim.
4. Serve the ham hot with Raisin, Orange or Tartare Sauce, or with mustard.

**YIELD**

100 3-oz. servings.


## GLAZED HAM

### Simmered Ham
### Brown Sugar
### Mustard

**METHOD**

1. Rub a mixture of brown sugar and mustard over the surface of the skinned ham, allowing 1 tsp. mustard to 1 cup of brown sugar.
2. Bake the ham in a hot oven until the glaze is a golden brown.
3. Serve with the same sauces as for boiled ham.

**NOTE**

1. Corn or Maple syrup may be substituted for half the brown sugar.
2. Whole cloves may be pushed into the ham after the glaze has been put on and before the ham is baked.

# DRY ROASTS

## MEAT SUITABLE FOR ROASTING

Only tender meat should be roasted. If there is any doubt because of the cut or the quality or age of the meat, it is always wiser to cook the meat by pot-roasting.

| BEEF | VEAL | LAMB | PORK | MUTTON |
|------|------|------|------|--------|
| Prime Ribs | Leg | Leg | Leg | Leg |
| Long Loin | Loin | Loin | Loin | Loin |
| Rump (variable) | Rib | Shoulder | Shoulder | (see note) |
| Beef Loaf | Shoulder | Patties | Spareribs | |
| Meat Balls | Veal Loaf | | Sausage-loaf | |

**NOTE**

Unless the mutton is of a very superior quality it should be simmered rather than roasted.

## TIME-TABLE FOR ROASTING ROLLED BONELESS MEAT

| Meat | Weight in lbs. | Oven temp. | No. of min. per inch of the diam. | Stage to which cooked | Internal temp. when cooked |
|------|------|------|------|------|------|
| Beef | 10-12 | 325°F. | 20 min. | Rare | 140°F. |
| | | 325°F. | 25 min. | Medium | 160°F. |
| | | 325°F. | 30 min. | Well-done | 170°F. |
| Lamb | 5-6 | 325°F. | 25 min. | Well-done | 180°F. |
| Mutton | 5-8 | 325°F. | 30 min. | Well-done | 180°F. |
| Pork | 10-12 | 325°F. | 45 min. | Well-done | 185°F. |
| Pork, smoked | 10-12 | 325°F. | 25 min. | Well-done | 170°F. |
| Pork, smoked, tenderized | 10-12 | 325°F. | 20 min. | Well-done | 170°F. |
| Veal | 5-8 | 325°F. | | Well-done | 180°F. |

## ROASTS OF MEAT

### Boneless Tender Meat, 35 lbs.

**METHOD**

1. Place the roasts in a greased pan.
2. If the meat is lean, coat with dripping or place pieces of suet on the top.
3. Bake in a slow oven, 300°-325°F., according to the table given for roasting meat. When cooked at this temperature, it is not necessary to baste the meat.

**YIELD**

100 4-oz. servings.

## DRESSINGS FOR ROAST MEAT

(For Lamb or Beef Dressing. see page 170.)

## VEAL DRESSING

| | | |
|---|---|---|
| 1½ pts. | Bacon or Chicken Fat | 1 lb., 8 oz. |
| 6 tbsp. | Finely Chopped Onions | |
| 6 tbsp. | Lemon Rind | |
| ½ pt. | Lemon Juice | 10 oz. |
| 3 gals. | Fresh Bread Crumbs | 7 lbs., 8 oz. |
| ½ c. | Salt | 5 oz. |
| 1 tbsp. | Pepper | |
| ½ c. | Thyme or Savoury | |

**METHOD**

1. Combine the ingredients as in making pork dressing.
2. Serve with roast veal or baked veal chops.

**NOTE**

1½ pts. Margarine or Butter (1 lb., 14 oz.) may be used in place of fat given above.

**YIELD**

100 1½-oz. servings.

## PORK DRESSING

| 1 pt. | Fat | 1 lb. |
|---|---|---|
| 2 c. | Finely Chopped Onions | 12 oz. |
| 8 qts. | Fresh Bread Crumbs | 5 lbs. |
| 12 | Medium Apples (diced) | 4 lbs. |
| 6 tbsp. | Salt | 4 oz. |
| 4 tsp. | Pepper | |
| 6 tbsp. | Sage | |

**METHOD**

1. Cook onions in the fat for 15 minutes or until tender.
2. Combine all ingredients.

**YIELD**

100 1½-oz. servings.

## DRESSED PORK TENDERLOIN

**Pork Tenderloins, 35 lbs.**
**Pork Dressing, 11 lbs.**

**METHOD**

1. Trim the fat and skin from the tenderloins.
2. Slit each tenderloin along the edge, so that it can be spread out flat.
3. Make several lengthwise cuts in the muscle, without slitting it through. When this is done, it can be formed into a roll more easily.
4. Cover half the tenderloins with dressing.
5. Put the other tenderloins on top. Arrange each pair so that the narrow end of one is placed at the wide end of the other. Tie securely.
6. Place in roasting pans. Brush lightly with fat. Cover and roast in a slow oven (300°-325°F.) for 1 to 1½ hours.

**NOTE**

When baked in uncovered pans, baste with boiling water to which dripping has been added (2 tbsp. dripping to 1 pt. water).

**YIELD**

100 5-oz. servings.

## STEAKS AND CHOPS

Tender steaks and chops are cooked by pan-broiling. The steaks and chops will have a better flavour and be more moist and tender if the fat which melts out from the meat is not allowed to collect in the pan, but is ladled or poured off when it becomes more than about $\frac{1}{8}''$ in depth.

When large quantities are being cooked, the steaks or chops may be browned by pan-broiling and then finished in the oven.

### MEATS WHICH CAN BE PAN-BROILED

| BEEF | VEAL | LAMB | MUTTON | PORK | SMOKED HAM |
|------|------|------|--------|------|------------|
| Steaks from long loin Steaks from prime rib Hamburgers | Chops Steaks | Rib chops Loin chops Shoulder chops Leg chops Patties | Loin chops | Loin chops Rib chops Sausages Sausage cakes | Sliced butt Sliced bacon |

## TIME-TABLE FOR PAN-BROILING

| Meat | Thickness | Rare | Medium | Well-done |
|------|-----------|------|--------|-----------|
| **BEEF** | | | | |
| Indiv. Steaks | ½" | 5 min. | 8 min. | 10 min. |
| Indiv. Steaks | 1" | 10 min. | 12 min. | 15 min. |
| Indiv. Steaks | 1½" | 20 min. | 25 min. | 30 min. |
| Indiv. Steaks | 2" | 30 min. | 35 min. | 40 min. |
| Hamburgers | ¼" | | 5 min. | 8 min. |
| Hamburgers | ½" | | 8 min. | 10 min. |
| Hamburg Steak | 1" | | 15 min. | 20 min. |
| **LAMB** | | | | |
| All chops | ½" | (Never | 10 min. | 15 min. |
| | 1" | served | 20 min. | 25 min. |
| Patties | 1" | rare) | | 20 min. |
| **MUTTON** | | | | |
| Loin chops | ½" | (Never | 10 min. | 15 min. |
| | 1" | rare) | 15 min. | 20 min. |
| **PORK** | | | | |
| Chops | ½" | (Never | (Never | 15 min. |
| | 1"– | rare) | medium) | 25 min. |
| Sausages | 1" | (Never | (Never | 12 min. |
| Sausage Cakes | 1"– | rare) | medium) | 25 min. |
| Ham Slices | ½" | (Never | (Never | 20 min. |
| | 1" | rare) | medium) | 25 min. |
| Bacon | ⅛" | (Never rare) | (Never medium) | 4-5 min. |
| **VEAL** | | | | |
| All Chops | ½" | (Never rare) | 8 min. | 10 min. |
| | 1" | (Never rare) | 12 min. | 20 min. |
| Steak (from leg) | ½" | (Never rare) | 12 min. | 15 min. |

## PAN-BROILED STEAK

**METHOD**

1. Trim and cut 100 5-oz. steaks suitable for broiling.
2. Heat heavy roasting pans or griddles and rub them over with trimmings of fat or suet, leaving only a thin film of grease in the pan.
3. Put the steaks in the pan. Leave without turning until the underside is browned.
4. Season with salt and pepper and turn.
5. Continue cooking until the steaks are done.
6. Steaks should be cooked quickly, but the pan should never become hot enough to cause the fat to smoke.
7. Cooking time:

|  | **ONE-INCH STEAK** | **ONE HALF-INCH STEAK** |
|---|---|---|
| Rare | 5-7 minutes | 3 minutes |
| Medium | 6-8 minutes | 4 minutes |
| Well done | 8-10 minutes | 5 minutes |

**NOTE**

When space on top of the stove is limited, the steaks may be cooked rare and finished in a moderate oven (6-8 minutes).

## SAUTÉD LIVER

|  |  |  |
|---|---|---|
|  | **Liver** | **25 lbs.** |
| 1/4 c. | **Salt** | **2 oz.** |
| 2 tbsp. | **Pepper** |  |
| 2 qts. | **Unsifted Pastry Flour** | **2 lbs., 8 oz.** |

**METHOD**

1. Cut liver into slices of 1/2 inch thickness, allowing 4 oz. per serving.
2. Add salt and pepper to flour.
3. Dip slices of liver into flour.
4. Sauté in hot fat, until the liver is well browned and cooked through to the centre. Turn once.
5. Serve with brown gravy, onion gravy or bacon.

**NOTE**

1. Liver becomes very hard and dry when overcooked or sautéd at too high a temperature.
2. Liver may be browned on top of the stove and the cooking finished in a moderate oven.

## BACON

**200 moderately thick slices, 12 lbs.**

**METHOD**

1. Arrange bacon in large pans with the slices slightly overlapping.
2. Cook in a moderate oven (350°F.) until the fat is a light brown.
3. Lift bacon from the fat and drain. Transfer to an ungreased pan. When possible, place paper on a rack in the pan in order to drain off the fat more thoroughly.

## BAKED HAM SLICES

|  | **Boneless Smoked Ham** | **25 lbs.** |
|---|---|---|
| **1 tbsp.** | **Ground Cloves** | |
| **1 tbsp.** | **Dry Mustard** | |
| **1 pt.** | **Brown Sugar** | **14 oz.** |
| **1½ qts.** | **Cider or Fruit Juice** | **3 lbs., 12 oz.** |

**METHOD**

1. Cut the ham into ¼" slices weighing approximately 3½ oz.
2. Place a single layer of slices in each roasting pan.
3. Combine the spices and sugar. Rub into the ham.
4. Pour the liquid around the ham. It should not cover the meat.
5. Bake in a slow oven (325°F.) for 30 to 45 minutes or until the top is browned.
6. Serve hot.

**YIELD**

100 3-oz. servings.

**VARIATIONS**

1. After rubbing in the sugar and spices, place on each slice of ham, either thin slices of unpeeled orange or half a cooked pear or peach, or 1 slice of pineapple. Baste occasionally with the liquid in the pan.
2. Omit spices and brown sugar, substitute Mustard Sauce (page 291).
3. Omit spices and sugar. Spread one of the following on each slice. Baste occasionally with the liquid in the pan.

**Cranberry and Honey** — 2½ qts. unsweetened cooked cranberries mixed with 4 c. honey.

**Cranberry Sauce** — 2½ qts. sweetened Cranberry Sauce mixed with 3 c. light corn syrup.

## BAKED PORK CHOPS

**100 6-oz. Chops**
**Recipe Pork Dressing (page 181)**

**METHOD**

1. Trim the pork chops, leaving about ¼″ fat or less.
2. Arrange in baking pans and spread with pork dressing (1″ deep).
3. Bake in a moderate oven (350°F.) until the chops are well done (30-40 minutes).

**YIELD**

100 6-oz. servings.

## PAN-BROILED SAUSAGES

**Sausages, 25 lbs.**

**METHOD**

1. Cut the sausage links. Prick each sausage with a fork.
2. Place sausages in heavy, hot, ungreased roasting pans over a moderate heat.
3. Cook on top of stove until done—10 to 12 minutes. Turn so that they brown evenly on all sides.
4. Ladle fat from pan as in cooking bacon.

**NOTE**

Sausages may be baked in a slow oven (325°F.). When done in this way, they do not need pricking. Ladle out fat when half done. Time—25 to 30 minutes.

**YIELD**

100 2- to 2½-oz. servings.

## SAUSAGES BAKED IN TOMATO SAUCE

|  | Sausages | 25 lbs. |
|---|---|---|
| 1½ gals. | Tomato Sauce (page 287) | 15 lbs. |

**METHOD**

1. Pan sausages and bake for 15 minutes in a moderate oven (350°F.).
2. Ladle off the fat.
3. Pour the hot Tomato Sauce over the half-cooked sausages.
4. Return to the oven, cover, and bake for 20 minutes.

**YIELD**

100 4½ to 5-oz. servings.

## SAUSAGE ROLLS

**25 lbs. Sausage**
**Standard Recipe for Pastry (page 216)**
**or**
**Standard Recipe for Tea Biscuits (page 340)**

**METHOD**

1. Separate the sausages.
2. Roll pie dough ⅛" thick or tea biscuit dough ¼" thick and cut into oblong pieces large enough to cover one or two sausages, depending on the size of the sausage.
3. Roll the sausage in the pastry dough, leaving the ends open. Seal the edge by moistening the under surface with water and pressing the upper edge on to it with a fork.
4. Place on baking sheets and cook in a hot oven (425°F.) until the pastry is brown and the sausage is cooked (20 to 30 minutes).
5. Serve hot with Chili, Tomato or Barbecue Sauce.

**YIELD**

100 to 150 rolls.

## SAUSAGE BAKED WITH SWEET POTATO AND APPLE

|          | Sausages or Sausage Meat | 20 lbs.        |
|----------|--------------------------|----------------|
|          | Sweet Potatoes or Yams   | 20 lbs.        |
| 3 gals.  | Cored, Sliced Apples     | 15 lbs.        |
| 2 qts.   | Brown Sugar              | 3 lbs., 8 oz.  |

**METHOD**

1. Par-cook sausages or sausage meat as directed on page 186.
2. Boil the sweet potatoes. When cool, peel and cut into half inch slices.
3. Cover the bottom of a greased baking dish with half the sweet potatoes. Sprinkle with salt.
4. Arrange the partly cooked sausages on top and cover them with the apples.
5. Sprinkle lightly with part of the brown sugar.
6. Place the rest of the sweet potatoes over the apples. Moisten with a little water, sprinkle with the remainder of the brown sugar and a small amount of salt.
7. Bake at 375°F. until the apples are tender and the sausages thoroughly cooked ($\frac{3}{4}$ to 1 hour).

**YIELD**

100 8-oz. servings.

## SAUSAGES BAKED WITH APPLE

|  | Sausages or Sausage Meat | 25 lbs. |
|---|---|---|
| 5 gals. | Cored Sliced Apples | 25 lbs. |
| 2 qts. | Brown Sugar | 3 lbs., 8 oz. |

**METHOD**

1. Simmer sausages for 10 minutes. Drain. If sausage meat is used, shape into 2-oz. patties and bake at 350°F. for 15 minutes. Ladle off the fat.
2. Spread half the sliced apples (cut one-quarter inch thick) on the bottom of the bake pans.
3. Arrange the partly cooked sausages on top and cover with the remaining apples.
4. Sprinkle with the brown sugar.
5. Bake at 400°F. for 10 minutes. Lower the heat to 375°F. and continue baking until the apples are tender and the sausage thoroughly cooked (about 15 minutes).

**YIELD**

100 8-oz. servings.


## HEAD CHEESE

|  | **A** |  |
|---|---|---|
|  | Pork Trimmings | 18 lbs. |
|  | **B** |  |
| 1 pt. | Diced Onion | 12 oz. |
| 1 | Small Bay Leaf |  |
|  | Celery Stalks and Leaves | 4 oz. |
| 2 tsp. | Sage |  |
| 2 cloves | Garlic |  |
|  | **C** |  |
| 1½ gals. | Boiling Water | 15 lbs. |
|  | **D** |  |
| 3⅓ c. | Gelatine | 1 lb., 4 oz. |
|  | **E** |  |
| 1½ qts. | Fresh Bread Crumbs | 1 lb. |
| 5 tbsp. | Salt | 3 oz. |
| 1 tbsp. | Pepper |  |

**METHOD**

Follow the method for Jellied Veal.

**YIELD**

100 4-oz. servings.

## JELLIED VEAL

|  | **A** |  |
|---|---|---|
|  | Lean Boneless Veal | 18 lbs. |
|  | **B** |  |
| 1 pt. | Diced Onion | 12 oz. |
| 1 | Small Bay Leaf |  |
|  | Celery Stalks and Leaves | 4 oz. |
|  | **C** |  |
| 1½ gals. | Boiling Water | 15 lbs. |
|  | **D** |  |
| 3⅓ c. | Gelatine | 1 lb., 4 oz. |
|  | **E** |  |
| 5 tbsp. | Salt | 3 oz. |
| 1 tbsp. | Pepper |  |

**METHOD**

1. Cut A into half inch dice.
2. Tie B in a thin bag.
3. Add A and B to C and simmer until A is tender (1½ to 2 hours).
4. Strain. Remove B. Dice or shred A.
5. Cool the stock and remove the fat.
6. Add the cool stock to D. Mix well and let stand until the gelatine is thoroughly moistened. Heat until the gelatine is completely dissolved. Add A and E. Stir well.
7. Pour into moistened moulds. Chill.
8. To serve, cut into one-quarter inch slices.

**NOTE**

One or more of the following may be added:
1. Finely chopped red or green peppers.
2. Diced ham.
3. Diced hard-cooked eggs.
4. Finely chopped parsley.
5. Sliced stuffed olives.

**YIELD**

100 4-oz. servings.

## BREADED VEAL CUTLET

|          | Boneless Veal Leg       | 38 lbs.        |
|----------|-------------------------|----------------|
| 3 tbsp.  | Salt                    | 2 oz.          |
| 2 tsp.   | Pepper                  |                |
| 1½ qts.  | Unsifted Pastry Flour   | 1 lb., 14 oz.  |
| 2        | Eggs                    |                |
| 1 qt.    | Milk                    | 2 lbs., 8 oz.  |
| 2 qts.   | Dry, Sifted Bread Crumbs | 2 lbs.        |

### METHOD

1. Cut the veal into 5-oz. servings, ½" thick.
2. Mix the salt and pepper with the flour.
3. Beat the eggs and add the milk.
4. Dip each piece of meat in the seasoned flour, then in the egg-wash and then in the sifted bread crumbs.
5. Brown the cutlets in the frying pan, having the fat ⅛" deep.
6. Drain. Arrange in a single layer in a baking pan, or stand the cutlets on edge. Do not pile them, as it spoils their appearance.
7. Cover closely. Bake in a slow oven (325°F.) until cooked through and tender.
8. Serve with Tomato or Barbecue Sauce.

### YIELD

100 4-oz. servings.

### VARIATIONS

A small amount of stock, gravy or tomato sauce may be placed in each baking pan. This will increase the tenderness but if much liquid is added it will spoil the finish.

## VEAL LOAF

|           | Minced Boneless Veal       | 25 lbs.        |
|-----------|----------------------------|----------------|
|           | Minced Lean Boneless Pork  | 5 lbs.         |
| ½ pt.     | Fat                        | 8 oz.          |
| 1 pt.     | Finely Chopped Onions      | 12 oz.         |
| 1½ gals.  | Fresh Bread Crumbs         | 4 lbs.         |
| 3 qts.    | Milk                       | 7 lbs., 8 oz.  |
| ½ c.      | Salt                       | 5 oz.          |
| 2 tsp.    | Pepper                     |                |

**METHOD**

1. Follow the directions given for making Beef Loaf.
2. Serve with Tomato, Spanish, Horseradish or Barbecue Sauce, gravy or vegetable gravy.

**NOTE**

If dried bread crumbs are used, reduce the amount to 3¾ qts. (3 lbs. 12 oz.) and
increase the milk to 1-1¼ gals.

**YIELD**

Approx. 100 5-oz. servings.

**VARIATIONS**

1. Add 1 qt. Finely Chopped Celery or Green Pepper.
2. Add ½ pt. lemon juice and reduce the milk by 1 c.
3. Add ½ c. Worcestershire Sauce.
4. Increase the veal to 30 lbs., omit the fresh pork and add 1 lb. salt pork, minced.
   When this is done, reduce the salt to 4 oz.

## VEAL PATTIES

**METHOD**

1. Prepare the Veal Loaf mixture.
2. Shape into 3 oz. patties 1″ thick.
3. Sauté until well-browned on both sides.
4. Arrange in roasting pans, add a small amount of water. Cover the pan closely.
5. Bake in a slow oven (325°F.) until tender (about 1 hour).
6. Serve with Tomato or Barbecue Sauce.

**YIELD**

200 patties.

## BEEF LOAF

| | | |
|---|---|---|
| 3 qts. | Dry Stale Bread | 3 lbs. |
| 1½ gals. | Milk or Water or Tomato Juice | 15 lbs. |
| 1½ pt. | Raw, Finely Chopped Onion | 1 lb., 2 oz. |
| ¼ c. | Fat | 2 oz. |
| | Minced Lean Beef from Chuck, Neck or Flanks | 35 lbs. |
| ¾ c. | Salt | 7 oz. |
| 1 tbsp. | Pepper | |
| 1 c. | Finely Chopped Parsley Stems | |

### METHOD

1. Break up the bread and soak in the liquid until it is nearly all absorbed. If necessary, stir to break up the lumps.
2. Cook the onions in the fat until tender.
3. Combine all the ingredients.
4. Pack tightly in greased bread tins or shape into 2-lb. loaves and place in roast pans.
5. Bake in a slow oven (325°F.) for 1 hour or until the meat is well-done.
6. Cut 10 slices per loaf. Serve 2 slices per order.
7. Serve with onion or vegetable gravy, Tomato or Chili Sauce.

### YIELD

100 4-oz. servings.

### VARIATIONS

1. One of the following may be substituted for an equal weight of meat:
   10 lbs. minced fresh pork, raw or cooked.
   10 lbs. minced kidney.
   4 lbs. green peas.
   4 lbs. cooked diced carrots.
   8 lbs. cubed cheddar cheese.
   8 lbs. cooked macaroni.
2. Spread Mock Duck dressing between two layers of the beef loaf mixture. This variation cannot be shaped into loaves but must be baked either in loaf tins or in roasting pans and will yield 100 6-oz. servings.
3. **Hamburg steaks.** Shape into flat 6-oz. cakes and panbroil or bake in a slow oven (325°F.). Lift from the pan to drain off the fat. Serve with brown gravy, onion gravy or Tomato Sauce.

## SAUSAGE MEAT

|          | Pork             | 24 lbs. |
|----------|------------------|---------|
|          | Beef             | 8 lbs.  |
| 1 gal.   | Dry Bread Crumbs | 4 lbs.  |
| 2 qts.   | Water            | 5 lbs.  |
| 2 tbsp.  | Sage             |         |
| 2 tbsp.  | Nutmeg           |         |
| 4 tbsp.  | Pepper           | 1 oz.   |
| 9 tbsp.  | Salt             | 6 oz.   |

**METHOD**

1. Grind the meat.
2. Mix remaining ingredients thoroughly.
3. Combine the two mixtures and regrind.
4. Use as sausage meat or make into sausages.

**YIELD**

40 lbs. raw sausage meat (approx.).

## SAUSAGE CAKES OR LOAF

|            | Minced Pork Cuttings  | 25 lbs.         |
|------------|-----------------------|-----------------|
|            | Minced Lean Beef      | 10 lbs.         |
| 3 qts.     | Unsifted Pastry Flour | 3 lbs., 12 oz.  |
| 3 qts.     | Dry Bread Crumbs      | 3 lbs.          |
| 1½ qts.    | Water                 | 3 lbs., 12 oz.  |
| 2 tsp.     | Sage                  |                 |
| 2 tsp.     | Nutmeg                |                 |
| ½ c.       | Salt                  | 5 oz.           |
| 2 tbsp.    | Pepper                |                 |

**METHOD**

1. Combine all the ingredients. Mix thoroughly.
2. Shape into 2-lb. loaves or 6-oz. cakes.
3. Bake in a moderate oven until thoroughly cooked.
Bake sausage loaves at 350°F. for approximately 1½ hours.
Pan broil sausage cakes or bake at 350°F. for approximately 15 minutes.
Serve with brown gravy or apple sauce.

**YIELD**

100 4-oz. servings.

## SCALLOPED BEEF AND RICE

|          |                           |              |
| -------- | ------------------------- | ------------ |
|          | **Lean Raw Beef**         | **20 lbs.**  |
| **1 pt.**    | **Fat**               | **1 lb.**    |
| **1 gal.**   | **Raw, Finely Diced Onions** | **6 lbs.** |
| **2½ qts.**  | **Raw Rice**          | **6 lbs., 4 oz.** |
| **1 gal.**   | **Strained Tomato**   | **10 lbs.**  |
| **1 gal.**   | **Stock**             | **10 lbs.**  |
| **½ c.**     | **Salt**              | **5 oz.**    |

**METHOD**

1. Cut the beef into ½-inch dice and braise for 1 hour.
2. Melt fat, add raw onion and rice. Cook for 10 minutes, stirring continuously.
3. Add hot tomato juice and stock to rice. Bring to boil.
4. Add braised beef, mix well and bake in a covered pan at 325°F. or simmer on top of the stove until tender.

**YIELD**

100 8-oz. servings.

## MEAT SAUCE FOR MACARONI OR SPAGHETTI

|              |                      |                |
| ------------ | -------------------- | -------------- |
|              | Lean Raw Beef        | 20 lbs.        |
| ½ c.         | Bacon Fat            | 4 oz.          |
| 3½ qts.      | Raw Minced Onions    | 5 lbs., 4 oz.  |
| 1 qt.        | Raw Diced Celery     | 1 lb., 4 oz.   |
| 1 clove      | Crushed Garlic       |                |
| ½ c.         | Salt                 | 5 oz.          |
| 2 tbsp.      | Pepper               |                |
| 2 #10 cans   | Tomatoes             | 12 lbs., 12 oz.|
| 2 #10 cans   | Tomato Purée         | 13             |
| 1 gal.       | Beef Stock           | 10             |

**METHOD**

1. Cut the meat into small dice or put through a coarse mincer. Braise in a moderate oven (350°F.) for 45 minutes.
2. Melt the bacon fat, add the onions, celery and garlic and cook slowly until the onions are lightly browned. Stir frequently.
3. Combine all the ingredients. Simmer for 2 to 3 hours.
4. Pour over hot boiled macaroni or spaghetti (page 40).

**YIELD**

Approx. 100 6-oz. servings.

# PREPARED MEATS
## BAKED

|           | Prepared Meat | 25 lbs.        |
|-----------|---------------|----------------|
| 1¾ pts.   | Brown Sugar   | 1 lb., 8 oz.   |
| 1 qt.     | Orange Juice  | 2 lbs., 8 oz.  |
| 2 qts.    | Water         | 5 lbs.         |

**METHOD**

1. Remove the meat from the tins without breaking it.
2. Place the loaves in baking pans and score on the surface.
3. Mix the sugar and orange juice and pour over the meat.
4. Add the water.
5. Bake in a moderate oven (350°F.) for 30 minutes. Baste occasionally.

**YIELD**

100 3 to 4-oz. servings.

**VARIATIONS**

Substitute 1 gal. of Tomato Sauce (page 287) or 1 gal. of Barbecue Sauce (page 288) for the orange juice and water.


## PAN-BROILED

**Prepared Meat, 25 lbs.**

**METHOD**

1. Cut the meat into ¼" slices.
2. Pan-broil until brown on both sides.
3. Serve very hot with Tomato, Spanish or Barbecue Sauce.

**YIELD**

100 3 to 4-oz. servings.

## WIENERS

### Wieners, 25 lbs.

**METHOD**

1. Have a steam-jacketed kettle or stock-pot one-third full of boiling water.
2. Put in the wieners. Cover the pot.
3. Lower the heat and cook below boiling for 5 minutes.

**YIELD**

Approx. 200 wieners.


## SPANISH WIENERS

| | | |
|---|---|---|
| 1 qt. | Finely Chopped Onions | 1 lb., 8 oz. |
| ½ pt. | Fat | 8 oz. |
| ¼ pt. | Vinegar | 5 oz. |
| ½ pt. | Brown Sugar | 8 oz. |
| 1 pt. | Lemon Juice | 1 lb., 4 oz. |
| 1 qt. | Quick Chili Sauce | 2 lbs., 8 oz. |
| 1 qt. | Tomato Purée | 2 lbs., 8 oz. |
| ½ c. | Prepared Mustard | 3 oz. |
| 1 qt. | Chopped Celery | 1 lb., 4 oz. |
| 2 qts. | Water | 5 lbs. |
| | Wieners | 25 lbs. |

**METHOD**

1. Braise the onion in the fat.
2. Add the other ingredients and simmer for 30 minutes.
3. Add the wieners. Cover tightly. Simmer for 30 minutes.

**NOTE**

2 qts. catsup may be substituted for the Quick Chili Sauce and the Purée.

**YIELD**

100 servings of 2 wieners plus 1½ oz. sauce.

## LEFT-OVER MEATS

### BAKED HASH

**A**

| | | |
|---|---|---|
| 3½ gals. | Raw Diced Potatoes | 21 lbs. |
| 1 gal. | Raw Diced Onions | 6 lbs. |
| 2 qts. | Brown Gravy | 5 lbs. |
| 2 qts. | Water | 5 lbs. |
| ½ c. | Salt | 5 oz. |

**B**

| | | |
|---|---|---|
| 2 gals. | Cooked Diced Meat | 16 lbs. |

**METHOD**

1. Combine A, bake in a hot oven (400°F.) or boil on top of the stove until the potatoes are almost tender.
2. Add the diced meat and continue cooking until the potatoes are tender and the meat is hot.

**YIELD**

100 6-oz. servings.


### SHEPHERD'S PIE

**A**

| | | |
|---|---|---|
| ½ pt. | Fat | 8 oz. |
| 1 qt. | Minced Raw Onions | 1 lb., 8 oz. |

**B**

| | | |
|---|---|---|
| 2½ gals. | Minced Cooked Meat | 25 lbs. |
| 3 tbsp. | Salt | 2 oz. |
| 1 tsp. | Pepper | |
| 2 qts. | Stock, Gravy or Tomato Juice | 5 lbs. |

**C**

| | | |
|---|---|---|
| 2½ gals. | Hot Mashed Potatoes (⅔ recipe) | 25 lbs. |

**METHOD**

1. Cook A for 10 minutes or until onion is tender.
2. Combine A and B.
3. Spread in baking pans and heat.
4. Cover with C. (The mashed potatoes should be quite dry).
5. Brush surface with fat and brown in the oven. Serve with Tomato or Chili Sauce or brown gravy.

**YIELD**

100 8-oz. servings.

## MEAT AND POTATO CAKE OR RISSOLE

| 2½ gals. | Mashed Potatoes | 25 lbs. |
| 10 | Eggs | 1 lb. |
| 1½ gals. | Minced Cooked Meat | 15 lbs. |
| 1½ c. | Minced Cooked Onions | 11 oz. |
| ½ c. | Salt | 5 oz. |
| 1 tbsp. | Pepper | |

**METHOD**

1. Combine all the ingredients thoroughly.
2. Mould into 6-oz. cakes.
3. Dip in flour and fry on a griddle or brush with fat and bake for 20 minutes in a hot oven at 400°F.

**NOTE**

1. For Rissole, dip cake in flour, egg wash and bread crumbs. Fry in deep fat at 370°F. till brown. Place in pan and finish heating in oven for 10 minutes.
2. 1 cup chopped parsley may be added.

**YIELD**

100 6-oz. cakes.

## MEAT TURNOVER

**Pie Crust, 20 lbs.**
**Shepherd's Pie Mixture, 20 lbs.**

**METHOD**

1. Roll the crust and cut into 5-inch squares.
2. Place three ounces of meat mixture on one-half of each square.
3. Wash edges with milk. Fold the other half over the meat, press edges of pastry together.
4. Bake on sheets in a hot oven (400°F.) for 30 minutes or until brown.
5. Serve with Tomato Sauce or Chili Sauce

**YIELD**

100 5-oz. turnovers.

## CORNED BEEF HASH I

| | | |
|---|---|---|
| 5 gals. | **Diced Raw Potatoes** | 30 lbs. |
| 2 qts. | **Diced Raw Onions** | 3 lbs. |
| 1 gal. | **Stock** | 10 lbs. |
| | **Canned Corned Beef** | 18 lbs. |

If canned corned beef is not used, buy 30 lbs. boneless corned beef. Cook, trim and remove excess fat.

#### METHOD

1. Combine potatoes, onion and stock.
2. Bake or cook on top of stove until tender.
3. Add diced meat and bake for 30 minutes at 325°F. or simmer on top of stove. If the canned corned beef is very fat, heat separately and pour off melted fat before adding the meat to the vegetables.

#### YIELD

100 8-oz. servings.

## CORNED BEEF HASH II

| | | |
|---|---|---|
| 2 qts. | **Minced Raw Onions** | 3 lbs. |
| 1 pt. | **Fat** | 1 lb. |
| 3½ gals. | **Dry Mashed Potatoes** | 35 lbs. |
| 3 gals. | **Minced Corned Beef** | 18 lbs. |
| | **Salt** | |
| | **Pepper** | |

#### METHOD

1. Cook the minced onion in the fat until tender.
2. Combine the potatoes, minced meat and cooked onion.
3. Add salt and pepper to taste.
4. Spread 2 inches to 3 inches deep in heavy, greased baking pans.
5. Bake in a hot oven until heated through and the under surface is well browned.
6. Cut into portions and serve with the browned side up.

#### YIELD

100 8-oz. servings.

## BAKED LIMA BEANS AND HAM

| | | |
|---|---|---|
| 9 qts. | Dried Lima Beans | 17 lbs. |
| | Cold Water to cover | |
| 3 gals. | Boiling Water | |
| 1 pt. | Raw Diced Onions | 12 oz. |
| 1 qt. | Brown Sugar | 1 lb., 12 oz. |
| 3 tbsp. | Salt | 2 oz. |
| 7½ qts. | Cooked Diced Ham | 15 lbs. |

**METHOD**

1. Pick over and wash the beans. Soak overnight in cold water to cover.
2. Do not drain before cooking. Add boiling water to cover (about 3 gals.) and boil gently until almost tender (1 to 2 hours). They must not be allowed to break up.
3. Drain.
4. Blanch the diced onions in boiling water. Drain.
5. Mix the salt and sugar.
6. Spread a layer of beans in greased baking pans, add a layer of diced ham, sprinkle with blanched onions and brown sugar. Repeat until the pans are full. The top layer should be brown sugar.
7. Bake in a slow oven (325°F.) for at least 1 hour or until the beans are tender. Cover during the first half of the baking, then remove the lid to permit browning.

**YIELD**

Approx. 100 7-oz. servings.

## DUMPLINGS FOR STEW

| | | |
|---|---|---|
| 5 qts. | **Unsifted Pastry Flour** | 6 lbs., 4 oz. |
| ¾ c. | **Baking Powder** | 6 oz. |
| 3 tbsp. | **Salt** | 2 oz. |
| 1½ pts. | **Butter or Shortening** | 1 lb., 8 oz. |
| 1½ qts. | **Milk** | 3 lbs., 12 oz. |

**METHOD**

1. Combine the ingredients as in making tea biscuits. Handle as little as possible. The dough should be soft but not sticky.
2. Scale in 1-oz. pieces. Drop on boiling stew. Cover tightly. Cook for at least 10 minutes without lifting the lid. Test with a skewer or by pressing lightly with the fingers. Serve very hot.

**NOTE**

1. Substitute 3 lbs. of chopped suet for shortening.
2. Steam dumplings on greased trays for 10-12 minutes.
3. Dumplings become tough and rubbery when over-mixed or when the dough is too stiff.

**YIELD**

200 1-oz. dumplings.

## YORKSHIRE PUDDING

| 4 qts. | **Unsifted Pastry Flour** | 5 lbs. |
| 5 tbsp. | **Salt** | 3 oz. |
| 30 | **Eggs at room temp.** | 3 lbs., 4 oz. |
| 5 qts. | **Milk at room temp.** | 12 lbs., 8 oz. |
| 1 pt. | **Beef Drippings** | 1 lb. |

**METHOD**

1. Sift the flour and salt.
2. Add the unbeaten eggs to the milk and beat well.
3. Add to the flour and beat until bubbles form.
4. Pour beef drippings into 5 roasting pans heated very hot.
5. Pour the mixture into the hot pans. Place immediately in a hot oven (425°F.). Bake for 15 minutes. Reduce heat to 325°F. and finish cooking (approximately 20 minutes longer).

**NOTE**

1. When made by hand, the pudding should be made in small amounts—one-quarter of the recipe at a time.
2. This batter **must** be at room temperature when it is mixed. Otherwise it will not puff.

**YIELD**

100 3-oz. servings.

# Muffins

## HINTS ON MUFFIN MAKING

A good muffin is even in shape, well-browned, has a rough, pebbly top and a coarse, even texture.

Muffins may be served hot for breakfast, at dinner with fruit or at supper with jam, honey or fruit. They are not supposed to be sweet, although occasionally a sweet muffin is desirable, and they should not be expected to resemble cake.

Most of the defects in muffins come from over-mixing. The object in mixing is merely to moisten the flour, not to produce a smooth creamy batter as in making cake. In fact, a muffin batter should be lumpy.

Muffins should never be beaten. Mixing of the dry and wet ingredients is done by drawing the flour into the liquid. For this reason the best muffins are made by hand.

When a muffin has a shiny surface, rises in peaks, or has large, uneven holes inside, it has been over-mixed.

### GENERAL METHOD FOR MIXING MUFFINS

1. Test the oven, to make certain it is hot (425°F.).
2. Grease the muffin tins or shallow baking pans (page 5).
3. Mix and sift the flour and baking powder.
4. Rub in the fat until the mixture is crumbly.
5. Mix salt, sugar, eggs and milk. Stir well to dissolve the sugar and salt.
6. Make a hollow in the centre of the dry ingredients.
7. Pour in all the liquid.
8. Stir very little—just enough to moisten the flour. The mixture should be lumpy.
9. Fill muffin tins ⅔ full.
10. Bake in a hot oven 20 to 25 minutes, until the muffins are well browned and firm on top.

## PLAIN MUFFINS

| | | |
|---|---|---|
| 7¾ qts. | Unsifted Pastry Flour | 9 lbs., 12 oz. |
| ½ pt. | Baking Powder | 8 oz. |
| 3 tbsp. | Salt | 2 oz. |
| 2½ pts. | Sugar | 2 lbs., 8 oz. |
| 1 qt. | Fat | 2 lbs., |
| 20 | Eggs | 2 lbs., 4 oz. |
| 3½ qts. | Milk | 8 lbs., 12 oz. |

**METHOD**

Make according to general method for muffins.

**YIELD**

200 medium-sized muffins.

### APRICOT MUFFINS

1. Add 3 lbs. washed, coarsely minced, dried apricots to the dry ingredients in the recipe for Plain, Whole Wheat or Rolled Oats Muffins.

### BACON MUFFINS

1. Omit sugar from muffin recipe.
2. Add 1½ lbs. crisp, cooked, drained bacon to the dry ingredients.
3. Serve hot for breakfast or supper.

### CHEESE MUFFINS

1. Omit sugar from muffin recipe.
2. Add 2 lbs. old cheese grated. Mix the cheese with the dry ingredients.
3. Serve hot for breakfast, dinner or supper.

### CRANBERRY MUFFINS

1. Increase the sugar in the Plain Muffin recipe to 3½ pts. (3 lbs. 8 oz.).
2. To the dry ingredients add 3 tbsp. grated orange rind and 2 qts. (2 lbs.) of raw cranberries which have been washed, picked over, dried and chopped.

### PRUNE MUFFINS

Add 3 lbs. washed, pitted and coarsely minced dried prunes to the dry ingredients, or use 1½ lbs. apricots and 1½ lbs. prunes.

### RAISIN MUFFINS

Add 3 lbs. washed, dried raisins to the dry ingredients after the fat has been worked in. Raisins may be added to Plain, Whole Wheat, Rolled Oats or Wheat Germ Muffins.

### ROLLED OATS MUFFINS

Substitute 3 lbs. of rolled oats for 3 lbs. of pastry flour.

### WHOLE WHEAT MUFFINS

Substitute 2 lbs. of whole wheat for 3 lbs. of pastry flour.

### WHEAT GERM MUFFINS

Add 1 pt. wheat germ to the dry ingredients in the muffin recipe.

## BANANA MUFFINS

| | | |
|---|---|---|
| 4 qts., 1 c. | **Sifted Cake Flour** | 4 lbs., 3 oz. |
| ½ c. | **Baking Powder** | 3 oz. |
| 1 tbsp. | **Baking Soda** | |
| 1½ pts. | **Sugar** | 1 lb., 8 oz. |
| 12 | **Eggs** | 1 lb., 6 oz. |
| 4 c. | **Shortening** | 1 lb., 10 oz. |
| | or | |
| 4 c. | **Margarine** | 2 lbs. |
| 2½ qts. | **Ripe Bananas, mashed** | |

**METHOD**

1. Follow the general method for making muffins, using the mashed bananas in place of the milk.

**YIELD**

200 small muffins.

## BRAN MUFFINS

### A

| 2 qts. | Unsifted Bread Flour | 2 lbs., 14 oz. |
| 1½ qts. | Unsifted Pastry Flour | 1 lb., 14 oz. |
| 7 qts. | Bran | 3 lbs., 8 oz. |
| 3 tbsp. | Salt | 2 oz. |
| ½ pt. | Baking Powder | 8 oz. |
| 1 qt. | Sugar | 2 lbs. |

### B

| 16 | Eggs | 1 lb., 12 oz. |
| 1 gal. | Milk | 10 lbs. |
| 1¼ pts. | Molasses | 2 lbs. |
| 3 pts. | Fat | 3 lbs. |

**METHOD**

Make according to the general method for muffins.

**YIELD**

200 medium-sized muffins.

**VARIATIONS**

1. **Raisin**—add 3 lbs. raisins.
2. **Date**—add 2 lbs. dates, chopped.

## WHEAT GERM MUFFINS

### A

| | | |
|---|---|---|
| 2½ qts. | Sifted Pastry Flour | 2 lbs., 8 oz. |
| 2½ qts. | Wheat Germ | 1 lb., 8 oz. |
| 4 tbsp. | Salt | 2½ oz. |
| 2 qts. | Brown Sugar | 3 lbs., 8 oz. |

### B

| | | |
|---|---|---|
| 2½ qts. | Sour Milk or Buttermilk | 6 lbs., 4 oz. |
| 12 | Eggs | 1 lb., 4 oz. |
| ¼ c. | Soda | 2 oz. |
| 1½ c. | Melted Shortening | 13 oz. |

### C

| | | |
|---|---|---|
| 1 pt. | Raisins or Dates | 12 oz. |

**METHOD**

1. Mix A together thoroughly.
2. Beat B together.
3. Gently fold A, B and C together.
4. Pour into greased muffin tins, filling about half full.
5. Bake at 425°F. for about 15 minutes.

**YIELD**

200 muffins.

## DATE BREAD

### A

| | | |
|---|---|---|
| 2½ qts. | Dates, stoned and chopped | 4 lbs., 6 oz. |
| 2½ tbsp. | Baking Soda | 1 oz. |
| 2½ pts. | Boiling Water | 3 lbs. |

### B

| | | |
|---|---|---|
| 1 qt. | Brown Sugar | 1 lb., 12 oz. |
| 6 | Eggs, beaten | 10 oz. |
| 6 tbsp. | Shortening | 3 oz. |
| 2 tbsp. | Vanilla | 1 oz. |

### C

| | | |
|---|---|---|
| 2 qts. | Unsifted Pastry Flour | 2 lbs., 8 oz. |
| 2 tbsp. | Salt | |
| 2½ tbsp. | Baking Powder | 1 oz. |

**METHOD**

1. Combine A. Mix well. Allow to cool.
2. Add B to A.
3. Mix and sift C and add to AB.
4. Pour into 6 well-greased bread pans.
5. Bake in a slow oven (270°-300°F.) until cooked through (approx. 1½ hours).
6. Cut each loaf into 17 or 18 slices. Serve with or without butter.

**YIELD**

100 slices.

## JOHNNY CAKE

| | | |
|---|---|---|
| 1¾ qts. | **Unsifted Pastry Flour** | 2 lbs., 3 oz. |
| 1¾ qts. | **Unsifted Bread Flour** | 2 lbs., 8 oz. |
| 1¼ qts. | **Cornmeal** | 2 lbs., 3 oz. |
| 4 tbsp. | **Salt** | 2½ oz. |
| 1 c. | **Baking Powder** | 6 oz. |
| 1 pt. | **Sugar** | 1 lb. |
| 16 | **Eggs** | 1 lb., 12 oz. |
| 2 qts. | **Milk** | 5 lbs. |
| 1¾ pts. | **Fat (melted)** | 1 lb., 12 oz. |

**METHOD**

1. Make according to general method for muffins.
2. Pour into well-greased muffin tins or cake pans.
3. Bake in a moderate oven (350°F.).

**YIELD**

100 servings.

## APRICOT BREAD

| | | |
|---|---|---|
| 3 c. | **Dried Apricots** | 1 lb. |
| 2½ qts. | **Sifted All Purpose Flour** | 3 lbs., 2 oz. |
| 6 tbsp. | **Baking Powder** | 2½ oz. |
| ½ tbsp. | **Salt** | |
| 4½ c. | **Sugar** | 1 lb., 13 oz. |
| 1 c. | **Margarine** | 8 oz. |
| 3 c. | **Raisins** | 15 oz. |
| ⅓ c. | **Grated Orange Rind** | |
| 12 | **Eggs** | 1 lb., 5 oz. |
| 2½ pts. | **Milk** | 3 lbs., 2 oz. |

**METHOD**

1. Pick over and wash apricots. Soak for one-half hour in warm water. Drain thoroughly, squeeze and then chop.
2. Combine ingredients as in making muffins. Add the fruit and rind before adding the liquid.
3. Pour into 6 well greased bread pans.
4. Bake at 350°F. for 50 to 60 minutes.
5. When cool cut each loaf into 17 slices. Serve with or without butter.

**YIELD**

100 slices.

## FRUIT BREAD

Follow the recipe for Apricot Bread but omit the apricots, raisins and orange rind. For these substitute:

| | | |
|---|---|---|
| 1½ c. | **Chopped Candied Citron Peel** | 7 oz. |
| ¾ c. | **Chopped Candied Lemon Peel** | 3 oz. |
| 1½ c. | **Raisins or Currants** | 8 oz. |
| ¾ c. | **Glacéed Cherries** | 4 oz. |
| 3 c. | **Chopped Nuts** | 12 oz. |

## LEMON LOAF

Follow the recipe for Apricot Bread but omit the apricots, raisins and orange rind. Add 1 qt. chopped nuts (1 lb., 5 oz.).

After removing from the oven, let the loaves stand in the pans for five minutes. Then pour over them a mixture of lemon and sugar, made by combining 2 cups of sugar with the juice of six lemons. Remove the bread from the pans while still warm.

## PANCAKES

### RECIPE I

| | | |
|---|---|---|
| 2½ qts. | Unsifted Pastry Flour | 3 lbs., 2 oz. |
| 1 c. | Baking Powder | 6 oz. |
| 2 tbsp. | Salt | |
| 3 qts. | Bread Crumbs (stale) | 3 lbs. |
| 1¼ gals. | Milk | 12 lbs., 8 oz. |
| 12 | Eggs | 1 lb., 4 oz. |
| 1 pt. | Melted Fat | 1 lb. |

**METHOD**

1. Mix and sift the dry ingredients together and add the bread crumbs.
2. Beat the eggs slightly. Add the milk and melted fat.
3. Stir this into the dry ingredients to make a smooth batter.
4. Pour batter into a hot well-greased frying pan, using 1½ oz. to a pancake.
5. Cook until bubbles break on the upper surface. Turn and brown on the other side. Keep the pan well greased.
6. Serve at once with bacon; butter and brown sugar; maple or corn syrup.

**YIELD**

200 pancakes.

### RECIPE II

| | | |
|---|---|---|
| 5 qts. | Sifted Pastry Flour | 5 lbs. |
| 1 c. | Baking Powder | 6 oz. |
| 2 tbsp. | Salt | |
| 1 qt. | Eggs | 2 lbs., 10 oz. |
| 5 qts. | Milk | 12 lbs., 8 oz. |
| 1½ c. | Melted Margarine | 13 oz. |

**METHOD**

See above.

**YIELD**

200 pancakes.

**NOTE**

1. Three cups of wheat germ may be substituted for 3 cups of flour.
2. Sour or buttermilk may be substituted for sweet milk by reducing the baking powder to ¾ cup (5 oz.) and adding 5 tsp. soda.

# Pies

## HINTS ON PASTRY MAKING

Good pastry is tender, flaky, golden brown and has a good flavour.

Too much handling makes pastry tough.

Too much water makes it hard, therefore add just enough to hold the mixture together in order to work with it.

The fat used should be firm. Soft fat makes pastry greasy. Very hard fat is difficult to blend with the flour.

When possible, use bread flour on the board for rolling pastry.

It is inadvisable to use a wash on the pastry as it tends to toughen the crust.

Pastry should be cooked in a hot oven.

## PASTRY

| 6½ qts. | Unsifted Pastry Flour | 8 lbs. |
| 1/3 c. | Salt | 3 oz. |
| 2 qts. | Fat | 4 lbs. |
| 1¾ qts. | Water (approx.) | |

**METHOD**

1. Mix salt and flour.
2. Rub ½ fat thoroughly into flour with fingers. Break remaining fat into ½-inch pieces and add.
3. Make a well in centre of flour mixture. Pour in 1½ quarts of the water.
4. Toss the flour mixture and water lightly together until the latter is evenly distributed. If the mixture does not hold together, add the remaining cup of water. The mixture must not be stirred or kneaded in any way.
5. Turn out on lightly floured board. Cut off ½ lb. pastry. Roll out to ⅛-inch thickness.

**NOTE**

When possible make the pastry the night before or at least several hours before using. Store in refrigerator or cool room.

**YIELD**

17 9-inch double crust pies.

## DOUBLE CRUST PIES

1. Place the rolled pastry on pie plate. Press down the edges.
2. Add the fruit filling.
3. Roll out the top crust, making it slightly larger than the size of the pie plate. Cut 2 or 3 slits in the centre.
4. Moisten the edge of the lower crust.
5. Place the upper crust on top. Press the edges of the two crusts together and trim.
6. For temperatures see individual pie recipes.

## PASTRY SHELLS

1. Place the rolled pastry on the pie plate. Press down the edges and trim
2. Prick the pastry thoroughly with a fork.
3. Bake in a very hot oven (450°-500°F.).

## TOP FOR DEEP DISH PIES

1. Fill the baking dish with the pie filling.
2. Roll out a sheet of pastry that is large enough to cover the dish and to press under the rim.
3. Put 3 or 4 slits in the top.
4. Bake at 400°-425°F. if the filling is precooked.
   Bake at 375°-400°F. if the filling is raw.

## APPLE PIE
### USING CANNED APPLES

| | | |
|---|---|---|
| 4 #10 tins | **Apples** | 26 lbs. |
| 5½ pts. | **Brown Sugar** | 5 lbs. |
| 1½ tbsp. | **Cinnamon** | |

**METHOD**

1. Mix apples, sugar, cinnamon.
2. Finish as fresh apple pie.

**YIELD**

17 9-inch pies.

## APPLE PIE
**USING EVAPORATED APPLES**

| | | |
|---|---|---|
| **2 gals.** | **Water** | **20 lbs.** |
| | **Dried Apples** | **5 lbs.** |
| **2 pts.** | **Sugar** | **2 lbs.** |
| **2 tbsp.** | **Cinnamon** | |
| **1 tbsp.** | **Salt** | |

**METHOD**

1. Soak apples in water, according to method, page 94.
2. Partially cook the apples. Add sugar, cinnamon and salt.
3. Finish as fresh apple pie.

**YIELD**

17 9-inch pies.


## APPLE PIE
**USING FRESH APPLES**

| | | |
|---|---|---|
| **6 gals.** | **Peeled Apples** | **30 lbs.** |
| **3 pts.** | **Sugar** | **3 lbs.** |
| **1 tbsp.** | **Salt** | |

**METHOD**

1. Partially cook the apples. Add sugar and salt. Cool.
2. Line pie plate with pastry. Allow 1½ lbs. filling for each pie.
3. Cover with pastry.
4. Bake in hot oven (425°F.) until the apples are tender and the pastry is browned.

**YIELD**

17 9-inch pies.

## APRICOT PIE

| | | |
|---|---|---|
| 2 gals. | **Dried Apricots** | 13 lbs., 8 oz. |
| 1½ gals. | **Water** | 15 lbs. |
| 1 gal. | **Sugar** | 8 lbs. |
| ⅓ c. | **Salt** | 3 oz. |
| 1 pt. | **Granulated Tapioca** | 13 oz. |
| ¾ | **Standard Recipe for Pastry** | |

### METHOD

1. Wash the apricots thoroughly. Put through the food chopper.
2. Heat the water to boiling.
3. Mix the sugar, salt and tapioca. Stir into the boiling water and boil for 2 to 3 minutes.
4. Add the apricots. Cool.
5. Pour into pie shells, allowing 2 lbs. per pie.
6. Arrange a lattice-work or strips of raw pastry (⅛″ thick x ¼″ to ⅜″ wide) over the top.
7. Bake in a hot oven (450°F.) for 30 minutes or until the pastry is thoroughly cooked.

### YIELD

17 9-inch pies.

### VARIATIONS

1. ¼ cup cinnamon (1 oz.) may be added with the sugar.
2. Add ½ pt. lemon juice and 2 tbsp. grated lemon rind after removing the filling from the heat.
3. Use half prunes and half apricots.

## BERRY PIE
**FOR UNSWEETENED (CANNED) FRUIT**

| | | |
|---|---|---|
| 4 #10 cans | **Blueberries, Blackberries** | |
| | **or Raspberries** | **26 lbs., 4 oz.** |
| 1½ gals. | **Water and Fruit Juice** | **15 lbs.** |
| 1¼ pts. | **Cornstarch** | **15 oz.** |
| 1 gal. | **Sugar** | **8 lbs.** |
| ½ pt. | **Lemon Juice** | **10 oz.** |
| | **Standard Recipe for Pastry** | |

**METHOD**

1. Drain the berries.
2. Add sufficient water to the juice to make 1½ gals. Bring to the boil.
3. Mix the cornstarch and sugar.
4. Add some of the hot liquid to the dry ingredients, mix well and then stir into the boiling juice.
5. Cook, stirring continuously until the mixture is clear and there is no taste of raw starch.
6. Remove from the heat. Add the fruit and lemon juice. Chill.
7. Allow approximately 2¼ lbs. of filling for each pie.
8. Finish according to the general method for double crust pies.
9. Bake in a hot oven (435°-450°F.) until the pastry is cooked and brown.

**NOTE**

1. The amount of sugar required will vary with the different fruits.
2. Lemon juice brings out the flavour of the fruit and helps to retain the colour. When not available, use grapefruit juice or powdered lemon juice.

**YIELD**

17 9-inch pies.

## FRESH BERRY PIE

|            | Raw Berries              | 30 lbs.        |
|------------|--------------------------|----------------|
| 5½ pts.    | Sugar                    | 5 lbs., 8 oz.  |
| ½ pt.      | Flour                    | 5 oz.          |
|            | Standard Recipe for Pastry |              |

**METHOD**

1. Pick over the berries.
2. Mix the sugar and flour. Sprinkle over the berries and mix carefully, without breaking.
3. Fill uncooked shells, allowing about 2¼ lbs. to each pie.
4. Finish according to general method for double crust pies.
5. Bake in a hot oven (435°-450°F.) until the pastry is cooked and brown.

**YIELD**

17 9-inch pies.


## CHERRY PIE

**4 #10 Cans Cherries**
or
**30 lbs. Fresh Cherries**
**Standard Recipe for Pastry**

**METHOD FOR CANNED CHERRIES**

1. Follow the recipe and method given for berry pie. If the canned cherries are sweetened, use only ¼ of the sugar given in the berry pie recipe. Add the cherries. Mix well, taste. Add more sugar if required.

**METHOD FOR FRESH CHERRIES**

1. Wash and pit the fresh cherries. Follow directions for fresh berry pie.

## BUTTERSCOTCH PIE

### A

| | | |
|---|---|---|
| 1 qt. | **Butter** | 2 lbs., 8 oz. |
| 5 qts. | **Brown Sugar** | 8 lbs., 12 oz. |
| 2 qts. | **Unsifted Pastry Flour** | 2 lbs., 8 oz. |
| | or | |
| 1 qt. | **Cornstarch** | 1 lb., 8 oz. |
| 2 tbsp. | **Salt** | |
| | | |
| 1½ gals. | **Hot Milk** | 15 lbs. |
| 24 | **Egg Yolks** | |
| 3 tbsp. | **Vanilla** | |

**METHOD**

1. Caramelize ingredients in A to a golden brown over the direct heat.
2. Heat milk over hot water or in a steam kettle. Add enough of the milk to A to give the consistency of a cream sauce. Pour this mixture back into the remaining milk, stirring constantly, and cook until there is no taste of raw starch.
3. Beat the egg yolks slightly. Add part of the hot mixture to the yolks, stirring as you add. Return this to the original mixture and continue cooking until there is no taste of raw yolk (about 5 minutes).
4. Remove from heat and cool slightly.
5. Add vanilla.
6. Pour into baked pie shells. Allow to set.
7. Top with meringue and brown in a moderate oven or serve plain or with whipped cream.

**YIELD**

17 9-inch pies.

## BUTTERSCOTCH BANANA PIE

### Butterscotch Pie Filling
### Peeled, Diced Bananas, 10 lbs.

**METHOD**

1. Prepare the Butterscotch Filling.
2. Finish as Banana Cream Pie (page 225), allowing 9 oz. diced bananas for each 9-inch pie shell, or 1½ oz. per serving if the pies are made in sheets.

**YIELD**

17 9-inch pies.

## CHOCOLATE PIE

| | | |
|---|---|---|
| **2 gals.** | **Hot Milk** | **20 lbs.** |
| **1½ qts.** | **Cocoa** | **1 lb., 8 oz.** |
| **1 qt.** | **Cornstarch** | **1 lb., 8 oz.** |
| **2 qts.** | **White Sugar** | **4 lbs.** |
| **2 qts.** | **Cold Milk** | **5 lbs.** |
| **2 tbsp.** | **Salt** | |
| **4 tbsp.** | **Vanilla** | |

**METHOD**

1. Heat the milk over hot water or in a steam kettle.
2. Mix the cocoa, cornstarch, sugar and salt and cold milk. Blend well together.
3. Add to the hot milk, stirring constantly. Cook until thick and there is no taste of raw starch.
4. Remove from heat. Add vanilla. Cool slightly.
5. Fill baked pie shells.
6. Top with meringue and brown in a moderate oven or serve plain or with whipped cream.

**YIELD**

17 9-inch pies.

## MERINGUE FOR PIES

| | | |
|---|---|---|
| **1 pt. (20)** | **Egg Whites** | **1 lb.** |
| **2 tbsp.** | **Cream of Tartar** | |
| **⅔ qt.** | **Fine White Sugar** | **1 lb., 5 oz.** |
| **½ tsp.** | **Salt** | |

**METHOD**

1. Have egg whites at room temperature.
2. Add the Cream of Tartar and beat until the whites are foamy.
3. Add the sugar **very** gradually, about ⅓ cup at a time, and continue to beat until the meringue is shiny and stands in soft peaks.
4. When spreading it on the pies, be sure that it touches the crust all the way round.
5. Bake in a moderate oven (350°F.) until a delicate brown.
6. Cool at room temperature, away from draughts.

**YIELD**

Meringue for 17 9-inch pies.

## CREAM PIE

| | | |
|---|---|---|
| 2 gals. | **Hot Milk** | **20 lbs.** |
| 2 qts. | **Sugar** | **4 lbs.** |
| 2 tbsp. | **Salt** | |
| 2 qts. | **Unsifted Pastry Flour** | **2 lbs., 8 oz.** |
| | or | |
| 1 qt. | **Cornstarch** | **1 lb., 8 oz.** |
| 2 qts. | **Cold Milk** | **5 lbs.** |
| 24 | **Egg Yolks** | |
| 4 tbsp. | **Vanilla** | |
| ½ pt. | **Butter** | **10 oz.** |

**METHOD**

1. Heat the milk in a double boiler or steam kettle.
2. Mix sugar, salt, cornstarch or flour and the cold milk. Blend well together.
3. Add this to the hot milk, stirring constantly. Cook until thick and until there is no taste of raw starch.
4. Beat the egg yolks slightly. Add part of the hot mixture slowly to the yolks, stirring as you add. Return this mixture to the thickened milk and cook for 5 minutes or until there is no taste of raw egg.
5. Remove from the heat and cool slightly.
6. Add vanilla and butter.
7. Pour into baked pie shells. Allow to set.
8. Top with meringue and brown in a moderate oven, or serve plain or with whipped cream.

**YIELD**

17 9-inch pies.

## COFFEE CREAM PIE

Mix 3¾ cups instant coffee with the dry ingredients before adding the milk. Omit the vanilla.

## CREAM PIE WITH CORNFLAKES

Empty 2 packages of cornflakes into a bowl, break up slightly. Sprinkle on top instead of meringue.

## BANANA CREAM PIE

**Cream Pie Filling**
**13 lbs.    Peeled, Diced Bananas**

**METHOD**

1. Spread ¾ lb. of diced bananas on each cooked 9-inch pie shell or allow 2 oz. per serving when the pies are made in sheets.
2. Pour the cooled filling over the bananas.
3. Finish as Cream Pie.

**NOTE**

1. Prepare the bananas just before the filling is to be poured over them.
2. The diced bananas may be carefully stirred into the lukewarm filling.

**YIELD**

17 9-inch pies.

## COCONUT CREAM PIE

**Cream Pie Filling**
**3¾ qts.    Moist Coconut    3 lbs.**

**METHOD**

1. Add 3 qts. of coconut to the filling, after removing it from the heat.
2. Add ¾ qt. of coconut to the meringue before putting the pies in the oven to brown.

**NOTE**

If the coconut has become dry, soak it in milk for ½ hour before using. Drain well before adding it to the filling or the meringue.

## DATE CREAM PIE

**Cream Pie Filling**
**1 gal.    Chopped Dates    7 lbs.**

**METHOD**

1. Add the washed, pitted chopped dates to the filling after it has been cooled.
2. Pour into cooked pie shells.
3. Finish as Cream Pie.

**YIELD**

17 9-inch pies.

## PEACH OR PEAR CREAM PIE

**Cream Pie Filling**

2 #10 Cans     **Dessert Peaches or Pears  13 lbs., 10 oz.**

**METHOD**

1. Drain the fruit and dice if the fruit is in halves. Drain the diced fruit.
2. Spread the fruit on the baked shells, allowing about 8 oz. per 9-inch pie.
3. Pour cooled cream filling over the fruit.
4. Finish as Cream Pie.

**NOTE**

1. The drained diced fruit may be carefully folded into the cooled filling before it is poured into the shells.
2. Save the juice from the fruit and use for jelly or for fruit sauce.

**YIELD**

17 9-inch pies.


## CUSTARD PIE

| | | |
|---|---|---|
| 48 | **Eggs** | 5 lbs. |
| 3 pts. | **Sugar** | 3 lbs. |
| 2½ gals. | **Cold Milk** | 25 lbs. |
| 2 tbsp. | **Vanilla** | |
| 1 tbsp. | **Salt** | |

**METHOD**

1. Beat the eggs slightly and add sugar. Stir well.
2. Add cold milk, vanilla and salt.
3. Pour into uncooked crusts and sprinkle with grated nutmeg.
4. Bake in a hot oven (450°F.) for 10 minutes. Reduce the heat to 325° and continue cooking until a knife inserted in the centre comes out clean.

**YIELD**

17 9-inch pies.

## LEMON PIE

| | | |
|---|---|---|
| 3 qts. | Sugar | 6 lbs. |
| 1 tbsp. | Salt | |
| 1½ qts. | Cornstarch | 2 lbs., 4 oz. |
| 2 gals. | Boiling Water | 20 lbs. |
| ½ pt. | Lemon Rind (grated) | 4 oz. |
| 24 | Egg Yolks | |
| 1½ qts. | Lemon Juice | 3 lbs., 12 oz. |
| 1 pt. | Butter | 1 lb., 4 oz. |

**METHOD**

1. Mix sugar, salt, and cornstarch. Blend well together.
2. Add the boiling water gradually, stirring as you add.
3. Cook until clear and there is no taste of raw starch.
4. Add the grated lemon rind.
5. Beat the egg yolks slightly. Add part of hot mixture to yolks. Return to original mixture and continue cooking until no taste of raw yolk remains (about 5 minutes).
6. Remove from heat, add lemon juice and butter and cool.
7. Pour into baked pie shells. Cover top with meringue and brown in a medium oven or serve plain or with whipped cream.

**YIELD**

17 9-inch pies.

## GRAHAM WAFER CRUST

| | | |
|---|---|---|
| 5 qts. | Finely Rolled Graham Wafers | 3 lbs., 12 oz. |
| 1 qt., 1 c. | Brown Sugar | 2 lbs. |
| 1 qt., 1 c. | Butter or Margarine | 3 lbs. |

**METHOD**

1. Thoroughly mix crumbs and sugar.
2. Melt butter, add the above and blend well.
3. Press a thin layer of this mixture on to bottoms and sides of the pie plates (not on the rims).
4. Chill for an hour before filling.

**YIELD**

17 9-inch crusts.

## LEMON SPONGE PIE

| | | |
|---|---|---|
| 3 c. | Butter | 1 lb., 8 oz. |
| 3 qts. | White Sugar | 6 lbs. |
| 3 c. | Unsifted Pastry Flour | 12 oz. |
| 3 tbsp. | Salt | 2 oz. |
| 3½ c. | Egg Yolks | 1 lb., 12 oz. |
| 5 c. | Lemon Juice | 2 lbs., 8 oz. |
| 6 tbsp. | Lemon Rind | |
| 7 qts. | Milk | 17 lbs., 8 oz. |
| 1 qt. | Egg Whites | 2 lbs., 10 oz. |

**METHOD**

1. Cream the butter and add sugar, flour and salt. Mix until smooth.
2. Add the egg yolks, lemon juice and rind. Blend thoroughly.
3. Add the milk slowly.
4. Fold in well-beaten egg whites.
5. Pour into unbaked pie shells. Bake in a hot oven (400°F.) for 30-40 minutes or until lightly browned.

**YIELD**

17 9-inch pies.

## APPLE DUMPLING

| | | |
|---|---|---|
| 100 | Medium Apples | |
| 3 qts. | Brown Sugar | 5 lbs. |
| 1½ tbsp. | Nutmeg | |
| 2 tbsp. | Cinnamon | |
| | Pie Pastry | 25 lbs. |

**METHOD**

1. Peel and core apples.
2. Mix sugar, nutmeg and cinnamon.
3. Roll out pastry to ⅛-inch thickness and cut into squares large enough to fold over apples.
4. Place apple in centre of each square. Fill core with sugar and spice mix. Fold opposite corners of dough over apple. Pinch edges together.
5. Place on baking sheets. Bake in hot oven (400°F.) until apples are tender and pastry brown.
6. Serve hot with Brown Sugar Sauce, Lemon Sauce or milk.

**YIELD**

100 orders.

## MINCEMEAT PIE

| 2 qts. | Chopped Suet | 2 lbs., 8 oz. |
| 1 qt. | Unsifted Pastry Flour | 1 lb., 4 oz. |

**A**

| 1 tsp. | Cinnamon | |
| 1 tsp. | Nutmeg | |
| 2 tsp. | Salt | |
| 1 qt. | Sugar | 2 lbs. |
| 5 pts. | Raisins | 4 lbs. |
| 5 pts. | Currants | 4 lbs. |

| 3 gals. | Apples (cored and peeled) | 15 lbs. |
| 2 qts. | Citron Peel | 3 lbs. |
| 1 qt. | Peel, Orange and Lemon | 1 lb., 8 oz. |

**METHOD**

1. Dredge suet with flour. Put through food chopper.
2. Add ingredients in A.
3. Chop peel and citron fine.
4. Chop or cut the apple into coarse pieces.
5. Add peel, citron and apple to the other ingredients.
6. Store in a keg for at least two weeks before using.
7. Keep the keg in a cool place.
8. Put 1 ½ lbs. filling into uncooked pastry shells. Cover with pastry and bake in a hot oven (425°F.).

**YIELD**

17 9-inch pies.

## PEACH PIE
(CANNED PEACHES)

| 4 #10 cans | Peaches | 27 lbs. |
|---|---|---|
| 1 gal. | Water and Peach Juice | 10 lbs. |
| ¾ pt. | Cornstarch | 8 oz. |
| 5 pts. | Sugar | 5 lbs. |
| | Standard Recipe for Pastry | |

**METHOD**

1. Drain the peaches.
2. Add sufficient water to the peach juice to make 1 gal. Heat to boiling.
3. Mix the sugar and cornstarch. Add a small amount of the hot liquid. Blend well, stir into the remainder of the boiling juice.
4. Cook, stirring continuously until the mixture thickens.
5. Remove from the heat. Add the fruit. Chill.
6. Finish according to the general directions for making double crust pies. Allow approximately 2¼ lbs. of filling to each pie.

**NOTE**

1. The flavour of peach pie is improved by the addition of grated orange rind. Mix ½ cup grated rind with the filling.
2. Deep-dish peach pie may be made from canned or Solid Pack peaches. Follow the general directions, page 217.

**YIELD**

17 9-inch pies.

**VARIATION**

Sweeten 4 #10 tins of Solid Pack peaches with 5 lbs. (5 pts.) of sugar. Use 2 lbs. of this filling per pie.

## PUMPKIN PIE

| | | |
|---|---|---|
| 7 #2½ cans | Pumpkin | 12 lbs., 11 oz. |
| 2 qts. | Brown Sugar | 3 lbs., 8 oz. |
| 4 tbsp. | Ground Ginger | |
| 6 tbsp. | Ground Cinnamon | |
| 1 tbsp. | Cloves | |
| 2 tbsp. | Nutmeg | |
| 2 tbsp. | Salt | |
| 1 qt. | Eggs (well beaten) | 2 lbs., 10 oz. |
| 1½ gals. | Milk | 15 lbs. |

### METHOD

1. Purée the pumpkin.
2. Mix sugar, spices and salt—add the pumpkin.
3. Add the beaten eggs and the milk. Mix thoroughly.
4. Pour into pie plates lined with pastry, allowing 2 lbs. filling per 9″ pie.
5. Bake in a hot oven (450°F.) for 10 minutes. Then cook in a slow oven (300°-325°F.) until a knife thrust into the centre comes out clean.

### NOTE

1. 12 oz. dried egg powder (1½ pts.) and 1½ pts. of water may be used in place of fresh eggs.
2. Use 2 #10 cans of pumpkin instead of the 2½ size.

### YIELD

17 9-inch pies.

## SQUASH PIE

Use cooked or canned squash instead of pumpkin. Add 4 tbsp. melted butter. Make as Pumpkin Pie.

## PUMPKIN CHIFFON PIE

### A

| ¾ c. | Gelatine | 4 oz. |
| 3 c. | Cold Water | 1 lb., 8 oz. |

### B

| 34 | Egg Yolks | 1 lb., 6 oz. |
| 4 c. | Sugar | 1 lb., 9 oz. |
| 3 qts. | Canned Pumpkin | |
| 6 c. | Milk | 3 lbs. |
| 2 tbsp. | Salt | |
| 2 tbsp. | Nutmeg | |
| 2 tbsp. | Ginger | |

### C

| 2 c. | Sugar | 12 oz. |

### D

| 34 | Egg Whites | 2 lbs., 4 oz. |

**METHOD**

1. Soak A.
2. Beat yolks slightly. Stir in remainder of B.
3. Cook over hot water until slightly thickened.
4. Add A. Stir until dissolved. Cool until partially set.
5. Add C.
6. Whip D until stiff and fold into the above.
7. Fill a baked pie shell or a graham cracker shell. Chill and serve with whipped cream.

**YIELD**

17 9-inch pies.

## RAISIN PIE I

| | | |
|---|---|---|
| 2 gals. | Raisins | 13 lbs. |
| 1½ gals. | Cold Water | 15 lbs. |

**A**

| | | |
|---|---|---|
| 3 pts. | Sugar | 3 lbs. |
| ⅔ qt. | Cornstarch | 1 lb. |
| 2 tbsp. | Salt | |
| ½ gal. | Cold Water | 5 lbs. |

**B**

| | | |
|---|---|---|
| 1 tbsp. | Cinnamon | |
| ½ pt. | Lemon Juice | 10 oz. |

**METHOD**

1. Wash raisins. Soak overnight in the cold water.
2. Bring raisins and water to a boil.
3. Mix ingredients in A and pour very slowly into the hot raisins. Cook until the mixture is clear and there is no taste of raw starch.
4. Remove from heat. Add B.
5. Pour into uncooked pie shells. Cover with pastry and bake in a hot oven (450°F.).

**YIELD**

17 9-inch pies.

## RAISIN PIE II

| | | |
|---|---|---|
| 2 gals. | Raisins | 13 lbs. |
| 2 qts. | White Sugar | 4 lbs. |
| 1 pt. | Lemon Juice | 1 lb., 4 oz. |
| ½ c. | Lemon Rind (grated) | 1½ oz. |
| 1 pt. | Dry Bread Crumbs | 8 oz. |

**METHOD**

1. Wash raisins. Soak for 1 hour in boiling water to cover. Drain well.
2. Add sugar, lemon juice, grated rind, and bread crumbs to the drained raisins.
3. Pour into uncooked pie shells. Cover with pastry. Bake in a hot oven (450°F.).

**YIELD**

17 9-inch pies.

## RHUBARB PIE

| | | |
|---|---|---|
| 5 gals. | Trimmed Raw Rhubarb | 25 lbs. |
| 4 qts. | Sugar | 8 lbs. |
| 1 qt. | Hot Water | 2 lbs., 8 oz. |
| 5 tsp. | Salt | 1 oz. |
| 1 qt. | Cornstarch | 1 lb., 8 oz. |
| 1 qt. | Cold Water | 2 lbs., 8 oz. |
| 5 tbsp. | Grated Orange Rind | |

**METHOD**

1. Wash and cut rhubarb into 1½-inch pieces.
2. Add sugar, hot water and salt. Bring to boil.
3. Mix cornstarch with cold water. Add to rhubarb, stirring gently to avoid breaking up the fruit. Cook until clear and there is no taste of raw starch.
4. Add orange rind. Cool.
5. Fill uncooked pie shells. Cover with pastry crust and bake in moderate oven (375°F.).

**YIELD**

17 9-inch pies.


## STRAWBERRY CHIFFON PIE

| | | |
|---|---|---|
| 6 qts. | Strawberries, Fresh | |
| 2½ qts. | Sugar | 5 lbs. |
| 1 c. | Gelatine | 5 oz. |
| 4 c. | Cold Water | 2 lbs. |
| 8 c. | Boiling Water | 4 lbs. |
| 1 c. | Fresh Lemon Juice | 8 oz. |
| 1½ qts. | Whipping Cream | |
| 34 | Egg Whites | 2 lbs., 4 oz. |
| 2 tsp. | Salt | |

**METHOD**

1. Wash, hull and slice strawberries. Add sugar and let stand for ½ hour.
2. Soak gelatine in cold water—dissolve in the boiling water.
3. Add lemon juice and berries. Chill until nearly set.
4. Whip cream until stiff, fold into above.
5. Fold in beaten whites and salt.
6. Fill shell and chill until serving time.

**YIELD**

17 9-inch pies.

## FRUIT TURNOVERS

### Pastry, 20 lbs.
### Cooked Fruit Filling

**Apple:** 20 lbs. of apple pie filling. Use 3 oz. per turnover.
**Raisin:** 20 lbs. of raisin filling. Use 3 oz. per turnover.
**Prune:** 16 lbs. of prune filling. Use 2½ oz. per turnover.
**Mincemeat:** 16 lbs. of filling. Use 2½ oz. per turnover.
**Jam:** 10 lbs. of jam filling. Use 1½ oz. per turnover.

**METHOD**

1. Roll out pastry to ⅛-inch thickness and cut in oblongs, approximately 5 inches by 7 inches.
2. Place the filling on one half of the pastry square. Make a slit in the other half and fold it over to cover the filling. Press the edges tightly.
3. Bake on sheets in a hot oven (425°F.).

**YIELD**

100 turnovers.

## BUTTER TARTS

| | | |
|---|---|---|
| 3 pts. | **Currants or Raisins** | 2 lbs., 10 oz. |
| 1 pt. | **Butter** | 1 lb., 4 oz. |
| 1 pt. | **Shortening** | 1 lb. |
| 4½ pts. | **Brown Sugar** | 4 lbs. |
| 14 | **Eggs** | 1 lb., 8 oz. |
| 3 | **Lemons (juice and rind)** | |
| 1 tbsp. | **Salt** | |
| | **Pie Pastry** | 10 lbs. |

**METHOD**

1. Cover currants with hot water. Let stand.
2. Cream butter, shortening and brown sugar together.
3. Add eggs and beat until light.
4. Add drained currants, lemon juice, rind and salt to the creamed mixture.
5. Roll out pastry ⅛-inch thick—cut in circles to fit tart tins.
6. Put 1½ oz. mixture in each shell. Bake in a moderate oven (325°F.).

**YIELD**

100 4½-inch tarts.

## SOME PIE TROUBLES

**Tough Pastry**—may be due to:

> Too much mixing while adding water.
> Too much handling after water has been added.
> Not enough fat.
> Milk or egg wash on crust.
> Too slow an oven.

**Greasy Pastry**—may be due to:

> Fat too warm.
> Too little water in proportion to fat.
> Too much fat.

**Hard Pastry**—may be due to:

> Too much water.
> The use of butter.

**Shrinkage during or after Baking**—may be due to:

> Improper mixing of fat and flour.
> Too much water.
> Over-mixing after water is added.

**Soggy Pastry**—may be due to:

> Under baking.
> Insufficient bottom heat.
> Too slow an oven.
> Too sweet a filling.
> Pouring a hot filling into a cooked shell.

# Poultry

## ROAST CHICKEN OR TURKEY

1. Clean, stuff and truss the birds.
2. Brush with melted fat.
3. Place on their sides in roasting pans.
4. Cook in a slow oven (300°-325°F.) until the meat is tender. Turn once or twice in order to brown evenly. Baste occasionally or brush with additional fat.
5. Serve with giblet or brown gravy made from the drippings in the pan.

**NOTE**

1. If the birds seem old, pour about ⅓″ water into the pan and cover for the first half of the cooking.
2. The bird is cooked if the leg-joint moves easily or breaks when the drumstick is grasped in the hand.

### TIME-TABLE FOR ROASTING POULTRY

| Kind | Weight | Min. per lb. Approx. | Cooking Temp. |
|------|--------|----------------------|---------------|
| Chicken | 3½ to 5 | 35 to 45 | 300° to 325° |
|  | 5 and over | 30 to 35 | ,,      ,, |
| Duck | 4 to 8 | 25 | ,,      ,, |
| Goose | 10 to 12 | 20 to 25 | ,,      ,, |
| Turkey | 12 to 18 | 18 to 20 | ,,      ,, |

## ROAST DUCK

1. Before drawing, scrub the skin with warm soapy water and a brush. Rinse the soap off thoroughly.
2. Clean, stuff, truss and weigh as in preparing chicken. Use chicken or apple stuffing.
3. Place in roasting pans, put strips of bacon over the breast.
4. Pour into the pans ½ pt. boiling water and 1 tsp. salt for each bird.
5. Roast in a slow oven (300°-325°F.). See Time-table on page 238. Baste frequently and turn at least once.
6. Serve hot with giblet gravy and apple sauce or steamed apple rings.

## ROAST GOOSE

1. Before drawing, scrub the skin with warm soapy water and a brush. Rinse the soap off thoroughly.
2. Clean, stuff, truss and weigh as in preparing chicken. Use apple or chicken dressing in which ¾ c. sage is used instead of savoury or thyme.
3. Place in pans and cover closely.
4. Cook in a slow oven (300°-325°F.) for about 1½ to 2 hours.
5. Pour off the grease which has collected in the pan.
6. Return to the oven. Cook uncovered until tender. See Time-table on page 238.
7. Baste frequently with the water in the pan.
8. Serve very hot with apple sauce.

### TO CUT RAW CHICKEN OR FOWL INTO SERVINGS

1. Clean and wash chicken.
2. Remove wing tips and cook with the giblets.
3. Cut off legs, separate the thigh from the drumstick.
4. Remove the wings, cutting around the joint close to the body.
5. Separate the breast from the back by cutting through the ribs.
6. Break the back in half cross-wise. Cut each half again, lengthwise.
7. Divide the breast into four pieces by cutting lengthwise and then across.

Chicken prepared in this way is used for baked, fricasseed and stewed chicken.

## GIBLET GRAVY

**METHOD**

1. Prepare giblets by washing and trimming.
2. Chop heart and gizzard finely or mince coarsely.
3. Cover with water and simmer for one hour.
4. Dice the liver and add. Continue to simmer until the giblets are tender.
5. Drain. Make brown gravy (page 284) from the drippings in the pan using the giblet stock as part of the liquid.
6. Add the cooked giblets. Reheat.

## DRESSING FOR ROAST CHICKEN OR TURKEY

| | | |
|---|---|---|
| 3 gals. | **Fresh Bread Crumbs** | 8 lbs. |
| 6 tbsp. | **Savoury or Thyme** | |
| ½ c. | **Salt** | 5 oz. |
| 2 tsp. | **Pepper** | |
| ½ pt. | **Chopped Parsley** | |
| 1½ pts. | **Melted Butter or Bacon Fat 1 lb., 14 oz.** | |

**METHOD**

1. Add the seasonings to the bread crumbs.
2. Add to the melted fat. Mix lightly.

**YIELD**

9 lbs. of dressing (approx. 1½ oz. per person).

**VARIATION**

Add 1 qt. of raisins or 1 qt. of diced celery.

**QUANTITIES**

A 15 lb. turkey requires 3 qts. (2¼ lbs.) of dressing.
A 5 lb. chicken requires 1 qt. (12 oz.) of dressing.

The dressing not used in stuffing the birds should be baked in a moderate oven (350°F.) for 1 hour. Brush the surface with melted fat to prevent drying out.

## APPLE DRESSING FOR ROAST GOOSE OR DUCK

| | | |
|---|---|---|
| ¾ pt. | Butter | 15 oz. |
| 2 qts. | Diced Raw Onions | 3 lbs. |
| 3 gals. | Fresh Bread Crumbs | 8 lbs. |
| 3 tbsp. | Salt | 2 oz. |
| 1 tsp. | Pepper | |
| 1 gal. | Sliced or Diced Apples | 5 lbs. |

**METHOD**

1. Melt the butter and sauté the onions until clear.
2. Combine the bread, salt and pepper.
3. Cut the apples into thick slices or dice coarsely and add.
4. Cook as directed on page 240.

**YIELD**

16 lbs. dressing (approx. 2½ oz. per serving).

**VARIATIONS**

1. Omit apples, add 5 lbs. cooked, drained prunes or dried apricots.
2. Use 5 lbs. apples and 3 lbs. raisins.

## SAUSAGE DRESSING FOR TURKEY

| | | |
|---|---|---|
| 3 gals. | Fresh Bread Crumbs | 8 lbs. |
| 2½ qts. | Sausage Meat | 6 lbs. |
| ¾ c. | Finely Chopped Parsley | |
| ⅓ c. | Salt | 3 oz. |
| 4 tsp. | Pepper | |
| ¾ pt. | Finely Chopped Onions | 9 oz. |
| ¾ c. | Butter or Bacon Fat | 6 oz. |
| 9 | Eggs, Beaten | 1 lb. |

**METHOD**

1. Mix the bread crumbs, sausage meat and seasonings.
2. Cook the onion in the fat until clear.
3. Add the beaten eggs, onion and fat to the other ingredients and mix well.

**NOTE**

Sausage dressing should not be made from frozen sausage.

**YIELD**

100 2-oz. servings.

## BRAISED FOWL

### Fowl 75-100 lbs., A.P.

1. Prepare the fowl for cooking.
2. Cut into servings as directed on page 239.
3. Simmer in water to cover until tender (1 ½ to 2 hours).
4. Drain. Save the stock.
5. When the fowl is cool enough to handle, coat with flour which has been seasoned with salt and pepper (see Fried Chicken).
6. Sauté until golden brown.
7. Serve hot with gravy made from the stock drained from the fowl and any drippings remaining in the pan.

**YIELD**

100 5- to 6-oz. servings.


## FRIED CHICKEN

|          | Chicken                    | 75-100 lbs. |
|----------|----------------------------|-------------|
| 3 qts.   | **Unsifted Pastry Flour**  | 4 lbs.      |
| ½ c.     | **Salt**                   | 5 oz.       |
| 2 tbsp.  | **Pepper**                 |             |
| 1 qt.    | **Bacon or Chicken Fat**   | 2 lbs.      |
|          | **Hot Water or Chicken Stock** |         |

**METHOD**

1. Prepare chicken for cooking.
2. Cut into servings.
3. Mix flour, salt and pepper.
4. Coat each piece of chicken with the seasoned flour.
5. Cook in the bacon fat until well browned.
6. Place in baking pans.
7. Add enough hot water to cover the bottom of the pans.
8. Cover closely.
9. Cook in a moderate oven (350°F.) until tender (2½ to 3½ hours).
10. Turn and baste several times during the cooking.
11. Make gravy from liquid left in pan.

**YIELD**

100 6- to 7-oz. servings.

## CHICKEN STEW

Chicken or Turkey used in pies, stews, creamed dishes, etc., must be cooked and served on the same day. Never prepare filling for chicken pie one day and make the pie on the day following.

|  | Chicken A.P. | 75 lbs. |
|---|---|---|
| 2¾ pts. | Raw Chopped Onions | 2 lbs. |
| 3 pts. | Raw Diced Celery | 2 lbs. |
| 1 qt. | Raw Diced Carrots | 1 lb., 8 oz. |
|  | Hot Water to cover |  |
| ⅓ c. | Salt | 3 oz. |
| 1 pt. | Rendered Chicken Fat | 1 lb. |
| 1 qt. | Unsifted Pastry Flour | 1 lb., 4 oz. |

**METHOD**

1. Prepare chicken for cooking. Cut into portions and place in a steam kettle.
2. Blanch the chopped onions by allowing them to stand in boiling water for 2 minutes. Drain.
3. Add the blanched onions, the celery, carrots and salt to the chicken.
4. Add the hot water. (There should be just enough to cover the chicken.)
5. Cover the kettle and simmer until the chicken is tender (3½ to 4 hours). Do not allow it to boil.
6. Make a roux with the fat and flour.
7. Drain off the chicken stock and measure. There should be 1½ gals. Make up to this amount with water or vegetable stock, if necessary, or if there is too much, concentrate it by cooking it in the steam-jacketed kettle.
8. Finish the gravy, using the chicken stock as liquid.
9. Pour the gravy over the chicken and vegetables. Reheat. Serve immediately on mashed potatoes, boiled rice or noodles.

**YIELD**

100 4- to 5-oz. servings.

## CHICKEN PIE I

**(BONE IN)**

**Recipe for Chicken Stew**
**½ Recipe for Pastry**
**or**
**½ Recipe for Tea Biscuits**

**METHOD**

1. Prepare Chicken Stew according to the recipe.
2. Pour into baking pans.
3. Cover with pie dough rolled ⅛" thick or with biscuit dough rolled ¼" thick.
4. Bake in a hot oven (425°F.) until the crust is brown on top (15 to 20 minutes).


## CHICKEN PIE II

**Recipe for Chicken Stew**
**Tea Biscuit Crust (½ recipe)**
**or**
**Pastry Crust (½ recipe)**

**METHOD**

1. Prepare chicken or fowl for cooking.
2. Leave whole but cook as directed for Chicken Stew.
3. Drain off the stock and make gravy, using the proportions and method given for Chicken Stew.
4. Remove cooked chicken from the kettle and separate the meat from the bones. (Use the fingers as little as possible in doing this.)
5. Cut the meat into large dice (1" to 1½").
6. Place the meat in baking pans, pour the gravy and vegetables over it.
7. Cover with biscuit dough rolled ¼" thick or pie dough rolled ⅛" thick.
8. Bake in a hot oven (425°F.) for 15 to 20 minutes.
9. Keep very hot and serve at once.

**NOTE**

To give larger servings, the vegetables may be increased 1 gal. onions (6 lbs.), ¾ gal. carrots (4 lbs.), ¾ gal. celery (3¾ lbs.).

**YIELD**

100 7-oz. servings.

## CHICKEN À LA KING

| | | |
|---|---|---|
| 1 qt. | Chicken Fat or Butter | 2 lbs. |
| | Sliced Mushrooms | 2 lbs. |
| 1½ gals. | Chicken Stock | 15 lbs. |
| 1 qt. | Diced Green Pepper | 1 lb., 8 oz. |
| 1½ gals. | Milk | 15 lbs. |
| ¼ c. | Onion Juice | |
| 2 qts. | Unsifted Pastry Flour | 2 lbs., 8 oz. |
| 1 pt. | Slightly beaten Eggs | 1 lb., 5 oz. |
| 1 qt. | Cut Pimiento | 2 lbs., 8 oz. |
| ⅓ c. | Salt | 3 oz. |
| 6 qts. | Chicken, cooked and cut into 1″ dice | 10 lbs. |

**METHOD**

1. Melt the fat and add the mushrooms. Cook for 5 minutes. Lift out the mushrooms.
2. Heat the chicken stock, add the green pepper and cook until tender.
3. Combine the hot stock, milk and onion juice.
4. Make a roux using the fat in which the mushrooms were cooked, and the flour. Cook 10 minutes.
5. Add the hot stock and milk and simmer for 10 minutes.
6. Stir about 1 pt. of the hot sauce into the beaten eggs.
7. Add the egg mixture to the sauce, stirring constantly.
8. Add the mushrooms, pimiento, salt and chicken. Reheat over hot water or in a steam-jacketed kettle with the steam pressure very low.
9. Serve immediately on toast, or on tea biscuits split in half.

**NOTE**

Mushrooms may be omitted altogether or 2 #2 cans of mushroom soup may be used in place of fresh mushrooms.

**YIELD**

100 7- to 8-oz. servings (approx. ½ pt.).

## CREAMED CHICKEN

| 7½ qts. | Cooked Chicken | 12 lbs. |
| 1½ gals. | Chicken Stock | 15 lbs. |
| 1½ gals. | Milk | 15 lbs. |
| 1 qt. | Chicken Fat or Butter | 2 lbs. |
| 2 qts. | Unsifted Pastry Flour | 2 lbs., 8 oz. |
| ⅓ c. | Salt | 3 oz. |
| ½ tsp. | Pepper | |

**METHOD**

1. Cut the cooked chicken into 1″ dice.
2. Make a cream sauce, using the chicken stock and milk as the liquid.
3. When the sauce is cooked, add the chicken and reheat.
4. Serve on Tea Biscuits, split in half; on toast, rice or noodles.

**NOTE**

Creamed chicken or turkey must be prepared only a short time before it is served or prepared in relays.

**YIELD**

100 7-oz. servings.

**VARIATIONS**

1. Use turkey instead of chicken.
2. Reduce chicken to 10 lbs. and add 2 doz. hard-cooked eggs, cut into quarters.
3. Cook 1 pt. finely chopped green pepper in the milk for 10 minutes before making the sauce.

# Rolls

## SWEET DOUGH

The Basic Sweet Dough recipe can be made up into a variety of rolls, buns and coffee cakes by cutting it into different shapes, adding fruit, spices, etc. A few suggestions for using it are given on the following pages, but there are many others which a baker can work out for himself.

The method of mixing and proofing is exactly the same as in making bread, but the dough should be slightly softer in order to permit rolling and shaping.

### PROOFING

Because of the higher percentage of fat this dough contains, the first proofing will take at least 2 hours, if the temperature of the dough is kept at about 80°F. The first proofing is completed when the fingers can be pressed into the dough to a depth of about 4″ without meeting much resistance.

The final proofing will take about 1 hour if the dough is kept at 80°F. The dough is ready for the oven if it retains a slight impression when touched lightly with the finger.

### BAKING

Products made from Sweet Dough brown more quickly than bread does and unless the oven temperature is carefully watched, a crust may form too quickly, with the result that the outside will have a good colour but the inside will be moist and doughy.

If the buns, rolls, etc., are closely packed on bun pans, they should be baked at 375°F. If there is a space between them, or if they are cooked in muffin tins, bake at 400°-425°F.

## BASIC SWEET DOUGH

| | | |
|---|---|---|
| 3 gals. | **Unsifted Bread Flour** | **17 lbs.** |
| 1½ pts. | **Butter** | **1 lb., 14 oz.** |
| 1½ pts. | **Shortening** | **1 lb., 8 oz.** |
| 3 pts. | **Sugar** | **3 lbs.** |
| ⅔ c. | **Salt** | **7 oz.** |
| 1 pt. | **Milk Powder** | **14 oz.** |
| | **Compressed Yeast** | **1 lb.** |
| 1 qt. | **(25) Eggs, beaten** | **2 lbs., 10 oz.** |
| 3 qts. | **Warm Water (90°F.)** | **7 lbs., 8 oz.** |

**NOTE**

1. 3 qts. of warm fluid milk (90°F.) may be substituted for the milk powder and warm water.
2. Use 24 envelopes or 7 oz. of dehydrated yeast in place of the 1 lb. of compressed yeast.

### GENERAL METHOD FOR MIXING BASIC SWEET DOUGH

1. Mix the flour and milk powder, add the fat and cut it into the dry ingredients as in making pastry.
2. Moisten the yeast in about 1 qt. of the warm water and stir until smooth.
3. Dissolve the sugar and salt in the remaining water.
4. Add the moistened yeast, the sugar and salt solution and the eggs to the flour.
5. Work the flour and liquid into a dough.
6. Knead the dough until it is elastic and full of bubbles.
7. Place the dough in a greased container, brush the top of the dough with water, cover lightly, put in a warm place and let rise (proof) until double in bulk. This will take about 2 hours. The dough should be kept at a temperature of 80°F.
8. Punch or cut down the dough and let it rest for 20 minutes.
9. Shape and finish as directed in the recipes following.

## CHELSEA BUNS

|              | Basic Sweet Dough Recipe         |              |
|--------------|----------------------------------|--------------|
| 6 tbsp.      | Cinnamon                         |              |
| 1½ pts.      | Brown Sugar                      | 1 lb., 5 oz. |
| 5 qts.       | Raisins                          | 8 lbs.       |
|              | Butter (melted)                  |              |
|              | Egg Wash                         |              |
|              | Brown Sugar and Butter           |              |
|              | for tins                         |              |

Prepare cake tins by greasing thoroughly and then sprinkling generously with brown sugar on the sides and bottom. Dot with pieces of butter.

### METHOD

1. Mix the sugar and cinnamon thoroughly.
2. Pick over, wash and dry or drain the raisins well.
3. Divide the proofed dough into 7 equal pieces.
4. Roll out each piece into an oblong shape ⅛" to ¼" thick and about 15" wide. Let rest for 10 to 15 minutes.
5. Brush with melted butter—be sure that the butter is spread right to the edge.
6. Sprinkle with the sugar, cinnamon and raisins.
7. Roll towards you like a jelly roll. Seal the edge.
8. Cut into slices about ¾" thick.
9. Place the pieces, cut side down, close together, in the cake tins.
10. Proof until double in bulk.
11. Bake in a hot oven (375°F.) for 15 to 20 minutes. Turn out of pans immediately.

### YIELD

235 buns.

## CINNAMON ROLLS

1. Prepare as Chelsea Buns.
2. Place on greased pans, omitting sugar and butter from the pans.
3. Finish as Chelsea Buns.

## HOT CROSS BUNS

|          | **Recipe for Basic Sweet Dough** |              |
|----------|----------------------------------|--------------|
| 6 tbsp.  | **Cinnamon**                     | 1 oz.        |
| 2 qts.   | **Raisins, washed and drained**  | 3 lbs., 4 oz. |

**METHOD**

1. Combine the ingredients in the Basic Sweet Dough Recipe as directed. Mix the cinnamon with the sugar, before adding to the other ingredients.
2. Add the fruit just before the mixing is completed.
3. After proofing, punch. Let rest for 20 minutes.
4. Divide the dough into 7 pieces. Roll out each piece to ¾" thickness.
5. Cut with a 3" cookie cutter. Make a cross on top by cutting with a knife.
6. Place on greased bun pans, about 1" or more apart. Brush the surface with water or butter.
7. Proof until double in bulk. Test by pressing with the finger.
8. Bake in a hot oven (400°F.).
9. At the end of 15 minutes baking, brush with a mixture of sugar and milk in order to glaze. Repeat 5 minutes later.

**GLAZE**

½ c. sugar mixed with 1 pt. milk.

**YIELD**

300 buns.

## COFFEE CAKE WITH TOPPING

**Basic Sweet Dough Recipe**
**7 lbs. Seedless Raisins washed and drained**
**3 lbs. Peel**

**METHOD**

1. Combine ingredients of Basic Sweet Dough recipe as directed.
2. Add the raisins and peel just before mixing is completed.
3. Allow to proof as in making Basic Sweet Dough. Punch. Let rest 20 minutes.
4. Cut into 5-lb. pieces, roll out to ½" thickness. Place on greased bun pans.
5. Roll lightly towards the sides of the pan until the whole pan is covered.
6. Brush with melted fat.
7. Spread with Cinnamon and Butter Topping or Streusel Topping (page 253).
8. Proof until double in bulk. Test by pressing lightly with the finger.
9. Bake at 375°F. for 20 to 25 minutes.
10. Remove from the oven, turn upside down on cake racks. Leave in this position until cool.

**YIELD**

200 servings.

# TOPPINGS FOR COFFEE CAKE

## CINNAMON AND BUTTER TOPPING

| | | |
|---|---|---|
| ¾ c. | Cinnamon | 2 oz. |
| 3 pts. | Sugar | 3 lbs. |
| 1½ pts. | Butter | 1 lb., 14 oz. |
| 1½ tsp. | Salt | |
| 1 pt. | (12) Eggs | 1 lb., 5 oz. |
| ¾ pt. | Flour | 7 oz. |
| 4 drops | Vanilla or Almond Flavouring | |

### METHOD

1. Cream butter, add sugar and cinnamon.
2. Add beaten eggs and salt.
3. Add flour and flavouring. Cream lightly.
4. Using a palette knife, spread on the coffee cake dough before the final proofing.

### YIELD

6 lbs. topping.

## STREUSEL TOPPING

| | | |
|---|---|---|
| 1 pt. | Shortening | 1 lb. |
| 1 pt. | Butter | 1 lb., 4 oz. |
| 1 qt. | Sugar (white or brown) | 2 lbs. |
| 2 tsp. | Salt | |
| | Honey or Corn Syrup | 6 oz. |
| 1 qt. | Flour | 1 lb., 4 oz. |

### METHOD

1. Cream the butter and shortening.
2. Add the sugar and salt. Cream together thoroughly.
3. Add the honey and syrup.
4. Add the flour and combine until the mixture becomes crumbly.
5. Sprinkle over the coffee cake dough before the final proofing.

### YIELD

8 lbs. of topping.

## YEAST-RAISED DOUGHNUTS

### Sweet Dough Recipe, page 249.

**METHOD**

1. When proofing is finished, punch and allow to rest for 15 to 20 minutes.
2. Cut the dough into 7 pieces. Roll each piece into a sheet ¼" thick.
3. Cut with a doughnut cutter. Place on a cloth-covered tray and proof until doubled in volume or until the dough retains the impression of the finger (about 30 minutes).
4. Fry and drain as directed on page 141.
5. While still warm, dust with icing sugar with which a little cinnamon has been mixed. (2 tbsp. cinnamon mixed with 1 c. icing sugar.)

**YIELD**

300 doughnuts.

## PLAIN ROLLS
(STRAIGHT DOUGH)

| | | |
|---|---|---|
| 1½ gals. | Unsifted Bread Flour | 8 lbs., 10 oz. |
| ½ pt. | Milk Powder | 8 oz. |
| ½ pt. | Shortening or Lard | 8 oz. |
| 3 tbsp. | Salt | 2 oz. |
| ½ gal. | Water | 5 lbs. |
| ½ pt. | Sugar | 8 oz. |
| | Compressed Yeast | 2¾ oz. |

#### METHOD

1. Follow the general method for making Basic Sweet Dough.
2. After punching the dough, allow it to rest for 30 minutes.
3. Scale off the rolls into 1-oz. pieces. (Tuck the cut edges underneath and work each roll until it has a smooth surface.)
4. Place in greased muffin tins or on greased baking sheets, 1″ apart. Brush with water or butter, cover lightly and proof until the dough retains the impression of the fingers when pressed.
5. Bake in a hot oven (375°-400°F.) until thoroughly cooked and browned (15 to 30 minutes).
6. Remove from oven, brush top surface with melted butter or milk, to give a tender crust.

#### YIELD

18 doz. rolls.

#### NOTE

Use 4 envelopes or 1 oz. of dehydrated yeast in place of 2¾ oz. of compressed yeast.

## PARKER HOUSE ROLLS

### Recipe for Plain Rolls

**METHOD**

1. After punching the dough and allowing it to proof for 30 minutes, roll it out to ¼″ thickness on a floured board. Roll only part of the dough at a time.
2. Lift the rolled dough from the board to let it shrink.
3. Replace on board and cut with a round or oval cutter.
4. Crease each piece across the centre with the back of a knife, brush melted butter over one half the piece.
5. Fold over, press edges together.
6. Finish as rolls.

**YIELD**

18 doz. rolls.


## APRICOT GLAZE

| 3 c. | **Apricot Nectar** | 1 lb., 8 oz. |
| 3 c. | **Sugar** | 1 lb., 3 oz. |

**METHOD**

1. Boil the nectar and sugar together until the syrup is thick.
2. Use as a glaze on sweet doughs, fruit breads etc., while they are still warm, after removal from the oven.

**NOTE**

This glaze will keep for months if stored in covered jars in a cool place.

**YIELD**

Approximately 1 qt.

# Salads

# GENERAL DIRECTIONS

## PREPARATION OF LETTUCE

Cut the entire core from the centre of head lettuce. Hold the head under the cold-water tap, allowing the water to run into the hole made by the removal of the core. This will separate the leaves.

Trim heads, cutting away all unusable outside leaves. Soak heads for 1 hour in cold water. Remove and place in a container in refrigerator in such a way as to permit them to drain. Cover heads and let stand for several hours to become crisp. Separate leaves and serve.

## PREPARATION OF CELERY HEARTS

Cut off leafy part of the stalks and keep for use in the soup stock.

Trim off the outer coarse stalks, wash and scrub them with a small brush and use diced in salads or sandwiches.

Wash and brush the remaining part of the celery. Trim the heart to a point and cut the head lengthwise into 4-6 pieces.

# BEET AND CELERY SALAD

| | | |
|---|---|---|
| 3 gals. | **Diced Cooked Beets** | 24 lbs. |
| 1½ gals. | **Diced Celery** | 7 lbs., 8 oz. |
| ½ pt. | **Finely Diced Onions** | 6 oz. |
| 3 pts. | **Cooked Dressing** | 3 lbs., 12 oz. |
| 1 pt. | **Vinegar** | 1 lb., 4 oz. |
| ⅓ c. | **Salt** | 3 oz. |
| 2 tsp. | **Pepper** | |

**METHOD**

1. Mix all ingredients together, having first chilled them.
2. Serve on lettuce with cold meat or other vegetable salad.

**NOTE**

½ cup grated horseradish will improve the flavour.

**YIELD**

100 5-oz. servings.

## CHICKEN SALAD

| | | |
|---|---|---|
| 2 gals. | Cooked Boneless Fowl | 13 lbs. |
| 5 qts. | Diced Celery | 6 lbs., 4 oz. |
| ⅓ c. | Salt | 3 oz. |
| 1½ qts. | Mayonnaise | 3 lbs., 12 oz. |
| 1 pt. | Diced Green Pepper or Pimiento | |

**METHOD**

1. Cut the chicken into ½″ cubes.
2. Add the diced celery, pepper or pimiento, and salt. Chill.
3. Add the mayonnaise, toss lightly and serve at once.

**YIELD**

100 4-oz. servings.

## COMBINATION SALAD

| | | |
|---|---|---|
| 1½ gals. | Cooked Diced Potatoes | 10 lbs., 8 oz. |
| 4 #2 tins | Peas | 4 lbs. |
| 4 #2 tins | Beans | 4 lbs. |
| 1 gal. | Diced Celery | 5 lbs. |
| 1 gal. | Diced Cooked Carrots | 8 lbs. |
| 1 pt. | Finely Diced Onions | 12 oz. |
| 3 qts. | Cooked Dressing | 7 lbs., 8 oz. |
| ⅓ c. | Salt | 3 oz. |
| 2 tsp. | Pepper | |

**METHOD**

1. Combine all ingredients. Mix carefully in order not to break up the vegetables. Chill.
2. Serve on lettuce with cold meat or other salads. Garnish with hard-cooked egg.

**YIELD**

100 5-oz. servings.

## SALAD GREENS

1. This is a salad composed mainly of coarsely shredded head or leaf lettuce, to which one or more of the following vegetables may be added. The greater the variety of ingredients the more attractive is the salad.

| | |
|---|---|
| Coarsely Shredded Spinach | Diced Cucumber |
| Finely Chopped Onion | Diced Tomatoes |
| Sliced Radishes | Water Cress |
| Finely Chopped Green Pepper | Finely Shredded Cabbage |

2. Marinate the greens in French dressing and chill in the refrigerator for ½ hour before serving.
3. Prepare 7 gallons for 100 servings.

## CABBAGE SALAD

| | | |
|---|---|---|
| 6 gals. | **Shredded Cabbage** | 18 lbs. |
| 1 pt. | **Vinegar** | 1 lb., 4 oz. |
| 2 qts. | **Mayonnaise** | 5 lbs. |
| 1½ pts. | **Cooked Dressing** | 2 lbs. |
| ⅓ c. | **Salt** | 3 oz. |
| 2 tsp. | **Pepper** | |

**METHOD**

1. Select firm, crisp cabbage. Remove the coarse outer leaves and the heart.
2. Wash thoroughly and drain.
3. Shred very fine and chill.
4. Add remaining ingredients just before serving.

**YIELD**

100 4-oz. servings.

## VARIATIONS — CABBAGE SALAD

Cabbage salad may be varied by substituting one or more of the following for an equivalent weight of cabbage.

| Ingredient | Preparation | Weight | Measure |
|---|---|---|---|
| **Celery** | Finely diced. | 5 lbs. | 1 gal. |
| **Celery Leaves** | Coarsely chopped. | 3 lbs. | |
| **Carrots** | Shredded or finely diced. | 3 lbs. | 2 qts. |
| **Onions** | Finely chopped. (Blanch after chopping by allowing to stand in boiling water for 2 minutes. Drain and chill before using.) | 3 lbs. | 2 qts. |
| **Green Peppers** | Remove the core and seeds. Dice the peppers fine. | | 6 to 8 |
| **Apples, raw** | Wash, core and cut into ½″ dice. Use unpeeled if the skin is red. | 5 lbs. | 1 gal. |
| **Raisins, Seedless** | Pick over, wash and drain. | 3 lbs. | 2 qts. |
| **Pineapple, canned** | Drain and dice. | 5 lbs. | 1 gal. |
| **Spinach, raw** | Coarsely chopped leaves. | 3 lbs. | |

## FRUIT SALAD

| 1¼ gal. | Diced Oranges | 12 lbs., 8 oz. |
| 3 qts. | Diced Pineapple | 8 lbs. |
| 2 gals. | Diced Apples | 10 lbs. |
| 2 qts. | Cooked Salad Dressing | 5 lbs. |
| | Lettuce | |

### METHOD

1. Prepare the oranges and pineapple.
2. As the apples are diced, add to the other fruit.
3. Chill.
4. Just before serving, drain. Save the juice.
5. Mix the drained fruit with the salad dressing and pile on lettuce or serve the dressing separately.

### NOTE

1. Any combination of fresh or canned fruit may be used but some citrus fruit should always be included. The total weight of fruit should be from 30 to 40 lbs. The total volume from 4 to 6 gallons.
2. When bananas are added, slice or dice just before serving, and drop into the other fruit or into the salad dressing as they are prepared. This prevents discolouration.

### YIELD

100 5-oz. servings.

## POTATO SALAD

| | | |
|---|---|---|
| 4 gals. | Cooked Diced Potatoes | 28 lbs. |
| 1 qt. | Finely Diced Onions | 1 lb., 8 oz. |
| 2 qts. | Mayonnaise | 5 lbs. |
| 1 qt. | Cooked Dressing | 2 lbs., 8 oz. |
| 1/3 c. | Salt | 3 oz. |
| 2 tsp. | Pepper | |

**METHOD**

1. Cut the potatoes in 1/2-inch dice.
2. Combine all ingredients carefully. Chill.
3. Serve on lettuce with cold meat.

**YIELD**

100 5-oz. servings.

**VARIATIONS**

Add one or a combination of the following when available:

| | |
|---|---|
| Diced Celery | Chopped Parsley |
| Diced Cucumber | Chopped Egg |
| Diced Radishes | Chopped Green Peppers |

## SALMON SALAD

| | | |
|---|---|---|
| 24 tins | Salmon (1 lb. tins) | 20 lbs. |
| 2 gals. | Diced Celery | 10 lbs. |
| 1/2 pt. | Finely Diced Onions | 6 oz. |
| 2 qts. | Cooked Dressing | 5 lbs. |
| 1/3 c. | Salt | 3 oz. |
| 2 tsp. | Pepper | |

**METHOD**

1. Remove skin and bones from salmon and flake. Add remaining ingredients. Chill before serving.
2. Serve on lettuce with vegetable salad.

**YIELD**

100 5-oz. servings.

## BASIC RECIPE FOR JELLIED FRUIT SALADS

### A

| | | |
|---|---|---|
| 1¼ c. | Gelatine | 6 oz. |
| 4 c. | Cold Water | 2 lbs. |
| | | |
| 1 gal. | Fruit Juice | 10 lbs. |
| 4 to 6 c. | Sugar | 1½ to 2½ lbs. |
| 4 c. | Lemon Juice | 2 lbs. |
| 5 qts. | Prepared Fruit | 11 lbs. |

**METHOD**

1. Soak A for 5 minutes.
2. Heat 2 qts. fruit juice, add A and the sugar. Stir until dissolved.
3. Add remaining juice and lemon juice.
4. Chill. When partly set, add the drained, diced or sectioned fruit.
5. Pour into moistened moulds. Chill.
6. Serve on lettuce with mayonnaise or cooked dressing or as part of a fruit salad or with cold meat.

**YIELD**

100 4-oz. servings.

**NOTE**

The larger amount of sugar is required with tart juices such as grapefruit. If the juice is very sour, increase the sugar to 8 c. or reduce the lemon juice.

### SUGGESTED COMBINATIONS

1. Use grapefruit juice and fold in grapefruit and orange sections or grapefruit sections and diced, cooked pineapple.
2. Use grapefruit juice and fold in shrimps and finely diced celery.
3. Use the juice from canned fruits and fold in diced canned fruit and chopped nuts.

# BASIC RECIPE FOR JELLIED VEGETABLE SALAD

### A

| | | |
|---|---|---|
| 1½ c. | **Gelatine** | 7 oz. |
| 4 c. | **Cold Water** | 2 lbs. |

### B

| | | |
|---|---|---|
| 1 gal. | **Boiling Water** | 10 lbs. |
| 4 c. | **Sugar** | 1 lb., 10 oz. |
| 8 tsp. | **Salt** | 2 oz. |

### C

| | | |
|---|---|---|
| 1 qt. | **Mild Vinegar** | 2 lbs., 8 oz. |

### D

| | | |
|---|---|---|
| 5 qts. | **Diced or Shredded Vegetables** | |

### METHOD

1. Soak A for 5 minutes.
2. Combine B, add A, stir until the gelatine, sugar and salt are dissolved.
3. Add C. Chill.
4. When partially set add D.
5. Pour into moistened moulds. Chill until set.
6. Serve on lettuce as salad, or as part of a vegetable plate or with cold meat or fish.

### YIELD

100 4-oz. servings (approx. ½ c.).

### VARIATIONS

1. Substitute 1 c. lemon juice or 1 c. tarragon vinegar for 1 c. vinegar.
2. Use vegetable stock as part of the liquid.
3. Reduce boiling water to 3 qts. and beat in 6 c. mayonnaise or cooked salad dressing when the mixture is cool but before it sets.
4. Green colouring may be added.

### SUGGESTED COMBINATIONS

1. Use finely shredded cabbage, diced celery, diced red and green peppers.
2. Use diced cooked beets, well drained, finely diced raw celery and horseradish.
3. Use diced cucumber, diced cooked pineapple, grated raw carrot.
4. Use grated raw carrot in #1 above instead of red pepper.

## CRANBERRY SALAD

| | | |
|---|---|---|
| 10 pkgs. (3 oz. size) | Lime Jelly Powder | 1 lb., 14 oz. |
| 1½ qts. | Boiling Water | 3 lbs., 12 oz. |
| 3 qts. | Sugar | 6 lbs. |
| 2 qts. | Pineapple Juice | 5 lbs. |
| 3 qts. | Raw Cranberries | 3 lbs. |
| 2 qts. | Finely Chopped Canned Pineapple | 5 lbs. |
| 2 qts. | Finely Chopped Celery Red Colouring | 2 lbs., 8 oz. |

**METHOD**

1. Add the jelly powder to the boiling water and stir until dissolved.
2. Add the sugar and stir until it melts.
3. Add pineapple juice. Chill until partially set.
4. Wash and pick over the cranberries, then mince them.
5. Stir the cranberries, pineapple and celery into the jelly. Add red colouring at the same time if it is needed.
6. Pour into oiled moulds and chill until set.
7. Serve on lettuce with cold fowl, ham or tongue.

**YIELD**

100 4-oz. servings.

## CRANBERRY-APPLE MOULD

| | | |
|---|---|---|
| 5 qts. | Raw Cranberries | 5 lbs. |
| 1½ gals. | Apple Juice | 15 lbs. |
| 1½ c. | Gelatine | 7 oz. |
| 2 qts. | Sugar | 4 lbs. |
| 1 tsp. | Salt | |
| ½ c. | Lemon Juice | 4 oz. |
| 1 qt. | Chopped Apples | 1 lb., 4 oz. |
| 1 qt. | Chopped Celery | 1 lb., 4 oz. |

**METHOD**

1. Pick over and wash cranberries.
2. Heat 2 qts. apple juice, add cranberries and simmer until the skins are tender. Purée.
3. Soak gelatine for 5 minutes in 1 qt. apple juice.
4. Reheat puréed cranberries, add softened gelatine, sugar, salt. Stir over heat until completely dissolved.
5. Add the remaining apple juice (3 qts.) and lemon juice, mix well. Chill until partially set.
6. Fold in the chopped apples and celery.
7. Pour into moulds which have been rinsed with cold water or brushed with oil. Chill until set.

**YIELD**

100 4-oz. servings.

## CUCUMBER JELLY

### A

| 1¾ c. | Gelatine | 8 oz. |
| 4 c. | Cold Water | 2 lbs. |

### B

| 2 qts. | Boiling Water | 5 lbs. |
| ¼ c. | Sugar | |
| ¼ c. | Salt | 2½ oz. |

### C

| 4 c. | Lemon Juice or White Vinegar | 2 lbs. |

### D

| 7 qts. | Grated or Minced Cucumber | 17 lbs., 8 oz. |
| | Green Food Colouring | |

**METHOD**

1. Soak A for 5 minutes.
2. Combine B, add A and stir to dissolve gelatine, sugar and salt.
3. Add C. Cool.
4. Stir in D. Add sufficient green colouring to make the jelly a delicate green.
5. Pour into moistened moulds. Chill until firm.
6. Serve on lettuce as salad or with cold meat or cold fish.

**YIELD**

100 4-oz. servings (approx. ½ c.).

**VARIATIONS**

1. Add 1 qt. very finely chopped celery leaves.
2. Add 1½ c. finely chopped pimiento.
3. Add 2 c. finely diced green pepper.
4. Use chicken stock instead of water.
5. Add ¼ c. onion juice or 2 tsp. powdered onion.

## CUCUMBER MOUSSE

1. Reduce the cucumbers in the Cucumber Jelly recipe to 5 qts.
2. When the jelly begins to set fold in
   1 qt. whipped cream
   1 qt. mayonnaise.
3. Finish as Cucumber Jelly.

## TOMATO JELLY

| | | |
|---|---|---|
| ⅔ pt. | Gelatine | 8 oz. |
| 1 pt. | Cold Water | 1 lb., 4 oz. |
| 8 #2½ tins | Tomatoes (1½ gals.) | 14 lbs. |
| 8 | Bay Leaves | |
| 5 | Cloves | |
| ½ tsp. | Cinnamon | |
| 1 pt. | Celery Leaves and Stalks | |
| 3 tbsp. | Salt | 2 oz. |
| 8 | Onion Slices | 6 oz. |
| ¾ c. | Sugar | 5 oz. |
| 1 c. | Vinegar | 8 oz. |
| 4 tbsp. | Lemon Juice | 2 oz. |

**METHOD**

1. Dissolve gelatine in cold water.
2. Simmer spices, celery, onion and 2 tins of tomatoes together for 20 minutes. Add gelatine. Continue to heat until all gelatine is dissolved. Strain. Add sugar and salt.
3. Purée remaining tomatoes and add to hot spiced mixture. Add vinegar and lemon juice.
4. Pour into moistened moulds or pans. Allow to set in a cool place.

**YIELD**

100 2½-oz. servings.

## TUNA SALAD MOUSSE

| | | |
|---|---|---|
| 1½ c. | Gelatine | 7 oz. |
| 1 qt. | Cold Water | 2 lbs., 8 oz. |
| 3 qts. | Hot Water | 7 lbs., 8 oz. |
| 1 qt. | Vinegar | 2 lbs., 8 oz. |
| | Canned Flaked Tuna Fish | 9 lbs. |
| 1 gal. | Finely Chopped Celery | 5 lbs. |
| 3 doz. | Hard Cooked Eggs | 4 lbs. |
| 1 qt. | Stuffed Olives | |
| 2 c. | Sweet Pickles | 10 oz. |
| 1 c. | Minced Onions | 5 oz. |
| 2 tbsp. | Salt | |
| 1 tsp. | Pepper | |
| ½ gal. | Mayonnaise | 5 lbs. |

**METHOD**

1. Soften the gelatine in the cold water.
2. Dissolve in the hot water.
3. Add vinegar and chill until partially set.
4. Chop finely the celery, eggs, olives and pickles.
5. Add these and the remaining ingredients to the gelatine mixture and combine well.
6. Chill in oiled moulds until the salad is firm.
7. Serve with raw vegetable salad.

**YIELD**

100 5-oz. servings.

## TUNA FISH SALAD

### A

| | | |
|---|---|---|
| 17 tins<br>(7 oz. size) | Tuna Fish | 7 lbs., 7 oz. |

### B

| | | |
|---|---|---|
| 4 c. | Chopped Green Pepper | 1 lb., 3 oz. |
| 1 c. | Blanched, Minced Onion | 5 oz. |
| 3 qts. | Crisp Shredded Cabbage | 2 lbs., 4 oz. |

### C

| | | |
|---|---|---|
| 8 c. | Salad Dressing | 4 lbs. |
| 2 c. | Vinegar | 1 lb. |

### D

| | | |
|---|---|---|
| 7 qts. | Potato Chips | 2 lbs., 3 oz. |

**METHOD**
1. Break the fish into coarse flakes. Drain off extra oil.
2. Add B to A and mix well.
3. Combine C and fold carefully into AB.
4. Just before serving add D and toss lightly.
5. Serve on crisp lettuce. Garnish with tomato sections, pimiento or radish roses.

**YIELD**
100 3-oz. servings.

## FRENCH DRESSING

| | | |
|---|---|---|
| ½ pt. | Vinegar | 10 oz. |
| 1 tbsp. | Salt | |
| 1 tsp. | Pepper | |
| 1 tsp. | Mustard | |
| 1 tbsp. | Onion Juice | |
| 1½ pts. | Salad Oil | 1 lb., 11 oz. |

**METHOD**
1. Mix all ingredients together.
2. Shake well before using.

**NOTE**
This dressing may be made in larger quantities and kept in a covered container in a cool, dark place.

**YIELD**
1 quart.

## MAYONNAISE

### A

| | | |
|---|---|---|
| 6 tbsp. | Pure Mustard | 1 oz. |
| 4 tbsp. | Salt | 2½ oz. |
| 4 tbsp. | Sugar | 2 oz. |

### B

| | | |
|---|---|---|
| ½ pt. | Vinegar | 10 oz. |

### C

| | | |
|---|---|---|
| 16 | Egg Yolks | 10 oz. |
| 2 tbsp. | Onion Juice | |

### D

| | | |
|---|---|---|
| 1 gal. | Salad Oil | 9 lbs., 8 oz. |

**METHOD**

1. Mix ingredients in A together.
2. Add B. Blend well.
3. Add C. Beat together.
4. Add D very gradually, beating constantly.

**NOTE**

A modified mayonnaise may be made by mixing together equal quantities of cooked dressing and mayonnaise.

**YIELD**

5 qts. (approx.).

## BLACKSTONE DRESSING

| | | |
|---|---|---|
| 1 qt. | Mayonnaise | 2 lbs., 8 oz. |
| ⅓ c. | Finely Chopped Pimiento | 1½ oz. |
| ⅓ c. | Finely Chopped Green Pepper | 1½ oz. |
| ⅓ c. | Finely Chopped Onions | 1½ oz. |
| 8 | Finely Chopped Hard-Cooked Eggs | 14 oz. |
| 1 pt. | Catsup | 1 lb., 4 oz. |

**METHOD**

1. Combine all the ingredients.

**YIELD**

2 qts. or 100 servings (1½ tbsp.).

## RUSSIAN DRESSING

| 1 qt. | Mayonnaise | 2 lbs., 8 oz. |
|---|---|---|
| ⅔ c. | Finely Chopped Pimiento | 3 oz. |
| ⅔ c. | Finely Chopped Green Pepper | 3 oz. |
| ⅔ c. | Finely Chopped Onions | 3 oz. |
| ⅔ c. | Finely Chopped Celery | 2 oz. |
| 1 pt | Catsup | 1 lb., 4 oz. |

**METHOD**

1. Combine all the ingredients.

**YIELD**

Approx. 2 qts. or 100 servings (1½ tbsp.).

## THOUSAND ISLAND DRESSING

| 1½ qts. | Mayonnaise | 3 lbs., 12 oz. |
|---|---|---|
| 6 tbsp. | Finely Chopped Pimiento | 2 oz. |
| 6 tbsp. | Finely Chopped Onions | 2 oz. |
| 6 | Finely Chopped Hard-Cooked Eggs | 10 oz. |
| ¾ c. | Chili Sauce | 6 oz. |
| ¾ c. | Catsup | 6 oz. |

**METHOD**

1. Combine all the ingredients.

**YIELD**

2 qts. or 100 servings (1½ tbsp.).

**NOTE**

Dressings which contain Catsup or Chili Sauce should be made in the amount required for immediate use as they ferment if stored for any length or time.

## MODIFIED MAYONNAISE

| | | |
|---|---|---|
| 6 tbsp. | Sugar | |
| ¾ pt. | Unsifted Pastry Flour | 8 oz. |
| 3 tbsp. | Salt | 2 oz. |
| 1 tbsp. | Mustard | |
| ¾ pt. | Vinegar | 15 oz. |
| 1½ qts. | Boiling Water | 3 lbs., 12 oz. |
| 6 | Egg Yolks | |
| 3 qts. | Salad Oil | 7 lbs., 2 oz. |

**METHOD**
1. Mix the dry ingredients.
2. Add the vinegar, 2 tbsp. of oil and the boiling water.
3. Cook until it thickens and there is no taste of raw flour. Stir constantly.
4. Cool. Add the egg yolks and beat well.
5. Add the oil and beat until thoroughly blended.

**YIELD**
1¼ gallons.

## COOKED SALAD DRESSING

| | A | | |
|---|---|---|---|
| 6 | Eggs | | 10 oz. |
| | **B** | | |
| 2½ c. | Sugar | | 1 lb. |
| 6 tbsp. | Salt | | 4 oz. |
| ½ c. | Mustard | | 1½ oz. |
| | **C** | | |
| 1½ pts. | Vinegar | | 1 lb., 14 oz. |
| 1 qt. | Milk | | 2 lbs., 8 oz. |
| 1½ pts. | Unsifted Pastry Flour | | 15 oz. |
| | **D** | | |
| 3 pts. | Hot Milk | | 3 lbs., 12 oz. |
| | **E** | | |
| 3 c. | Butter | | 1 lb., 8 oz. |

**METHOD**
1. Beat A in a mixer until thick.
2. Add B and beat well.
3. Add C and continue beating.
4. Add D and cook over hot water, stirring constantly until there is no taste of raw flour.
5. Remove from heat, cool slightly, and beat in E.

**YIELD**
1 gal.

# Sandwiches

## GENERAL DIRECTIONS

### QUANTITIES

**Bread:** It is impossible to state the exact amount required.

> For meals—4 to 6 thick slices per person
> For parties—3 to 4 thin slices

**Butter:** ¼ lb. to a 1½-lb. loaf of bread
**Filling:** ¾ lb. to a 1½-lb. loaf of bread

### MAKING THE SANDWICHES

1. Handle the bread as little as possible.
2. Use a palette knife or one with a broad blade that is not sharp.
3. Arrange several slices of bread in pairs on a clean surface.
4. Use only one or two strokes of the knife for spreading.
5. Cover the entire slice of bread with butter and filling.

### STORING THE SANDWICHES

Line a clean box with brown or waxed paper, pile the sandwiches in neatly and cover with paper. If they are to be kept for several hours, spread a clean damp cloth on top of this paper before putting the lid on the box. When possible, store in a cool place.

### BREAD

The bread for sandwiches should be fresh but firm enough to slice easily. The thickness of the slices will depend upon the purpose for which the sandwiches are intended.

> Substantial sandwiches—20 slices to a 1½-lb. loaf
> Small sandwiches      —28 slices to a 1½-lb. loaf

### BUTTER AND MARGARINE

The butter or margarine used in sandwiches should be creamed until it is soft enough to spread easily but should never be melted.

For large quantities, hard butter or margarine may be put through a mincer with the filling. Use a coarse blade and put through twice.

### SEASONED BUTTER OR MARGARINE

By adding seasonings to creamed butter or margarine, the flavour of many sand- wiches is greatly improved.

To 1 lb. of butter or margarine, add any one of the following and beat until thoroughly mixed.

| | |
|---|---|
| ½ pt. | **Chili Sauce** |
| 1 tbsp. | **Horseradish (moist)** |
| 2 tbsp. | **Lemon Juice** |
| 1 tbsp. | **Prepared Mustard** |
| 1 tbsp. | **Grated Onion** |
| ½ c. | **Chopped Parsley** |

# FILLINGS

Sandwich fillings should be moist but not wet. They should be well seasoned. Chopping the ingredients is preferable to mincing, but when making large quantities a mincer will probably be necessary. In this case, always use a coarse blade so that the ingredients will be in small pieces rather than in a paste.

## CHEESE FILLING

Grate or put through a mincer. Moisten with salad dressing or prepared mustard.

## TOASTED OPEN-FACED CHEESE FILLING

1. Prepare cheese filling.
2. Spread on toast or on thin slices of bread.
3. Place on baking sheets and cook in a hot oven until the cheese melts.
4. Serve very hot with cooked bacon on top.

## EGG FILLING

Cook eggs. Chop fine and moisten with salad dressing.
Additions:
1. A small quantity of minced onion with the egg.
2. A small quantity of grated or minced cheese.
3. Diced celery, pimiento or green pepper.

## FISH FILLING
**(FOR 1 LOAF BREAD, 10 SANDWICHES)**

| 1 #1 tall tin | Salmon | 1 lb. |
| | or | |
| 2 7-oz. tins | Tuna | 14 oz. |
| ½ pt. | Finely Diced Celery | 5 oz. |
| | Salt to taste | |
| | Salad Dressing | |

**METHOD**
1. Drain fish, remove skin and bones. Crush bones, flake fish.
2. Using a fork, combine the fish, crushed bones and the other ingredients to make a mixture that will spread.

**ADDITIONS**
1. 1 oz. finely chopped green pepper.
2. 1 oz. finely chopped sweet pickle
3. 1 tbsp. lemon juice.

## SARDINE FILLING
(FOR 1 LOAF BREAD, 10 SANDWICHES)

**Sardines, 20 oz.**
**Lemon Juice**

**METHOD**

1. Drain fish well and break into pieces with a fork. Do not mince or flake.
2. Spread on buttered bread and sprinkle with lemon juice.


## CHICKEN SALAD FILLING
(FOR 1 LOAF BREAD, 10 SANDWICHES)

| | | |
|---|---|---|
| 1 pt. | **Cooked Boned Chicken** | 1 lb. |
| ½ pt. | **Finely Chopped Celery** | 5 oz. |
| | **Mayonnaise** | |
| | or | |
| | **Cooked Salad Dressing** | |
| | **Salt to taste** | |
| ¼ pt. | **Chopped Green Pepper** | |
| ¼ c. | **Chopped Pimiento** | |

**METHOD**

1. Chop the chicken fine.
2. Add the celery, green pepper, pimiento, and sufficient salad dressing to moisten.
3. Spread on buttered bread and use within a short time.

**YIELD**

10 luncheon sandwiches or 14 afternoon tea sandwiches.

**NOTE**

The salad dressing must not be added to the chicken until just before the filling is to be used.
The chicken must be kept in the refrigerator.
The sandwiches must also be kept in the refrigerator until they are served.

**VARIATIONS**

1. Concentrate chicken stock and add gelatine to make a firm jelly. Chop this jelly and substitute 1 cup jelly for 1 cup of chicken.
2. Beef, veal, pork or turkey may be substituted for chicken.
3. When meat other than chicken or turkey is used, relish or finely chopped pickle may be added.

## PEANUT BUTTER FILLING
(FOR 1 LOAF BREAD, 10 SANDWICHES)

| | | |
|---|---|---|
| ½ pt. | Peanut Butter | 1 lb. |
| 3 tbsp. | Butter | 1½ oz. |
| ¼ #1 can | Evaporated Milk | 3 oz. |
| | Salt to taste | |

#### METHOD

1. Beat the peanut butter, butter and milk together in a mixer (slow speed) until smooth and creamy.
2. Add salt as required.

      or

Work the peanut butter with a knife until soft. Cream the butter. Mix the peanut butter, butter and milk together until blended.

#### YIELD

10 luncheon sandwiches or 14 afternoon tea sandwiches.

#### VARIATIONS

1. Use ½ cup Chili Sauce instead of the evaporated milk.
2. Spread both slices of bread with a thin layer of peanut butter filling. Spread marmalade on one slice before putting the sandwich together.
3. Spread both slices of bread with a thin layer of peanut butter filling. Cover one slice with sliced banana before putting the sandwich together. These sandwiches will keep fresh for only a short time.


## PEANUT BUTTER AND BACON FILLING
(FOR 1 LOAF BREAD, 10 SANDWICHES)

**Peanut Butter Filling**
**¼ lb. Chopped Bacon**

1. Prepare the peanut filling.
2. Cook the chopped bacon until crisp.
3. Drain. Add to the filling.

#### YIELD

Approx. 2 oz. per sandwich.

## LIVER FILLING

| | Beef Liver | 10 lbs. |
|---|---|---|
| 1 tsp. | Powdered Onion | |
| ½ tsp. | Powdered Garlic | |
| ½ c. | Worcestershire Sauce | |
| ½ tsp. | Pepper | |
| ¼ c. | Grated Horseradish | |
| 1 to 1½ qts. | Salad dressing or Chili Sauce or Chutney | |

**METHOD**

1. Simmer (do not boil) the liver until it is firm (about 15 minutes).
2. Trim off membrane and coarse tissue.
3. Put through a fine meat chopper twice.
4. Add the remaining ingredients and stir until of spreading consistency.
5. Use 2½ tbsp. of filling per sandwich.

**NOTE**

1. A combination of part salad dressing and part Chili Sauce or Chutney may be used.
2. ¼ c. onion juice may be substituted for the onion powder.

**YIELD**

Approximately 3 qts. of filling.

# STALE BREAD

## BUTTERED BREAD CRUMBS

| 1 gal. | **Fresh Bread Crumbs** | 2 lbs., 8 oz. |
| 1 pt. | **Butter** | 1 lb., 4 oz. |

#### METHOD

1. Use bread three or four days old. Break into fine crumbs.
2. Melt fat in a pan large enough to hold all the crumbs.
3. Add crumbs. Mix lightly until fat is evenly distributed.

#### USE

1. On the top of scalloped dishes.
2. As a basis for meat, fish or poultry dressing.
3. Apple or Rhubarb Betty.

## MELBA TOAST

1. Cut stale bread into $\frac{1}{4}$-inch slices.
2. Place on pans at the back of the stove or in a spent oven, until the corners begin to curl.
3. Continue drying in a very slow oven until the colour changes to a golden brown.

#### USE

Serve at any meal in which there is no other crisp food.

#### VARIATION

Grated cheese may be sprinkled on the bread before drying.

## DRY BREAD CRUMBS

Save all crusts, stale bread, Melba toast, etc. Place in pans and dry out in a very slow oven, or cover with paper or a cloth and dry on the back of the stove. When very crisp but not browned, put through a meat grinder. Keep in a perfectly dry, covered container in a dry place.

**USE**

1. For breading food that is to be sautéd or fried in deep fat. It should be sifted before being used.
2. In suet puddings.
3. In fruit pies to prevent absorption of liquid by pastry.
4. In meat loaf.

# Sauces

FOR MEAT, FISH, AND VEGETABLES

## GRAVY STOCK

|           | Bones                        | 25 lbs. |
|-----------|------------------------------|---------|
|           | Celery Leaves and Stalks     | 8 lbs.  |
|           | Sliced Onions                | 8 lbs.  |
| 3 gals.   | Hot Water or Soup Stock      | 30 lbs. |

**METHOD**

1. Break bones into small pieces. Brown for two hours in oven.
2. Add vegetables and brown for an additional ½ hour.
3. Add hot water or soup stock. Simmer for 1 hour in oven.
4. Strain off liquid and simmer until it reduces to 1½ gallons.
5. Use as liquid in making brown gravy.

## BROWN GRAVY

|           | Renderings from Meat         | 1 lb., 4 oz. |
|-----------|------------------------------|--------------|
| 1 pt.     | Renderings from Meat         | 1 lb., 4 oz. |
| 1 qt.     | Unsifted Pastry Flour        | 1 lb., 4 oz. |
| 1½ gal.   | Hot Water or Gravy Stock     | 15 lbs.      |
| 5 tsp.    | Salt                         | 1 oz.        |

**METHOD**

1. If there is not 1 pint renderings in the pan, add dripping to bring up to this amount. If there is more than a pint, pour off the excess fat.
2. Brown the renderings in the pan on top of the stove if the colour is not a dark brown.
3. Add flour and salt, mix thoroughly and cook for 3 minutes, stirring constantly.
4. Add the hot water or stock gradually, stirring until smooth.
5. Cook until there is no taste of raw flour.

**YIELD**

100 2½-oz. servings.

## CURRY SAUCE

| | | |
|---|---|---|
| 1 pt. | Fat | 1 lb. |
| 1 qt. | Chopped Vegetables | |
| | (carrots, onions, celery) | 1 lb., 4 oz. |
| 1 qt. | Chopped Fruit | |
| | (apples plums, rhubarb) | 1 lb., 8 oz. |
| ½ c. | Curry Powder | 2 oz. |
| 1 pt. | Unsifted Pastry Flour | 10 oz. |
| 1 gal. | Water or Stock | 10 lbs. |
| 2 tbsp. | Pickling Spice | |

**METHOD**

1. Melt fat.
2. Add fruit and vegetables and pickling spice. Cook until the vegetables are almost tender.
3. Add curry powder and continue cooking until the vegetables are soft.
4. Add flour.
5. Add liquid slowly, stirring constantly.
6. Simmer gently for ½ hour or longer, and purée.
7. Add salt to taste.

**NOTE**

This sauce may be used for curried meats or rice.

**YIELD**

1 gallon.


## ONION GRAVY

| | | |
|---|---|---|
| ½ pt. | Fat | 8 oz. |
| 3 qts. | Diced Raw Onions | 4 lbs., 8 oz. |
| 1½ gals. | Gravy | 15 lbs. |

**METHOD**

1. Cook onions in fat till evenly browned.
2. Add to gravy.

**YIELD**

100 2½-oz. servings.

## VEGETABLE GRAVY

| | | |
|---|---|---|
| 1¼ gal. | Gravy | 12 lbs., 8 oz. |
| ½ gal. | Cooked Vegetables | 4 lbs. |

**METHOD**

Add gravy to diced cooked vegetables (carrots, peas, onions, celery). Heat and serve.

**YIELD**

100 2½-oz. servings.


## ORANGE SAUCE

| | | |
|---|---|---|
| ½ pt. | Vinegar | 10 oz. |
| ½ pt. | Brown Sugar | 7 oz. |
| 3 qts. | Hot Brown Gravy | 7 lbs., 8 oz. |
| 4 | Oranges | |
| 5 tsp. | Salt | 1 oz. |
| 1 tsp. | Pepper | |

**METHOD**

1. Bring vinegar and sugar to the boil and add to the hot gravy.
2. Grate outside skin of oranges and squeeze out the juice. Add these to the gravy.
3. Add seasonings. Serve with baked ham.

**YIELD**

100 1½-oz. servings.


## RAISIN SAUCE

Substitute 1½ pints sultana raisins (1¼ lbs.) for the orange juice and rind.

## QUICK CHILI SAUCE

| | | |
|---|---|---|
| 1½ pts. | Diced Onions | 1 lb., 2 oz. |
| 3 qts. | Tomatoes (canned) | 7 lbs., 8 oz. |
| 1½ pts. | Vinegar | 1 lb., 14 oz. |
| 1½ tbsp. | Cinnamon | |
| 3 tbsp. | Salt | 2 oz. |
| 1½ pts. | Sugar | 1 lb., 8 oz. |

**METHOD**
1. Mix all ingredients together and cook 30 minutes.

**YIELD**
1 gallon or 100 1½-oz. servings.

**VARIATION**
One green pepper or 1 pint diced celery (10 oz.) may be added before cooking.
Serve with meats—hot or cold—meat cakes, rissoles or fish.

## TOMATO SAUCE

### A

| | | |
|---|---|---|
| ¼ c. | Butter or Bacon Fat | 2 oz. |
| 1 pt. | Chopped Onion | 12 oz. |
| 1 pt. | Chopped Celery | 8 oz. |
| 1 tbsp. | Whole Cloves | |
| ½ tbsp. | Allspice Berries | |
| 2 | Bay Leaves | |

### B

| | | |
|---|---|---|
| 1 gal. | Tomato Juice | 10 lbs. |
| 1 gal. | Stock | 10 lbs. |

### C

| | | |
|---|---|---|
| 1 qt. | Water | 2 lbs., 8 oz. |
| 1½ c. | Cornstarch | 7½ oz. |
| 3 tbsp. | Salt | 2 oz. |

**METHOD**
1. Braise ingredients in A.
2. Heat B and add to A.
3. Blend ingredients in C and add slowly to A and B, stirring constantly. Continue to cook until sauce is thickened and there is no taste of raw starch.
4. Strain and serve hot with meat loaf, hamburg steak or fish.

**YIELD**
100 2½-oz. servings.

## BARBECUE SAUCE

| | | |
|---|---|---|
| 1 qt. | Diced Onions | 1 lb., 8 oz. |
| ½ pt. | Bacon Fat | 8 oz. |
| ½ pt. | Flour | 5 oz. |
| ½ c. | Dry Mustard | 2 oz. |
| 2 tbsp. | Ground Cloves | |
| ⅓ c. | Salt | 3 oz. |
| 1 tbsp. | Pepper | |
| ½ pt. | Brown Sugar | 7 oz. |
| ½ gal. | Vinegar (see note below) | 5 lbs. |
| ½ gal. | Meat Stock | 5 lbs. |
| 1½ #10 tins | Tomato Purée | 10 lbs. |
| 1 pt. | Worcestershire Sauce | 1 lb., 4 oz. |

**METHOD**

1. Cook the onions in the fat until they are clear.
2. Mix the flour, seasonings and sugar. Add to the fat and onions and stir well.
3. Add the vinegar, stock, purée and sauce. Stir.
4. Heat to boiling. Simmer for 15 minutes.
5. Serve with meat, fish, boiled beans or macaroni.

**NOTE**

If the vinegar is very strong, use ¼ gallon and dilute with ¼ gallon of water.

**YIELD**

1½ gals. or 100 3-oz. servings.

## SPANISH SAUCE

| | | |
|---|---|---|
| ½ pt. | Butter or other Fat | 8 oz. |
| 2½ qts. | Lean, Raw, Diced Ham | 3 lbs. |
| 1 qt. | Finely Chopped Onions | 1 lb., 8 oz. |
| 1 qt. | Finely Chopped Celery | 1 lb., 4 oz. |
| 1 qt. | Finely Chopped Green Pepper | 1 lb., 7 oz. |
| ½ pt. | Unsifted Pastry Flour | 5 oz. |
| 2 #10 tins | Tomatoes, Hot | 12 lbs., 12 oz. |
| 2½ tbsp. | Salt | |

**METHOD**

1. Melt fat, add ham and diced vegetables. Cook until the onions are tender. Stir while cooking.
2. Stir in the flour and cook for two to three minutes. Add the hot tomatoes and the salt, stir until thoroughly blended. Bring to boil.
3. Serve with roast veal, lamb, pork chops, omelet.

**YIELD**

100 2½-oz. servings.

## MINT SAUCE

| | | |
|---|---|---|
| ½ gal. | Chopped Fresh Mint | |
| 1½ pts. | Sugar | 1 lb., 8 oz. |
| 1 qt. | Hot Water | 2 lbs., 8 oz. |
| 2 qts. | Vinegar | 5 lbs. |
| 4 tsp. | Salt | |

**METHOD**

1. Remove mint leaves from stems.
2. Wash thoroughly, drain and chop very fine.
3. Add the sugar and hot water. Let stand until the water is cool.
4. Add the vinegar.
5. Serve with lamb.

**YIELD**

Approx. 1 gal. or 100 1½-oz. servings.

## PREPARED MUSTARD

| | | |
|---|---|---|
| 1 pt. | Flour | 10 oz. |
| 1 pt. | Dry Mustard | 6 oz. |
| 2 tbsp. | Turmeric Powder | |
| 1 tsp. | Salt | |
| 1 tbsp. | Sugar | |
| 1 pt. | Salad Oil | 1 lb., 4 oz. |
| 1 qt. | Prepared Mustard | 1 lb., 4 oz. |
| 1½ pts. | Water | 1 lb., 14 oz. |
| 1 qt. | Vinegar | 2 lbs., 8 oz. |

**METHOD**

1. Mix all the dry ingredients.
2. Heat the salad oil and add to the dry ingredients. Mix to a smooth paste. Add the prepared mustard.
3. Heat water and vinegar to boiling.
4. Add to the mustard paste.
5. Cook for 10 minutes, stirring constantly.

**YIELD**

Approx. 3 qts.

## MUSTARD SAUCE I

| | | |
|---|---|---|
| 1½ qts. | Mayonnaise | 3 lbs. |
| ¾ pt. | Horseradish (prepared) | 12 oz. |
| ½ c. | Prepared Mustard | 2½ oz. |

**METHOD**

1. Blend thoroughly.
2. Serve with ham, meat loaf, tongue or simmered beef.

**NOTE**

If dried horseradish is used, refresh according to directions given on the bottle.

**YIELD**

1 tbsp. per person.

## MUSTARD SAUCE II

| | A | |
|---|---|---|
| 1½ c. | Mustard | 3½ oz. |
| 1 c. | Sugar | 6 oz. |
| 1 c. | Unsifted Pastry Flour | 4 oz. |
| 6 tsp. | Salt | |
| | **B** | |
| 1 qt. | Water | 2 lbs., 8 oz. |
| ½ pt. | Vinegar | 10 oz. |
| | **C** | |
| 5 | Eggs | 8 oz. |
| | **D** | |
| 2 c. | Salad Oil | 1 lb. |

**METHOD**

1. Combine A in a saucepan.
2. Heat B and add gradually to A, stirring constantly.
3. Cook and stir until the mixture thickens.
4. Beat C sufficiently to mix. Stir in a small quantity of the hot mixture and then pour back into the saucepan. Stir and cook over a low heat for about 2 minutes.
5. Add D and beat until well mixed.

**YIELD**

100 1-oz. servings.

## CRANBERRY SAUCE

| 5 qts. | Cranberries | 5 lbs. |
| 1½ qts. | Water | 3 lbs., 12 oz. |
| 2 qts. | Sugar | 4 lbs. |

**METHOD**

1. Wash the cranberries, remove the stems and discard any berries that are soft.
2. Add to the water, cover.
3. Bring to the boil and cook over a moderate heat until the skins burst and become tender.
4. Add the sugar, stir until dissolved.
5. Pour into enamel or china bowls to set.
6. Serve with chicken or turkey.

**NOTE**

If a thinner sauce that will not mould is desired, increase the water to 2½ qts.

**YIELD**

100 1½- to 2-oz. servings.

## CRANBERRY RELISH

| 5 qts. | Cranberries | 5 lbs. |
| 10 | Oranges | 5 lbs. |
| 2½ qts. | Sugar | 5 lbs. |

**METHOD**

1. Wash the cranberries, remove stems and discard any soft berries.
2. Wash the oranges, quarter and remove seeds.
3. Put cranberries and orange quarters through a coarse mincer. Collect the juice and add to the minced fruit.
4. Add the sugar, mix well.
5. Let stand for 24 hours before using.
6. Serve with chicken or turkey.

**YIELD**

100 2-oz. servings.

## BEET AND HORSERADISH RELISH

| | | |
|---|---|---|
| 1 gal. | Cooked Beets | 7 lbs. |
| 2 tsp. | Salt | |
| 1 tsp. | Cinnamon | |
| 1 tsp. | Cloves | |
| 1 pt. | Brown Sugar | 14 oz. |
| 1 qt. | Boiling Water | 2 lbs., 8 oz. |
| 1½ pts. | Vinegar | 1 lb., 14 oz. |
| 3 qts. | Raw Minced Cabbage | 4 lbs. |
| ½ c. | Grated Horseradish | 2 oz. |

**METHOD**

1. Mince the cooked beets or chop fine.
2. Add the salt, spices and brown sugar to the water. Cool. Add the vinegar.
3. Pour over the beets.
4. Chop or mince the cabbage.
5. Add the cabbage and horseradish to the beets. Mix well.
6. Serve with cold meat.

**NOTE**

1. Left-over spiced beets may be used up in this way. Omit the spiced syrup and vinegar, mix the beets with the cabbage and horseradish.
2. If dried horseradish is substituted, use about 2 tbsp. moistened in ⅓ cup of water.

**YIELD**

100 servings (approx. ¼ cup).

## RAISIN SAUCE

| 1 pt. | Seedless Raisins | 13 oz. |
| 2 qts. | Boiling Water or Ham Stock | 5 lbs. |
| 1½ pts. | Brown Sugar | 1 lb., 5 oz. |
| 3 tbsp. | Mustard | ½ oz. |
| 6 | Whole Cloves | |
| ¾ pt. | Vinegar | 15 oz. |
| 1 pt. | Grape or a tart Jelly | 1 lb., 9 oz. |

**METHOD**

1. Pick over and wash the raisins. (Add the boiling water or stock and let stand for 10 minutes.)
2. Simmer for 10 minutes.
3. Mix the sugar, mustard and cloves. Add the vinegar and raisin water. Boil until it forms a syrup.
5. Add the jelly and stir until it dissolves.
6. Add the drained raisins. Reheat.
7. Serve with ham or tongue.

**YIELD**

100 1-oz. servings.


## MUSHROOM SAUCE

| | Mushrooms | 2 lbs., 8 oz. |
| ⅔ c. | Butter | 5 oz. |
| ¾ c. | Finely Chopped Onions | 5 oz. |
| 3 qts. | Gravy | 7 lbs., 8 oz. |
| 5 tsp. | Salt | 1 oz. |
| ½ tsp. | Pepper | |
| ¼ c. | Parsley | |

**METHOD**

1. Wash the mushrooms. Remove stems and cut very fine. Dice the caps.
2. Melt the butter. Add the mushrooms and onions. Cook for 10 to 12 minutes.
3. Add the gravy, salt and pepper. Simmer for 10 minutes.
4. Add the parsley, finely chopped, just before serving.

**YIELD**

100 1½-oz. servings.

## MEDIUM CREAM SAUCE

| 1 pt. | Fat | 1 lb. |
|---|---|---|
| 1½ pts. | Unsifted Pastry Flour | 1 lb. |
| 6 qts. | Hot Milk or Milk and Stock | 15 lbs. |
| 3 tbsp. | Salt | 2 oz. |

**METHOD**

1. Melt the fat. (Use butter, dripping or shortening.)
2. Add the flour, blending well. Heat until the mixture froths.
3. Add the hot liquid gradually, stirring as you add.
4. Cook over hot water about 15 minutes or until there is no taste of raw starch.

**YIELD**

1½ gallons.

**VARIATIONS**

1. **Cheese:** Add 1½ quarts grated cheese (1½ lbs.).
2. **Egg:** Add 1 dozen chopped hard-cooked eggs.
3. **Parsley:** Add 2 cups chopped parsley.
4. **Vegetable Sauce:** Use at least half vegetable stock as part of the liquid.
5. **With Bacon:** Add ½ lb. finely diced bacon, cooked until crisp.

## THICK CREAM SAUCE

| 1½ pts. | Fat | 1 lb., 8 oz. |
|---|---|---|
| 1¼ qts. | Unsifted Pastry Flour | 1 lb., 9 oz. |
| 6 qts. | Hot Milk or Milk and Stock | 15 lbs. |
| 3 tbsp. | Salt | 2 oz. |

**METHOD**

Make according to the method given above for Medium Cream Sauce.

## BÉCHAMEL SAUCE

| | | |
|---|---|---|
| ½ pt. | Chopped Carrots | 6 oz. |
| 2 | Bay Leaves | |
| 1 gal. | White Stock (Veal or Chicken) | 10 lbs. |
| 1 pt. | Butter | 1 lb., 4 oz. |
| ½ pt. | Chopped Onions | 6 oz. |
| 1½ pts. | Flour | 15 oz. |
| 5 tsp. | Salt | 1 oz. |
| 2 tsp. | Thyme | |
| 2 tsp. | Pepper | |
| 2 qts. | Hot Milk | 5 lbs. |

### METHOD

1. Simmer the carrots and bay leaves in the stock for 10 minutes.
2. Cook the chopped onions in the butter until they are clear.
3. Make a roux by cooking the flour and remaining seasonings with the onions and butter.
4. Add the stock slowly. Cook until there is no taste of raw flour.
5. Strain into the milk, mix thoroughly and reheat.
6. Serve on croquettes or fish.

### YIELD

100 2-oz. servings.

### VARIATION

Add 1 pt. chopped, drained sweet pickles. Serve on fish.

## YELLOW BÉCHAMEL SAUCE

Reduce the flour to 1 pt. When the sauce is cooked, add one qt. gradually to 16 egg yolks, slightly beaten. Stir the egg mixture into the sauce and continue stirring for 2 to 3 minutes. Serve on fish.

## MOCK HOLLANDAISE SAUCE

| | | |
|---|---|---|
| 1 qt. | **Butter** | **2 lbs., 8 oz.** |
| 1½ pts. | **Flour** | **1 lb.** |
| 2 qts. | **Hot Milk** | **5 lbs.** |
| 1 pt. | **Egg Yolks (beaten)** | **1 lb., 5 oz.** |
| ½ pt. | **Lemon Juice** | **10 oz.** |
| 5 tsp. | **Salt** | **1 oz.** |
| 1 tbsp. | **Pepper** | |
| 1 tbsp. | **Paprika** | |

**METHOD**

1. Melt the fat, add the flour, blend well and cook for two to three minutes.
2. Add the milk slowly, stirring as you add.
3. Add a small amount of the hot sauce to the beaten eggs, mix well.
4. Stir the egg mixture slowly into the cream sauce.
5. Add the lemon juice gradually.
6. Simmer for 10 to 15 minutes, beating constantly with a whip.
7. Serve with fish or vegetables.

**YIELD**

100 1½-oz. servings.

## TARTARE SAUCE

| | | |
|---|---|---|
| 3 qts. | **Mayonnaise** | **7 lbs., 8 oz.** |
| 1 qt. | **Finely Chopped Pickles** | **1 lb., 11 oz.** |

**METHOD**

Add the pickles to the mayonnaise. Serve with fried cod, haddock, halibut, etc.

**YIELD**

1 gal. of sauce, 100 servings (2 tbsp.).

**VARIATIONS**

1. Substitute diced olives, green peppers or pimiento in place of part of the pickles.
2. Add ½ cup of finely chopped parsley.
3. Add ½ cup of capers.
4. Add ¼ cup of freshly grated onion.

## SAUCE REMOULADE

| | | |
|---|---|---|
| 3 qts. | Mayonnaise | 7 lbs., 8 oz. |
| ⅔ c. | Chopped Olives | 3 oz. |
| 2 c. | Chopped Pickles | 10 oz. |
| ⅔ c. | Chopped Parsley | 2 oz. |
| 1¾ c. | Chopped Hard-Cooked Eggs | 11 oz. |

**METHOD**

Combine all the ingredients.

**YIELD**

1 gal. sauce, 100 servings (2 tbsp.).

## CLEOPATRA SAUCE

| | | |
|---|---|---|
| 3 c. | Browned Butter | 1 lb., 8 oz. |
| | Chopped Anchovies | 6 oz. |
| 6 tbsp. | Capers | |
| 6 tbsp. | Chopped Pimiento | 2 oz. |
| 6 tbsp. | Chopped Green Pepper | 2 oz. |
| 2 c. | Lemon Juice | 1 lb. |
| 1 qt. | Hot Gravy | 2 lbs., 8 oz. |
| 1 tbsp. | Salt | |
| ¾ tsp. | Pepper | |

**METHOD**

1. Combine all the ingredients. Reheat.
2. Serve on hot fish.

**YIELD**

100 servings (1 tbsp. each).

## CHUTNEY

| | | |
|---|---|---|
| 4 c. | Chopped Seeded Raisins | 1 lb., 4 oz. |
| 4 c. | Tart Apples | 1 lb., 4 oz. |
| 2 c. | Chopped Onions | 10 oz. |
| ½ c. | Salt | 5 oz. |
| 3½ pts. | Brown Sugar | 3 lbs. |
| 1 qt. | Cider Vinegar | 2 lbs., 8 oz. |
| 1 #10 tin | Tomatoes, drained | |
| 1 tsp. | Indian Curry Powder | |
| 4 | Minced Cloves of Garlic | |
| | White Mustard Seed | 8 oz. |
| | Finely Chopped Preserved | |
| | Ginger | 4 oz. |
| ¼ tsp. | Cayenne | |

**METHOD**

1. Combine ingredients and cook slowly for 3 hours. Stir frequently.
2. Seal in sterile jars.
3. Serve with hot or cold meats.

**YIELD**

4½ pts.


## SAUCE MEUNIÈRE

| | | |
|---|---|---|
| 3 c. | Butter | 1 lb., 8 oz. |
| 2 c. | Lemon Juice | 1 lb. |
| 6 c. | Gravy | 3 lbs. |
| 1 tbsp. | Salt | |
| ¾ tsp. | Pepper | |

**METHOD**

1. Melt the butter. Add the other ingredients. Heat.
2. Serve with beef or fish.

**YIELD**

100 servings.

## COCKTAIL SAUCE

### A

| | | |
|---|---|---|
| ¾ c. | **Raw Onions** | 4 oz. |
| ¾ c. | **Sweet Red Pepper** | 4 oz. |
| ¾ c. | **Green Pepper** | 4 oz. |

### B

| | | |
|---|---|---|
| 1 c. | **Fresh Grated Horseradish** | 6 oz. |
| 6 c. | **Catsup** | 3 lbs., 8 oz. |
| ¼ c. | **Worcestershire Sauce** | 2 oz. |

**METHOD**

1. Chop A very fine.
2. Combine A and B and mix well.
3. Use on veal cutlet, pork chops, hot or cold fish.

**NOTE**

If fresh horseradish is not available, use ¾ oz. of dried or 6 oz. bottled.

**YIELD**

100 servings (1½ tbsp.).


## SAUCE BÈRCY

| | | |
|---|---|---|
| 3 c. | **Butter** | 1 lb., 8 oz. |
| 1 pt. | **Very finely Chopped Onions** | 12 oz. |
| 2 c. | **Lemon Juice** | 1 lb. |
| 3 c. | **Tomato Juice** | 1 lb., 8 oz. |
| 3 c. | **Gravy** | 1 lb., 8 oz. |
| 1 tbsp. | **Salt** | |
| ¾ tsp. | **Pepper** | |

**METHOD**

1. Cook onion in butter.
2. Combine all ingredients and heat.
3. Serve with fish.

**YIELD**

100 1-oz. servings.

## CREOLE SAUCE

### A

| | | |
|---|---|---|
| ¾ c. | **Butter or Margarine** | 6 oz. |
| 1 qt. | **Finely Diced Onion** | 1 lb.,.8 oz. |
| 1½ qt. | **Thinly Sliced Mushrooms** | 1 lb., 8 oz. |
| 1¼ c. | **Finely Diced Green Pepper** | 6 oz. |
| 1¼ c. | **Finely Diced Pimiento** | 10 oz. |
| 1 pt. | **Finely Diced Ham** | 13 oz. |

### B

| | | |
|---|---|---|
| 1½ qts. | **Tomato Juice** | 3 lbs., 12 oz. |

### C

| | | |
|---|---|---|
| ¾ c. | **Water** | 6 oz. |
| ⅔ c. | **Cornstarch** | 3 oz. |
| 2 tbsp. | **Salt** | |
| 5 tbsp. | **Sugar** | 2 oz. |

**METHOD**

1. Melt fat, and remaining ingredients in A and cook until tender.
2. Add B. Heat.
3. Combine C. Pour gradually into AB, stirring constantly. Continue stirring until the sauce thickens and is clear.
4. Simmer for one-half hour.
5. Serve with veal, fish, cheese soufflé, omelet.

**YIELD**

100 1-oz. servings.

**NOTE**

Mushrooms and/or ham may be omitted.

## RAVIGOTTI SAUCE

| 3 c. | Butter | 1 lb., 8 oz. |
|---|---|---|
| 1 c. | Very Finely Chopped Onion | 5 oz. |
| 3 tbsp. | Capers | |
| 6 tbsp. | Finely Chopped Cooked Beets | |
| 2 c. | Lemon Juice | 1 lb. |
| 3 c. | Gravy | 1 lb., 8 oz. |
| 3 c. | Tomato Juice | 1 lb., 8 oz. |
| 1 tbsp. | Salt | |
| ¾ tsp. | Pepper | |

**METHOD**

1. Cook onions in butter until tender.
2. Add all the other ingredients and heat.
3. Serve with meat or fish.

**YIELD**

100 1-oz. servings.

## SAUCE BAYONNAISE

| 3 qts. | Mayonnaise | 7 lbs., 8 oz. |
|---|---|---|
| ⅔ c. | Chopped Olives | 3 oz. |
| 1¼ c. | Chopped Pickles | 7 oz. |
| ⅔ c. | Chopped Parsley | 2 oz. |
| 1 c. | Chopped Hard-Cooked Eggs | 6 oz. |
| 1½ c. | Diced Ham | 8 oz. |

**METHOD**

Combine all the ingredients.

**YIELD**

1 gal. sauce, 100 servings (2 tbsp.).

# Soups

## GENERAL DIRECTIONS FOR SOUPS

Crack and use all meat bones except those of pork for soup stock. Use ham bones, bacon rind and cuttings for dried bean and pea soup.

Use water from boiled and canned vegetables as part of the soup stock.

The flavour of soup will be improved and there will be less odour in the kitchen if the diced onions are blanched in boiling water before being added to the soup.

Season soup carefully just before serving. Add the salt and pepper gradually, tasting soup after each addition.

Introduce variety into soups by using vegetables in season.

Enhance flavour by using monosodium glutamate.

## MEAT STOCK

|          | Bones       | 30 lbs. |
|----------|-------------|---------|
| 6 gals.  | Cold Water  | 60 lbs. |
|          | Onions      | 3 lbs.  |
|          | Carrots     | 3 lbs.  |
| 6 tbsp.  | Salt        | 4 oz.   |

**METHOD**
1. Break the bones to expose the marrow.
2. Add unpeeled washed vegetables, cut in pieces.
3. Add the water to the bones and vegetables.
4. Cover and heat to simmering, continue cooking just below boiling point for at least 8 hours.
5. Strain.
6. Cool slightly and skim off the fat. Use for soup, gravy or meat and vegetable sauces.

**NOTE**
1. Celery leaves, stalks and trimmings will improve the flavour of the stock.
2. Left-over vegetables may be used in making stock or may be added to the soup after straining the stock.
3. Part of the vegetables may be browned in fat before being added—this improves the flavour and colour of the stock.

**YIELD**
5 gals.

## BEAN SOUP

| | | |
|---|---|---|
| 2 gals. | Water | 20 lbs. |
| 1 gal. | Dried Beans | 8 lbs. |
| 3 gals. | Hot Stock | 30 lbs. |
| 1⅓ qts. | Raw Diced Onions | 2 lbs. |
| 1⅓ qts. | Raw Diced Celery | 1 lb., 10 oz. |
| 1⅓ qts. | Raw Diced Carrots | 2 lbs. |
| ½ c. | Salt | 5 oz. |
| | Ham Bones or Bacon Rind | |

**METHOD**

1. Soak the beans in the cold water overnight.
2. Add the hot stock. Cook for approximately 1 hour until very soft. Purée if possible.
3. Add the remaining ingredients and cook for 1 hour.

**YIELD**

100 8-oz. servings.

**VARIATIONS**

1. Use split peas or lentils instead of beans.


## THICK PURÉE (Beans, Peas, Lentils)

**METHOD**

1. Use the above recipe but increase the dried vegetable to 10 lbs.
2. After soaking, cook all the ingredients except the stock until the vegetables are sufficiently tender to purée.
3. Purée, add the stock. Simmer 1 hour.

# BEEF AND BARLEY
OR
# LAMB AND BARLEY

### A

| | | |
|---|---|---|
| ½ pt. | Barley | 10 oz. |
| 1 qt. | Water | 2 lbs., 8 oz. |

### B

| | | |
|---|---|---|
| 3½ gals. | Hot Stock (beef or lamb) | 35 lbs. |
| 1½ pt. | Raw Diced Onions | 1 lb., 2 oz. |
| 1 qt. | Raw Diced Celery | 1 lb., 4 oz. |
| 1½ pt. | Raw Diced Carrots | 1 lb., 2 oz. |
| 1 pt. | Raw Diced Turnips | 12 oz. |

### C

| | | |
|---|---|---|
| 2 qts. | Cold Water | 5 lbs. |
| 1 qt. | Unsifted Pastry Flour | 1 lb., 4 oz. |

### D

| | | |
|---|---|---|
| 2 qts. | Canned Tomato | 5 lbs. |
| ½ c. | Salt | 5 oz. |

**METHOD**

1. Cook A for 1 hour.
2. Combine A and B and cook for ten minutes.
3. Mix C and strain. Add slowly to soup, stirring constantly.
4. Add D and cook for 1 hour.

**YIELD**

100 8-oz. servings.

## BEEF CONSOMMÉ

| | | |
|---|---|---|
| 6 gals. | Clear Soup Stock | 60 lbs. |
| 1 #10 tin | Tomato Juice | 6 lbs., 8 oz. |
| | Lean Raw Beef | 10 lbs. |
| 20 | Egg Whites and Shells | |
| ½ tsp. | Pepper Berries | |
| 1 | Bay Leaf | |
| 1 | Clove Garlic | |
| 6 | Whole Cloves | |
| ½ c. | Salt | 5 oz. |
| | Onions | 1 lb. |
| | Carrots | 1 lb. |
| | Celery | 1 lb. |

**METHOD**

1. Make soup stock the previous day and chill thoroughly.
2. Mix the cold stock, tomato juice, beef, egg whites and crushed shells together.
3. Add the peeled, whole vegetables and the seasonings.
4. Heat to simmering point, stirring once or twice. Cover and simmer for 4 hours. Do not boil and do not stir.
5. Strain through a fine cloth, reheat and serve.

**NOTE**

1. Save the meat from the soup to use in croquettes.
2. Veal or chicken consommé may be made by the same method, but the tomato juice should be omitted.

**YIELD**

100 8-oz. servings.

## BEEF BROTH WITH RICE

### A

| 4½ gals. | Hot Beef Stock | 45 lbs. |
| 1½ pts. | Raw Diced Onions | 1 lb., 2 oz. |
| 1 qt. | Raw Diced Celery | 1 lb., 4 oz. |
| 1½ pts. | Raw Diced Carrots | 1 lb., 2 oz. |
| 1 pt. | Raw Diced Turnips | 12 oz. |

### B

| 1½ pts. | Raw Rice | 1 lb., 14 oz. |

### C

| 2 #2 tins | Peas | 2 lbs., 8 oz. |
| ½ c. | Salt | 5 oz. |

**METHOD**

1. Simmer A for 1 hour in a covered pot.
2. Add B. Cook for an additional 20 minutes.
3. Add C. Reheat.

**YIELD**

100 8-oz. servings.

## CREOLE SOUP

### A

| 2 c. | Margarine | 1 lb. |
| 6 c. | Sliced Mushrooms | 1 lb., 8 oz. |
| 1½ qts. | Raw, Diced Onions | 2 lbs., 4 oz. |

### B

| 1 qt. | Raw, Diced Celery | 1 lb., 4 oz. |
| 1½ qts. | Diced Green Pepper | 2 lbs., 4 oz. |
| 1½ gals. | Hot Canned Tomatoes | 15 lbs. |

### C

| 3 gals. | Hot Stock | 30 lbs. |
| ½ c. | Salt | 5 oz. |
| ¼ c. | Sugar | |
| 1¼ pts. | Raw Rice (washed) | 1 lb., 9 oz. |

**METHOD**

1. Braise A for 15 minutes. Add B.
2. Add C. Boil for 10 to 15 minutes.
3. Add rice. Boil until the rice is tender (about 20 minutes).

**YIELD**

100 8-oz. servings.

## MULLIGATAWNY SOUP

| | | |
|---|---|---|
| 2½ pts. | Raw Diced Onions | 1 lb., 14 oz. |
| 2½ pts. | Raw Diced Celery | 1 lb., 9 oz. |
| 2½ pts. | Raw Minced Carrots | 1 lb., 14 oz. |
| 16 | Medium Apples, Chopped | |
| 1½ pts. | Fat | 1 lb., 8 oz. |
| ¾ c. | Curry Powder | 3 oz. |
| 1 tbsp. | Mace | |
| 1½ qts. | Unsifted Pastry Flour | 1 lb., 14 oz. |
| 4 gals. | Meat Stock | 40 lbs. |
| 6 #2½ tins | Tomatoes | 10 lbs. |
| 30 | Whole Cloves | |
| ½ c. | Salt | 5 oz. |

**METHOD**

1. Braise the vegetables and apples in the melted fat.
2. When almost finished add the curry powder and mace. Cook for 2 minutes.
3. Add the flour, to make a roux.
4. Add the stock and tomatoes.
5. Place the cloves in a small piece of thin cotton and add to the soup.
6. Boil for 1 hour. Remove the cloves.
7. Purée the soup.
8. Add the salt and reheat.

**YIELD**

Approx. 100 8-oz. servings.

**VARIATIONS**

1. 1 c. diced green pepper may be added with the other vegetables.
2. 1 pt. finely chopped parsley may be added just before serving.

## CHICKEN AND RICE SOUP

| | | |
|---|---|---|
| 4½ gals. | Chicken Stock | 45 lbs. |
| 1½ pts. | Raw Diced Onions | 1 lb., 2 oz. |
| 1 pt. | Raw Rice | 1 lb., 4 oz. |
| 2 qts. | Raw Diced Celery | 2 lbs., 8 oz. |
| 1½ pts. | Chicken Fat | 1 lb., 8 oz. |
| 1¼ qts. | Unsifted Pastry Flour | 1 lb., 8 oz. |
| ½ c. | Salt | 5 oz. |
| 1 tbsp. | Pepper | |

**METHOD**

1. Heat the chicken stock to boiling.
2. Blanch the raw diced onions for 2 minutes in boiling water to cover. Drain.
3. Wash the rice thoroughly.
4. Add the onions, rice and celery to the stock. Cook until tender.
5. Make a roux of the chicken fat and flour. Add to the soup and cook until there is no taste of raw starch (10 minutes).
6. Add seasonings. Reheat.

**YIELD**

Approx. 100 8-oz. servings (1 c.).

**VARIATION**

1 pt. finely diced raw green pepper may be added with the seasonings.

## POTAGE JACKSON

| | | |
|---|---|---|
| 3½ qts. | Raw Diced Onions | 5 lbs., 4 oz. |
| 2 qts. | Raw Diced Celery | 2 lbs., 8 oz. |
| 1¾ qts. | Raw Diced Carrots | 2 lbs., 8 oz. |
| 1½ pts. | Raw Diced Turnips | 1 lb., 2 oz. |
| 1¾ gals. | Raw Diced Potatoes | 10 lbs., 8 oz. |
| 2 #2 tins | Peas | 2 lbs., 8 oz. |
| 2 #2 tins | Corn | 2 lbs., 8 oz. |
| 2 gals. | Stock | 20 lbs. |
| 1 gal. | Canned Tomatoes | 10 lbs. |
| ½ c. | Salt | 5 oz. |

**METHOD**

1. Add the vegetables to the stock and cook for 1 hour.
2. Purée the soup.
3. Add the tomatoes and salt. Cook for 10 minutes.

**YIELD**

100 8-oz. servings.

## RICE AND TOMATO

### A

| | | |
|---|---|---|
| 3½ gals. | Hot Stock | 35 lbs. |
| 1 pt. | Raw Diced Onions | 12 oz. |
| 1 pt. | Raw Diced Carrots | 12 oz. |
| 1 pt. | Raw Diced Celery | 10 oz. |
| 1½ pts. | Raw Rice | 1 lb., 14 oz. |

### B

| | | |
|---|---|---|
| 1½ gals. | Canned Tomatoes | 15 lbs. |
| ½ c. | Salt | 5 oz. |
| ½ c. | Sugar | 3 oz. |

**METHOD**

1. Combine ingredients in A. Cook for 1 hour.
2. Add B and cook for an additional 10 minutes.

**YIELD**

100 8-oz. servings.

## SCOTCH SOUP

| | | |
|---|---|---|
| 1½ c. | Fat | 10 oz. |
| 3 qts. | Thinly Sliced Onions | 4 lbs., 8 oz. |
| 1½ pts. | Unsifted Pastry Flour | 15 oz. |
| 3 gals. | Hot Stock | 30 lbs. |
| 1½ qts. | Rolled Oats | 1 lb., 8 oz. |
| 3 qts. | Raw Diced Potatoes | 4 lbs., 8 oz. |
| 2 gals. | Tomatoes | 20 lbs. |
| 6 tbsp. | Salt | 4 oz. |

**METHOD**

1. Melt fat. Add the onions and cook until they are tender.
2. Add the pastry flour and blend well.
3. Add the stock slowly, stirring as you add.
4. When the thickened stock is boiling, sprinkle in the rolled oats slowly.
5. Add the potato and cook until tender.
6. Just before serving, add the tomatoes and salt. Reheat.

**YIELD**

100 8-oz. servings.


## TOMATO BOUILLON

| | | |
|---|---|---|
| 2 gals. | Tomato Juice or Strained Canned Tomatoes | 20 lbs. |
| 3 gals. | Hot Stock | 30 lbs. |
| 1 pt. | Raw Diced Carrots | 12 oz. |
| 1 pt. | Raw Diced Onions | 12 oz. |
| 1 pt. | Raw Diced Celery | 10 oz. |
| 2 | Bay Leaves | |
| 4 | Cloves | |
| 1 qt. | Crushed Egg Shells | |
| ½ c. | Salt | 5 oz. |

**METHOD**

1. Combine ingredients.
2. Simmer 1 hour.
3. Strain.

**YIELD**

100 8-oz. servings.

## VEGETABLE SOUP

### A

| | | |
|---|---|---|
| 4 gals. | Hot Stock | 40 lbs. |
| 1½ pts. | Raw Diced Onions | 1 lb., 2 oz. |
| 1 qt. | Raw Diced Celery | 1 lb., 4 oz. |
| 1½ pts. | Raw Diced Carrots | 1 lb., 2 oz. |
| 1 pt. | Raw Diced Turnips | 12 oz. |
| 1 pt. | Diced Green Peppers | 12 oz. |

### B

| | | |
|---|---|---|
| 2 #2 tins | Peas | 2 lbs., 8 oz. |
| 2 #2 tins | Corn | 2 lbs., 8 oz. |
| ½ c. | Salt | 5 oz. |

**METHOD**

1. Cook A for 1 hour.
2. Add B. Cook for an additional 10 minutes.

**NOTE**

1. Stock may consist of meat or vegetable stock or a combination of the two.
2. When vegetable stock is used, taste the soup before adding the salt.
3. Use any vegetables available (with the exception of beets), allowing 2 to 3 lbs. to 1 gallon of liquid.
   The above list is merely a suggestion.
4. Soup may be thickened with flour, using ½ cup (2 oz.) to 1 gallon soup.

**YIELD**

100 8-oz. servings.

**VARIATION**

Omit peas and corn and add 1 lb. raw macaroni to A and cook with the vegetables.

## CHOWDER POLONAISE

### A

| 2 qts. | Kidneys | 5 lbs. |
| 2 qts. | Water | 5 lbs. |

### B

| 3½ gals. | Hot Stock | 35 lbs. |
| 1½ pts. | Raw Diced Carrots | 1 lb., 2 oz. |
| 1½ pts. | Raw Diced Onions | 1 lb., 2 oz. |
| 1 qt. | Raw Diced Celery | 1 lb., 4 oz. |
| 1½ pts. | Diced Green Peppers | 1 lb., 2 oz. |
| 3½ pts. | Raw Diced Potatoes | 2 lbs., 10 oz. |

### C

| 2 qts. | Cold Water | 5 lbs. |
| 1 qt. | Unsifted Pastry Flour | 1 lb., 4 oz. |

### D

| 1 qt. | Canned Tomatoes | 2 lbs., 8 oz. |
| ½ c. | Salt | 5 oz. |
| 1 pt. | Diced Cooked Beets | 1 lb. |

**METHOD**

1. Trim kidneys and dice. Simmer A for half an hour or until tender. Drain and rinse.
2. Combine ingredients in B. Simmer for 1 hour in a covered pot. Add kidneys.
3. Mix C and strain. Add slowly to B, stirring constantly.
4. Add D and cook for 10 minutes.

**YIELD**

100 8-oz. servings.

## CLAM CHOWDER

| | | |
|---|---|---|
| 2 bus. | Clams | |
| 2 gals. | Water | 20 lbs. |
| | Diced Bacon or Salt Pork | 2 lbs. |
| 1½ pts. | Raw Sliced Onions | 1 lb., 2 oz. |
| 2 gals. | Raw Sliced Potatoes | 14 lbs. |
| 1 qt. | Unsifted Pastry Flour | 1 lb., 4 oz. |
| 1 gal. | Milk | 10 lbs. |
| ½ c. | Salt | 5 oz. |
| 1 tbsp. | Thyme | |
| | Whole Soda Biscuits | |

**METHOD**

1. Wash the sand from the clams, using 3 waters. Throw away all clams that float.
2. Add 2 gals. of water to the washed clams, bring quickly to the boil and then strain off the liquid into another saucepan.
3. Remove clams from their shells, beard them, then chop coarsely.
4. Cook the diced pork or bacon over a low heat.
5. Add the onions and cook until they are lightly browned.
6. Add the potatoes and the clam liquid and cook until the potatoes are nearly tender.
7. Blend the flour and milk and strain into the mixture, stirring as you add.
8. Cook for 5 minutes. Add thyme and salt, cook 5 minutes longer.
9. Add the chopped clams. Reheat.
10. Serve the chowder with whole soda biscuits.

**NOTE**

8 oz. of butter may be added just before serving.

**YIELD**

100 8-oz. servings.

## CORN CHOWDER

### A

| | | |
|---|---|---|
| 8 #2 tins | Corn (cream style) | 10 lbs. |
| 1½ pts. | Raw Diced Onions | 1 lb., 2 oz. |
| 1 qt. | Raw Diced Celery | 1 lb., 4 oz. |
| 2 | Diced Green Peppers | |
| 3 qts. | Raw Diced Potatoes | 4 lbs., 8 oz. |
| 3 gals. | Hot Stock | 30 lbs. |

### B

| | | |
|---|---|---|
| ½ gal. | Cold Water | 5 lbs. |
| 1 pt. | Unsifted Pastry Flour | 10 oz. |

### C

| | | |
|---|---|---|
| ½ c. | Salt | 5 oz. |
| 1 tbsp. | Savoury | |

**METHOD**

1. Simmer A for 1 hour in a covered pot. Purée.
2. Mix B and strain. Add to A, stirring constantly, and cook for 20 minutes.
3. Add C.

**YIELD**

100 8-oz. servings.

## CORN AND TOMATO CHOWDER

### A

| | | |
|---|---|---|
| 1 qt. | Butter or Margarine | 2 lbs., 8 oz. |
| 1 pt. | Raw Diced Onions | 12 oz. |
| 1 pt. | Raw Diced Celery | 10 oz. |
| 1 qt. | Unsifted Pastry Flour | 1 lb., 4 oz. |

### B

| | | |
|---|---|---|
| 1 gal. | Stock | 10 lbs. |

### C

| | | |
|---|---|---|
| 6 qts. | Canned Tomatoes | 15 lbs. |
| 8 #2 tins | Corn (cream style) | 10 lbs. |
| ½ c. | Salt | 5 oz. |

### D

| | | |
|---|---|---|
| 1 gal. | Milk | 10 lbs. |

**METHOD**

1. Make according to general method for Cream Soups, page 320.

**YIELD**

100 8-oz. servings.

## VEGETABLE CHOWDER

### A

| | | |
|---|---|---|
| 3 gals. | Hot Stock | 30 lbs. |
| 1 qt. | Raw Diced Onions | 1 lb., 8 oz. |
| 2½ pts. | Raw Diced Celery | 1 lb., 9 oz. |
| 1 qt. | Raw Diced Carrots | 1 lb., 8 oz. |
| 1 pt. | Raw Diced Turnips | 12 oz. |
| 1 pt. | Diced Green Peppers | 12 oz. |
| 1½ qts. | Raw Diced Potatoes | 2 lbs., 4 oz. |

### B

| | | |
|---|---|---|
| 2 qts. | Water | 5 lbs. |
| 1 qt. | Unsifted Pastry Flour | 1 lb., 4 oz. |

### C

| | | |
|---|---|---|
| 2 qts. | Tomatoes | 5 lbs. |
| 2 #2 tins | Peas | 2 lbs., 8 oz. |
| 2 #2 tins | Corn | 2 lbs., 8 oz. |
| ½ c. | Salt | 5 oz. |

**METHOD**

1. Cook A for 1 hour.
2. Mix B and strain. Add slowly to A, stirring constantly.
3. Add C and cook for an additional 10 minutes.

**YIELD**

100 8-oz. servings.

## FISH STOCK

|         | Fish Bones and Heads | 15 lbs.        |
| ------- | -------------------- | -------------- |
| 4 gals. | Boiling Water        | 40 lbs.        |
|         | Onions               | 1 lb., 8 oz.   |
|         | Celery Tops          | 8 oz.          |
|         | Carrots              | 1 lb., 8 oz.   |
| 1 only  | Bay Leaf             |                |
| 2 only  | Cloves               |                |

**METHOD**
1. Add fish bones and heads to boiling water.
2. Add unpeeled washed vegetables cut in pieces and heat to simmering point.
3. Cover and simmer for about ½ hour.
4. Strain and use in fish soups.

**YIELD**
3 gals.

## FISH CHOWDER

|           | **A**                |                |
| --------- | -------------------- | -------------- |
|           | Raw Diced Fish       | 5 lbs.         |
| 1½ pts.   | Raw Diced Onions     | 1 lb., 2 oz.   |
| 1 qt.     | Raw Diced Celery     | 1 lb., 4 oz.   |
| 1½ pts.   | Diced Green Peppers  | 1 lb., 2 oz.   |
| 3 qts.    | Raw Diced Potatoes   | 4 lbs., 8 oz.  |
| 3 gals.   | Hot Fish Stock       | 30 lbs.        |
|           | **B**                |                |
| ½ gal.    | Cold Water           | 5 lbs.         |
| 1 qt.     | Unsifted Pastry Flour | 1 lb., 4 oz.  |
|           | **C**                |                |
| ½ c.      | Salt                 | 5 oz.          |
| 1 tbsp.   | Savoury              |                |

**METHOD**
1. Simmer A for 1 hour.
2. Mix B and strain. Add slowly to A, stirring constantly. Cook for an additional 20 minutes.
3. Add C.

**NOTE**
Green peppers and savoury may be omitted.

**YIELD**
100 8-oz. servings.

## CREAM SOUPS

A cream soup should be of smooth texture and should have the consistency of whipping cream. The flavour of the main vegetable from which it is made should predominate.
Cream soups may be made from a combination of milk, vegetable stock and puréed vegetables; or meat stock may be substituted for all or part of the vegetable stock.

### GENERAL METHOD

A. Melt the fat. Add chopped onion and celery. Cook 10 minutes. Add flour and blend thoroughly.
B. Heat the stock. Add it gradually to the above, stirring constantly. Cook for 20 minutes.
C. Add the salt and the cooked vegetables which have been either puréed or put through a meat grinder.
D. Heat the milk and add.
E. Reheat before serving. Cream soups should be made only a short time before they are to be served. They will curdle if allowed to stand in a steam-table or steam-jacketed kettle for any length of time.

## CREAM OF CARROT SOUP
## CREAM OF PEA SOUP

### METHOD

1. Follow the recipe for Corn Soup, using 10 lbs. of the cooked vegetable (approx. 1 gallon), in place of corn.
2. Use the vegetable water as part of the stock.

## CREAM OF ASPARAGUS SOUP
## CREAM OF SPINACH SOUP
## CREAM OF ONION SOUP

### METHOD

1. Follow the recipe for Corn Soup, using 10 lbs. of the cooked vegetable (approx. 1 gallon) in place of corn.
2. Increase flour in Corn Soup recipe to 1½ qts. (1 lb. 14 oz.).
3. Use the vegetable water as part of the stock.

## CREAM OF CELERY SOUP

|              | **A¹**                              |                 |
| ------------ | ----------------------------------- | --------------- |
| 1½ bus.      | Celery Tops                         | 15 lbs.         |
| 3 gals.      | Hot Water                           | 30 lbs.         |
|              | **A**                               |                 |
| 1 qt.        | Butter or Margarine                 | 2 lbs., 8 oz.   |
| 1 pt.        | Raw Diced Onion                     | 12 oz.          |
| 1 pt.        | Raw Diced Celery                    | 10 oz.          |
| 2 qts.       | Unsifted Pastry Flour               | 2 lbs., 8 oz.   |
|              | **B**                               |                 |
| 2½ gals.     | Milk                                | 25 lbs.         |
|              | **C**                               |                 |
| ½ c.         | Salt                                | 5 oz.           |
|              | Puréed Vegetable and Stock from A¹  |                 |

**METHOD**

1. Boil A¹ for 20 minutes. Strain and use liquid (there should be 3 gallons) as stock in the soup.
2. Finish according to general method for Cream Soups, page 320.

**YIELD**

100 8-oz. servings.

## CREAM OF CORN SOUP

|              | **A**                  |                 |
| ------------ | ---------------------- | --------------- |
| 1 pt.        | Butter or Margarine    | 1 lb., 4 oz.    |
| 1 pt.        | Raw Diced Onions       | 12 oz.          |
| 1 pt.        | Raw Diced Celery       | 10 oz.          |
| 1 qt.        | Unsifted Pastry Flour  | 1 lb., 4 oz.    |
|              | **B**                  |                 |
| 2½ gals.     | Stock                  | 25 lbs.         |
|              | **C**                  |                 |
| 8 #2 tins    | Corn (cream style)     | 10 lbs.         |
| ½ c.         | Salt                   | 5 oz.           |
|              | **D**                  |                 |
| 1½ gals.     | Milk                   | 15 lbs.         |

**METHOD**

1. Make according to general method for Cream Soups, page 320.

**YIELD**

100 8-oz. servings.

## CREAM OF CHICKEN SOUP

| | | |
|---|---|---|
| 1½ pts. | Chicken Fat | 1 lb., 8 oz. |
| 1 pt. | Raw Diced Onions | 12 oz. |
| 1½ pts. | Raw Diced Celery | 1 lb. |
| 1½ qts. | Unsifted Pastry Flour | 1 lb., 14 oz. |
| 2½ gals. | Chicken Stock | 25 lbs. |
| 2½ gals. | Hot Milk | 25 lbs. |
| ½ c. | Salt | 5 oz. |

**METHOD**

Prepare according to the general method for Cream Soups, page 320.

**NOTE**

The diced onions and celery may be strained out or puréed before serving.

**YIELD**

Approx. 100 8-oz. servings.


## CREAM OF POTATO SOUP

### AI

| | | |
|---|---|---|
| 1½ gals. | Raw Potatoes | 9 lbs. |
| 2½ gals. | Stock or Water | 25 lbs. |

### A

| | | |
|---|---|---|
| 1 pt. | Butter or Margarine | 1 lb., 4 oz. |
| 1 qt. | Raw Diced Onions | 1 lb., 8 oz. |
| 1 qt. | Raw Diced Celery | 1 lb., 4 oz. |
| 1 pt. | Unsifted Pastry Flour | 10 oz. |

### B

| | | |
|---|---|---|
| ½ c. | Salt | 5 oz. |
| | Puréed Vegetables and Stock from AI | |

### C

| | | |
|---|---|---|
| 1½ gals. | Milk | 15 lbs. |

**METHOD**

1. Cook AI. Measure the liquid after cooking and make up to 2½ gallons with water. Purée the potatoes.
2. Finish according to the general method for Cream Soups, page 320.

**YIELD**

100 8-oz. servings.

## POTATO AND CHEESE SOUP

### A

| | | |
|---|---|---|
| 2 gals. | Raw Sliced Potatoes | 12 lbs. |
| 1 gal. | Raw Diced Onions | 6 lbs. |
| 1 pt. | Raw Diced Celery | 10 oz. |
| 3 gals. | Stock | 30 lbs. |

### B

| | | |
|---|---|---|
| 1 gal. | Milk | 10 lbs. |

### C

| | | |
|---|---|---|
| 1¼ qts. | Grated Cheese | 1 lb., 4 oz. |
| ½ c. | Salt | 5 oz. |

**METHOD**
1. Boil A for 30 minutes and purée.
2. Heat B and add to A.
3. Add C slowly, stirring to avoid lumps. Simmer for 10 minutes.

**YIELD**
100 8-oz. servings.

## POTATO AND ONION SOUP

### A¹

| | | |
|---|---|---|
| 1½ gals. | Raw Sliced Potatoes | 9 lbs. |
| 1 gal. | Raw Diced Onions | 6 lbs. |
| 1½ gals. | Water | 15 lbs. |

### A

| | | |
|---|---|---|
| 1 pt. | Butter or Margarine | 1 lb., 4 oz. |
| 1 pt. | Raw Diced Celery | 10 oz. |
| 1 pt. | Unsifted Pastry Flour | 10 oz. |

### B

| | | |
|---|---|---|
| 1½ gals. | Stock | 15 lbs. |
| 1 gal. | Milk | 10 lbs. |

### C

| | | |
|---|---|---|
| ½ c. | Salt | 5 oz. |
| | Puréed Vegetable and Stock from A¹ | |

**METHOD**
1. Cook A¹. Measure the liquid after cooking and make up to 1 gallon with water. Purée the vegetables.
2. Finish according to general method for Cream Soups, page 320.

**YIELD**
100 8-oz. servings.

## CREAM OF MIXED VEGETABLE SOUP

| | | |
|---|---|---|
| 2 qts. | Raw Diced Onions | 3 lbs. |
| 2 qts. | Raw Diced Carrots | 3 lbs. |
| 2½ qts. | Raw Chopped Celery Leaves and Stalks | 3 lbs. |
| 1½ gals. | Boiling Water | 15 lbs. |
| 1 qt. | Butter or Margarine | 2 lbs., 8 oz. |
| 1½ qts. | Unsifted Pastry Flour | 2 lbs. |
| 3 gals. | Hot Milk | 30 lbs. |
| 3 #2 cans | Green Peas | 3 lbs., 12 oz. |
| ½ c. | Salt | 5 oz. |

**METHOD**

1. Blanch the onions for 2 minutes in boiling water. Drain.
2. Add the blanched onions, the carrots and celery to the boiling water and boil until tender (about 20 minutes).
3. Drain off the liquid and measure. There should be 1 gal.
4. Finish as Cream Soup, using the hot vegetable stock as part of the liquid.
5. Add the canned peas with their liquid, the cooked vegetables and salt. Reheat.

**YIELD**

Approx. 100 8-oz. servings.

**VARIATIONS**

1. Tomato juice may be used as part of the liquid.
2. Other combinations of vegetables may be used.
3. Left-over vegetables may be used in this way. If no vegetable stock is available, substitute 1 gal. of meat stock.

# CREAM OF SPLIT PEA SOUP

| | | |
|---|---|---|
| 1 gal. | Green or Yellow Split Peas | 8 lbs. |
| | Cold Water to cover | |
| 1½ gals. | Boiling Water | 15 lbs. |
| ½ pt. | Butter or Margarine | 10 oz. |
| 1 pt. | Chopped Onions | 12 oz. |
| 1 pt. | Unsifted Pastry Flour | 10 oz. |
| 4 gals. | Milk | 40 lbs. |
| ½ c. | Salt | 5 oz. |
| | Ham Bones, Bacon Rind or 8 oz. Salt Pork | |

**METHOD**

1. Pick over and wash the peas.
2. Soak overnight in cold water to cover (about 2 gals.).
3. Without draining, add the boiling water and cook until very tender. Cook the bones, rind or pork with the peas.
4. Drain off the liquid and measure—there should be 1 gal.
5. Purée the cooked peas.
6. Finish as cream soup.

**NOTE**

Marrowfat peas may be substituted for split peas.

**YIELD**

Approx. 100 8-oz. servings.

**VARIATIONS**

2 bay leaves may be cooked with the peas.

## CREAM OF TOMATO SOUP

### A

| 1 qt. | Butter or Margarine | 2 lbs., 8 oz. |
| 1 pt. | Diced Onions | 12 oz. |
| 1 pt. | Diced Celery | 10 oz. |
| 1½ qts. | Unsifted Pastry Flour | 1 lb., 14 oz. |

### B

| 1¾ gals. | Stock | 17 lbs., 8 oz. |
| 2 gals. | Tomato Juice or Canned Tomatoes | 20 lbs. |
| ½ c. | Salt | 5 oz. |
| ½ c. | Sugar | 3 oz. |
| 1½ tbsp. | Pepper | |

### C

| 1 gal. | Hot Milk | 10 lbs. |

**METHOD**

1. Make according to general method for Cream Soups, page 320.

**NOTE**

1. One quart of tomato purée added to the soup will improve the flavour.
2. The soup will have a better colour and flavour and will be less apt to curdle if the hot thickened tomato is poured into the hot milk.

**YIELD**

100 8-oz. servings.

## CREAM SOUPS WITH BACON

| | Cream Soup Recipe |
| 1½ lbs. | Finely Diced Bacon cooked until crisp. |

**METHOD**

Add the well-drained cooked bacon to the soup just before serving.

# Supper Dishes

## BACON CHOWDER

|            | Potatoes, A.P. | 28 lbs.  |
|------------|----------------|----------|
|            | Onions, A.P.   | 3 lbs.   |
|            | Bacon          | 6 lbs.   |
| 12 #2 tins | Corn           | 15 lbs.  |
| 2 #10 tins | Tomatoes       | 13 lbs.  |
| 4 tbsp.    | Salt           | 2½ oz.   |
| 2 tsp.     | Pepper         |          |

**METHOD**

1. Prepare the potatoes and cut into ½-inch cubes. Parboil and drain well.
2. Chop the onions, dice the bacon, then brown and fry together until the onions are tender.
3. Combine all the ingredients, heat to simmering point and continue cooking for 15 minutes.

**YIELD**

100 8-oz. servings.


## BAKED BEANS WITH TOMATO

|            | Dried Beans     | 18 lbs.        |
|------------|-----------------|----------------|
| 9 qts.     | Dried Beans     | 18 lbs.        |
| 1 qt.      | Sliced Onions   | 1 lb., 8 oz.   |
| 1½ pts.    | Fat             | 1 lb., 8 oz.   |
| 2¼ gals.   | Canned Tomatoes | 22 lbs., 8 oz. |
| ¾ c.       | Salt            | 7 oz.          |
| 1 tbsp.    | Pepper          |                |

**METHOD**

1. Soak and cook the beans according to the general method, page 369. Drain thoroughly.
2. Cook the sliced onion in the fat until tender.
3. Arrange the ingredients in layers in bean pots. Cover.
4. Bake in a slow oven (300°-325°F.) for two hours or more.

**YIELD**

100 8-oz. servings.

## BAKED BEANS IN TOMATO SAUCE

| | | |
|---|---|---|
| 9 qts. | Dried Beans | 18 lbs. |
| 1 gal. | Water | 10 lbs. |
| 2½ gals. | Tomatoes | 25 lbs. |
| 1 qt. | Fat | 2 lbs. |
| 1 qt. | Sliced Onions | 1 lb., 8 oz. |
| 1½ qts. | Unsifted Pastry Flour | 1 lb., 14 oz. |
| 2 tbsp. | Mustard | |
| 2 tbsp. | Pepper | |
| ¾ c. | Salt | 7 oz. |

**METHOD**

1. Soak and cook beans according to the general method, page 369. Drain thoroughly.
2. Add the gallon of water to the tomatoes and heat to boiling.
3. Melt fat, add the onions and cook until tender.
4. Mix the flour and seasonings and add to the fat and onions. Blend well and continue cooking until the mixture froths.
5. Add the hot tomatoes gradually, stirring as you add. Cook and stir until the sauce thickens.
6. Push through a sieve until only the tomato seeds and onions remain.
7. Place the cooked beans and the tomato sauce in bean pots. Cover. Bake for at least 2 hours in a slow oven (300°-325°F.).

**YIELD**

100 12-oz. servings.

## BOSTON BAKED BEANS

| | | |
|---|---|---|
| 9 qts. | Dried Beans | 18 lbs. |
| 1 pt. | Sugar | 1 lb. |
| ¾ c. | Salt | 7 oz. |
| ¼ c. | Mustard | |
| 1 pt. | Molasses | 1 lb., 12 oz. |
| 2 qts. | Boiling Water | 5 lbs. |
| 5 qts. | Diced Fat Pork | 10 lbs. |

**METHOD**

1. Soak and cook the beans according to the general method, page 369.
2. Mix the dry ingredients together, then add the molasses and boiling water.
3. Place the cooked beans and the diced pork in bean pots. Pour the mixture over them.
4. Bake in a slow oven (300°-325°F.) for several hours. Keep them closely covered. Add water as required to keep them almost covered with liquid.

**YIELD**

100 6-oz. servings.

## BOSTON BROWN BREAD

| | | |
|---|---|---|
| 1½ qts. | Cornmeal | 2 lbs., 10 oz. |
| 2 qts. | Unsifted Rye Flour | 2 lbs. |
| 2 qts. | Unsifted Graham Flour | 2 lbs. |
| ⅓ c. | Salt | 3 oz. |
| 5 tbsp. | Baking Soda | 2 oz. |
| 1½ pts. | Molasses | 2 lbs., 10 oz. |
| 1 gal. | Buttermilk | 10 lbs. |
| 2 qts. | Raisins | 3 lbs., 4 oz. |

**METHOD**

1. Mix and sift the dry ingredients—add the raisins.
2. Make a well in the centre and pour in the liquids. Mix just sufficiently to moisten the dry ingredients.
3. Pour into greased baking pans or tins to a depth of about 1½ inches. Cover and steam for 3 hours.
4. Slice and serve hot with baked beans.

**YIELD**

100 servings.

## MACARONI AND CHEESE

| 5 qts. | Macaroni | 6 lbs., 4 oz. |
|---|---|---|
| | **A** | |
| 1½ pts. | Fat | 1 lb., 8 oz. |
| 1½ qts. | Unsifted Pastry Flour | 1 lb., 14 oz. |
| 6 tbsp. | Salt | 4 oz. |
| 3 gals. | Milk | 30 lbs. |
| 1½ gals. | Grated Cheese | 6 lbs. |
| 1 gal. | Buttered Crumbs | 3 lbs., 12 oz. |

**METHOD**

1. Cook the macaroni according to the general method, page 40. Drain well.
2. Combine A as a cream sauce.
3. When cooked, add the grated cheese and stir until it is melted.
4. Add the cooked macaroni.
5. Pour into greased baking pans.
6. Cover with buttered crumbs (page 281).
7. Brown in a slow oven (300°-325°F.).

**NOTE**

1. Macaroni and cheese may be served without baking in the oven, in which case the buttered crumbs are omitted.
2. Spaghetti may be substituted for macaroni.
3. If old cheese is used, reduce the quantity to 3 lbs.

**YIELD**

100 10-oz. servings.

## MACARONI, TOMATO AND CHEESE

| | | |
|---|---|---|
| 5 qts. | Macaroni | 6 lbs., 4 oz. |
| 1½ qts. | Sliced Onions | 2 lbs., 4 oz. |
| 1 qt. | Fat | 2 lbs. |
| 1½ qts. | Unsifted Pastry Flour | 1 lb., 14 oz. |
| ¾ c. | Salt | 7 oz. |
| 1 tbsp. | Pepper | |
| 2½ gals. | Hot Canned Tomatoes | 25 lbs. |
| 1½ gals. | Grated Cheese | 6 lbs. |

**METHOD**

1. Cook the macaroni according to the general method, page 40. Drain well.
2. Cook the sliced onion in the fat until tender.
3. Add the flour and seasonings to the fat and onion, and continue cooking until the mixture froths.
4. Add the hot canned tomatoes, slowly, stirring constantly until it thickens.
5. Add the grated cheese and stir until it is melted.
6. Combine with cooked macaroni.
7. This may be served without further cooking or it may be covered with buttered crumbs and baked in a slow oven (300°-325°F.) until browned on top.

**NOTE**

Spaghetti may be substituted for macaroni.

**YIELD**

100 9-oz. servings.

## MACARONI AND MEAT BALLS

### A

| 1 pt. | Fat | 1 lb. |
| 1 gal. | Raw Diced Onions | 6 lbs. |

### B

| 1 gal. | Hot Canned Tomatoes | 10 lbs. |
| ¾ gal. | Hot Stock, Vegetable or Meat | 7 lbs., 8 oz. |

### C

| 1 c. | Cornstarch | 5 oz. |
| | or | |
| 2 c. | Unsifted Pastry Flour | 8 oz. |
| 6 tbsp. | Salt | 4 oz. |
| 1 qt. | Cold Stock | 2 lbs., 8 oz. |

### D

| 3½ qts. | Raw Macaroni | 4 lbs., 6 oz. |

**METHOD**

1. Cook ingredients in A together for 10 minutes.
2. Add to B and bring to the boil.
3. Mix ingredients in C and add gradually to the above, stirring constantly until it boils. Continue cooking for 20 minutes or until there is no taste of raw starch.
4. Add the macaroni cooked according to the general method, page 40.

### MEAT BALLS

#### Meat Loaf Mixture, 30 lbs.

**METHOD**

1. Form the meat into walnut-sized balls.
2. Place in greased baking pans and bake in a moderate oven until meat balls are cooked through (about 15 minutes).
3. Lift the meat balls from the pan, allowing any fat to drain off. Add to the macaroni and sauce.
4. Serve very hot.

**YIELD**

100 9-oz. servings.

## MACARONI WITH TOMATO AND MEAT

| | | |
|---|---|---|
| 13 qts. | Diced Raw Meat | 26 lbs. |
| 1½ qts. | Sliced Onions | 2 lbs., 4 oz. |
| 6 qts. | Raw Macaroni | 7 lbs., 8 oz. |
| 1 pt. | Fat | 1 lb. |
| 1 qt. | Flour | 1 lb., 4 oz. |
| 6 tbsp. | Salt | 4 oz. |
| 2 tbsp. | Pepper | |
| 4 gals. | Tomato Juice | 40 lbs. |
| 1 qt. | Tomato Paste | 2 lbs., 8 oz. |

**METHOD**

1. Braise the meat for 45 minutes at 350°F.
2. Add the sliced onions and braise 15 minutes longer. Drain off the melted fat.
3. Cook the macaroni according to the general method, page 40.
4. Make a tomato sauce, using the remaining ingredients.
5. Lift the meat and onions from the pan and add to the sauce. Cover and cook over a low heat or bake in a moderate oven (350°F.) until the meat is tender.
6. Add the cooked macaroni and reheat.

**YIELD**

100 13-oz. servings.


## CHEESE RAREBIT

| | | |
|---|---|---|
| | Thick Cream Sauce | 1½ times recipe |
| 10 qts. | Grated Cheese | 10 lbs. |
| ½ c. | Lea & Perrin's Sauce | |
| 5 tbsp. | Mustard | |

**METHOD**

1. Add the cheese to the hot cream sauce. Stir until the cheese is melted, and add the seasonings.
2. Serve hot on crisp toast or crackers.

**YIELD**

100 6-oz. servings.

## SPANISH RICE

| 2½ qts. | Rice | 6 lbs. |
| 1½ gals. | Stock or Water | 15 lbs. |
| 1 pt. | Fat | 1 lb. |
| 1½ qts. | Sliced Onions | 2 lbs., 4 oz. |
| 2 gals. | Canned Tomatoes | 20 lbs. |
| ½ c. | Salt | 5 oz. |
| 2 tbsp. | Pepper | |
| 1½ gals. | Grated Cheese | 6 lbs. |

**METHOD**

1. Add rice to the hot stock and either boil or bake for 20 minutes. Drain.
2. Melt fat, add sliced onions and cook for 10 minutes.
3. Combine all ingredients, including fat in which onion was cooked.
4. Bake in a moderate oven (350°F.) ½ hour or longer.

**YIELD**

100 7-oz. servings.

**VARIATIONS**

1. Add 3 lbs. diced cooked bacon.
2. Add 1 quart chopped green pepper or diced celery. Cook in the fat with the onion.
3. Reduce rice by 2 lbs. and add 7 lbs. diced, cooked meat.

# CHILI CON CARNE

| | | |
|---|---|---|
| 2 gals. | Dried Kidney Beans | 15 lbs. |
| 2¼ gals. | Boiling Water | 22 lbs., 5 oz. |
| 2 qts. | Finely Chopped Onions | 3 lbs. |
| 3 qts. | Minced Raw Meat | 7 lbs., 8 oz. |
| 5 tbsp. | Chopped Garlic | 1½ oz. |
| 2 c. | Mexican Chili Powder | 9 oz. |
| | Chilies | 1½ oz. |
| 3 tbsp. | Oregano | |
| 3 tbsp. | Thyme | |
| 3 tbsp. | Marjoram | |
| 3 tbsp. | Basil | |
| 1 pt. | Chopped Green Pepper | 12 oz. |
| 1½ qts. | Tomato Purée | 3 lbs., 12 oz. |
| 1 c. | Salt | 10 oz. |

**METHOD**

1. Soak beans overnight in water to cover.
2. Drain. Add the boiling water and other ingredients.
3. Cook slowly until the beans are tender.

**YIELD**

100 8-oz. servings.

## EGG CASSEROLE

### A

| | | |
|---|---|---|
| 1½ pts. | Butter or Margarine | 1 lb., 14 oz. |
| 1 pt. | Finely Chopped Onion | 12 oz. |
| 6 c. | Unsifted Pastry Flour | 1 lb., 8 oz. |
| 1 gal. | Chicken Stock | 10 lbs. |
| 1 gal. | Milk | 10 lbs. |
| 4 tsp. | Pepper | |
| ¼ c. | Salt | |

### B

| | | |
|---|---|---|
| 2½ qts. | Sautéed Mushrooms | 2 lbs. |
| 4 c. | Chopped Pimientos | 2 lbs. |

### C

| | | |
|---|---|---|
| 100 | Hard-Cooked Eggs | 11 lbs. |

**METHOD**

1. Combine A as in making Cream Sauce. Cook the onion in the fat before adding the flour.
2. When A is cooked, stir in B.
3. Cut C in halves lengthwise and spread in a single layer in greased baking dishes.
4. Pour sauce over C and heat in a moderate oven (350°F.).
5. Serve, very hot, on toast, tea biscuits or rice.

**NOTE**

If chicken stock is not available, use all milk for the sauce.

**YIELD**

100 6-oz. servings.

# Tea Biscuits

## GENERAL DIRECTIONS FOR TEA BISCUITS

A good tea biscuit should double in bulk as it cooks, should be golden brown on top and bottom and should be fine grained and rather flaky inside.

When insufficiently mixed they have a rough, mottled surface and do not rise properly. When over-mixed they are tough.

### TEA BISCUIT METHOD

1. Grease the pans.
2. Mix and sift dry ingredients (A in recipe).
3. Work in the fat (B in recipe) with the fingers. The fat should be evenly divided into pieces about the size of a green pea. Shake the bowl occasionally so that the pieces of fat come to the top and then work on those that are too large.
4. Add the milk (C in recipe) gradually to moisten all the dry ingredients.
5. When all the milk has been added, mix the whole thing together. It should be very moist, but not too sticky to handle.
6. Turn on to a lightly floured table and knead for about 1 minute.
7. Roll or pat to $\frac{1}{2}$-inch thickness. Cut with a cookie cutter or knife.
8. Place close together on the greased baking pans.
9. Allow to stand at room temperature for 20 minutes.
10. Bake in a hot oven (450°F.) for 15 to 20 minutes.
11. When biscuits have doubled in bulk and are golden brown in colour, test by breaking one open to be sure that it is cooked through to the centre.

## TEA BISCUITS

### A

| | | |
|---|---|---|
| 6½ qts. | **Unsifted Pastry Flour** | 8 lbs. |
| 1 c. | **Baking Powder** | 6 oz. |
| 4 tbsp. | **Salt** | 2½ oz. |

### B

| | | |
|---|---|---|
| 1 qt. | **Fat** | 2 lbs. |

### C

| | | |
|---|---|---|
| 2 qts. | **Milk** | 5 lbs. |

### METHOD

Make according to general method for tea biscuits. For the best results make in batches of this size or smaller.

### YIELD

200 medium-sized tea biscuits.

## QUICK TEA BISCUITS

Use the standard recipe. Drop from a spoon onto the greased sheet, in place of kneading and cutting.

## CHEESE TEA BISCUITS

To the standard recipe add 3 quarts of grated cheese (3 lbs.). Reduce fat to 1 lb.

## ORANGE TEA BISCUITS

To the standard recipe

| (1) add | 1 qt. | **Grated Orange Rind** | 1 lb. |
| | 1 pt. | **Orange Juice** | 10 oz. |
| | ½ pt. | **Sugar** | 8 oz. |

(2) Reduce Milk to 1½ qts.

## RAISIN TEA BISCUITS

To the standard recipe add 2½ pts. raisins (2 lbs.).

## PLAIN SCONES

To the standard recipe

| (1) add | 1½ pts. | **White Sugar** | 1 lb., 8 oz. |
| | | **Eggs** | 14 oz. |

(2) Reduce Milk to 1¾ qts.

### METHOD
Follow general method for making tea biscuits and, after rolling dough to a thickness of ½ inch, place in pie plates or baking pans and mark into triangles.

## RAISIN SCONES

To the plain scone recipe add 2½ pints raisins (2 lbs.).

## BUTTERSCOTCH BISCUITS

|            | **Scone Dough, page 341.** |                |
|------------|----------------------------|----------------|
| **2 qts.** | **Brown Sugar**            | **3 lbs., 8 oz.** |
| **1 pt.**  | **Butter**                 | **1 lb., 4 oz.**  |

**METHOD**

1. Make scone dough.
2. Roll on floured board and cut into strips 6 inches wide.
3. Cream butter and sugar.
4. Spread sugar mix on dough.
5. Roll like a jelly roll and cut into slices 1 inch wide.
6. Bake at 425°F. in greased pans with the cut surface up.

**YIELD**

200 biscuits.


## MARMALADE TEA BISCUITS

1. Make standard tea biscuit dough. Divide into 4 equal pieces.
2. Roll each piece into strips, 6" wide, ¼" thick and as long as the quantity permits.
3. Spread with marmalade.
4. Roll like a jelly-roll and cut into ½" slices.
5. Place on well-greased baking sheets with the cut surface up.
6. Let proof for 15 minutes.
7. Bake in a hot oven (450°F.) for 10 to 15 minutes.

**YIELD**

200 biscuits.

# Vegetables

## COOKING FRESH VEGETABLES

Vegetables should be cooked by methods that will retain the food value and that will also produce an appetizing appearance.

### TO AVOID LOSS OF FOOD VALUE IN COOKING

1. Prepare vegetables only a short time before they are to be cooked. Try to plan your work so that they will not have to be left standing in cold water for several hours.
2. Whenever possible, leave the skin on. When paring, remove only a very thin skin.
3. Arrange the cooking time so that the vegetables will not stand for more than a few minutes before serving.
4. Bake or steam vegetables when it is possible to do so.
5. Although it is necessary to cover pared potatoes with cold water to prevent discolouration, they should be left in the water for only a short time.

### TO AVOID LOSS OF FOOD VALUE WHEN VEGETABLES ARE BOILED

If equipment is limited, boiling is usually the most practicable method for cooking vegetables. The loss in boiling is greater than in baking or steaming, but with care this loss can be greatly reduced.

1. Observe the first three general rules given above.
2. Unless the time required for cooking will be too greatly prolonged, leave the vegetables whole or cut into large-sized pieces. This does not apply to cabbage or turnips because the colour and flavour of these two vegetables will be spoiled by long cooking.
3. Vegetables should be cooked quickly. Have the water boiling when the vegetable is added and keep it boiling throughout the cooking period.
4. Boil gently to prevent the vegetable from breaking.
5. Drain as soon as tender.
6. Use as much of the vegetable water as possible for gravy, soups and sauces.

## GENERAL METHOD FOR BOILING VEGETABLES

For the purpose of boiling, vegetables are classified according to colour, into white, yellow, green and red.

**White Vegetables**

Potatoes
Parsnips
Celery

**Yellow Vegetables**

Carrots
Squash
Yellow Beans

**Red Vegetables**

Beets

**Green Vegetables**

Beet Greens
Broccoli
Green Beans
Green Cabbage
Green Celery
Green Peas

There are a few vegetables that have a very strong flavour. These are all boiled by the same method, regardless of their colour.

**Strong-Flavoured Vegetables**

Cauliflower
Cabbage
Leeks

Onions
Turnips

### METHOD FOR WHITE AND YELLOW VEGETABLES

1. Wash the vegetables thoroughly.
2. Pare or scrape if necessary.
3. Leave whole, cut in half or in medium-sized pieces or dice, according to the vegetable.
4. Add boiling water to $\frac{1}{3}$ the depth of the vegetable.
5. Add salt.
6. Cover with a tight-fitting lid and boil gently.
7. Drain as soon as tender. Do not over-cook.

### METHOD FOR GREEN AND STRONG-FLAVOURED VEGETABLES

1. Wash the vegetable thoroughly.
2. Cook in a large volume of boiling water.
3. Leave the lid off the saucepan.
4. Cook for as short a time as possible in order to retain the colour.
5. Add the salt when half-cooked.
6. It may be necessary to add more water.

## QUANTITIES

The following amounts yield 100 4- to 5-oz. servings.

|  | Potatoes | 50 lbs., A.P. |
|  | Fresh Green Peas | 50 lbs., A.P. |
| ½ c. | Salt | 5 oz. |
|  | Other Vegetables | 35 lbs., A.P. |
| ⅓ c. | Salt | 3 oz. |

Salt should be added to the water before the vegetables.

## TIME REQUIRED FOR COOKING

No definite time can be given for cooking, as this depends on the age of the vegetable, the size and shape of the pot and the heat of the stove.

Arrange the cooking time so that the vegetables will stand only a few minutes before they are served.

## POINTS TO REMEMBER

1. Pare as thinly as possible or cook with the skins on.
2. If vegetables are old or withered, it may be necessary to soak them overnight in cold water before paring.
3. Cook according to methods that will retain their food value and that will produce an appetizing appearance.
4. Save vegetable water for soup stock, except in the case of strong flavoured vegetables.
5. Cook only until tender and serve immediately.

## FRESH GREEN BEANS

### 35 lbs.

1. Remove ends and strings of beans.
2. Cut into thin strips, either lengthwise or diagonally. If the beans are long, cut the lengthwise pieces into halves or thirds.
3. Cook according to the general method for green vegetables.
4. Add melted butter and serve very hot.

**VARIATIONS**

1. Mix ¾ tsp. of nutmeg with the melted butter before pouring it over the beans.
2. Sauté 2 lbs. fresh mushrooms (sliced). Pour over the hot cooked beans and mix together lightly.
3. Sliver 3 c. blanched almonds. Bake in a slow oven until very lightly browned. Add to the beans with the butter and mix together gently.

## BOILED BEETS

### 35 lbs.

1. Cut off the leaves about ½ inch from the beet.
2. Scrub beets thoroughly.
3. Cook in boiling water to cover.

              Time: Young Beets     40 minutes
                    Old Beets       Indefinitely

4. When tender, plunge in cold water for a minute. Slip skins off. Slice or dice and reheat in a small quantity of the beet stock.

To avoid loss of colour while cooking, the skin of raw beets must not be broken.

## HARVARD BEETS

|              |              |
|--------------|--------------|
| **35 lbs.**  | **Raw Beets** |

SAUCE

|               |                |
|---------------|----------------|
| **¾ qt.**     | **Sugar**      |
| **½ c.**      | **Cornstarch** |
| **1½ qts.**   | **Beet Stock** |
| **1 qt.**     | **Vinegar**    |

**METHOD**

1. Boil beets, slice.
2. Mix cornstarch and sugar.
3. Add boiling beet stock gradually, stirring all the time.
4. Boil until clear and there is no taste of cornstarch.
5. Add vinegar.
6. Pour over boiled, sliced beets. Reheat.


## PICKLED BEETS

|              |              |
|--------------|--------------|
| **35 lbs.**  | **Raw Beets** |

SAUCE

|              |                |
|--------------|----------------|
| **2 qts.**   | **Beet Stock** |
| **1 pt.**    | **Vinegar**    |
| **⅓ c.**     | **Sugar**      |

**METHOD**

1. Boil beets, slice.
2. Dissolve sugar in vinegar and beet stock.
3. Pour over beets.
4. Serve hot or cold.

## BROCCOLI

### Broccoli, A.P. 50 lbs.

1. Wash Broccoli, remove leaves and discard.
2. Cut off stems leaving only about $\frac{1}{2}$ inch attached to the flower.
3. Discard any very coarse, fibrous stems, peel those remaining and split length-wise into $\frac{1}{4}$-inch strips. When necessary cut these across into 3- or 4-inch lengths.
4. Tie the stems together in bundles and place in a large volume of boiling, salted water. Cook uncovered.
5. When the stems have cooked for ten minutes, add the flowers and cover with a thin cloth, placed on the surface of the water.
6. Boil gently until the flowers are tender.
7. Lift out the flowers, with a fine strainer or egg-lifter, drain thoroughly and place carefully in serving dishes.
8. Drain the stems, remove strings and add to flowers.
9. Serve immediately with melted butter.

**YIELD**

100 3-oz. servings.

## CABBAGE

Cooked cabbage should be slightly crisp, dry and either bright green in colour (young cabbage, Savoy cabbage) or white (Winter cabbage). Over-cooked cabbage is yellow or brown in colour, soggy, and has a strong flavour.

Cabbage must be cooked quickly, drained very thoroughly and served at once. For large numbers, cooking should be done in relays. Cook in a steam-jacketed kettle when this is available.

### Cabbage, A.P. 30 lbs.

**PREPARATION FOR COOKING**

1. Trim off the heavy outer leaves.
2. Wash thoroughly, cut into quarters and remove the core. Wash again if the inside leaves require it.

**METHOD FOR COOKING NEW CABBAGE**

1. Cut the quarters into 1″ wedges or smaller.
2. Cook in a small amount of boiling, salted water, until tender (6 to 8 minutes). The lid should be on the pot and cabbage should be turned once.
3. Drain at once and serve immediately.
4. When available, melted butter (1 lb.) may be poured over the cabbage before serving.

**METHOD FOR COOKING OLD CABBAGE**

1. Cut the quarters into very thin slices ($\frac{1}{8}$″ or less) or shred.
2. Cook in a large volume of boiling salted water until tender (10 to 12 minutes). The pot should be uncovered.
3. Drain at once and serve immediately with melted bacon fat (5 oz.) or butter (1 lb.) or a Cream Sauce (1$\frac{1}{2}$ gals.) or Bacon Cream Sauce (page 295).

**NOTE**

Times given are for cooking in a steam-jacketed kettle.

**YIELD**

100 3$\frac{1}{2}$-oz. servings.

# CARROTS

**35 lbs.**

1. Scrub carrots thoroughly.
2. Scrape or pare.
3. Cut large carrots in uniform pieces of medium size. Cook small or medium carrots whole.
4. Cook according to the general method for yellow vegetables.
5. Carrots may be served diced, mashed or creamed or with vegetable sauce.

## DICED CARROTS

1. Cut pared carrots into ½-inch dice.
2. When cooked and drained, add butter and seasonings.

## MASHED CARROTS

1. Mash hot, freshly cooked carrots.
2. Add ½ lb. butter and salt and pepper to taste.

## MASHED CARROTS AND PARSNIPS

**18 lbs. Carrots, A.P.**
**18 lbs. Parsnips, A.P.**

1. Cook carrots and parsnips separately, following the general method for yellow and white vegetables.
2. Mash together and season.

**YIELD**

100 4-oz. servings.

## PARSLIED CARROTS

1. Prepare 25 lbs. carrots, A.P. Cook as directed.
2. Brown 1½ lbs. of butter, add 1 cup finely chopped parsley and pour over the carrots.

# CORN

## Corn, A.P., 50 lbs.

**METHOD**

1. Remove husks and silk.
2. Steam (7 minutes) or cook in boiling water to cover (3 to 4 minutes).
3. Serve very hot, with butter.

**YIELD**

100 4½- to 5-oz. servings.

# CAULIFLOWER

## Cauliflower, A.P., 50 lbs.

Cooked cauliflower should be snowy white, slightly crisp, and the flowerets should not be broken.

**METHOD**

1. Cut off any discoloured parts from the cauliflower and remove the leaves and stalk.
2. Wash thoroughly and separate into flowerets of a uniform size.
3. Soak in salted water (2 tbsp. salt to 1 gal. of cold water) for 15 minutes.
4. Cook according to the General Method for Strong-Flavoured Vegetables. Time carefully—the cauliflower will change colour, develop a strong flavour and break up if over-cooked.
5. Drain and serve at once with butter or with Cream Sauce.

**YIELD**

100 4-oz. servings.

### CREAMED CAULIFLOWER

Serve 1½ gals. Cream Sauce with the boiled cauliflower.

**VARIATIONS**

1. Add 1 lb. grated cheese (1 qt.) to the cream sauce served on the cauliflower.
2. Add 1½ qts. sautéed mushrooms to the cream sauce.

**YIELD**

100 5½-oz. servings.

## CELERY

### Celery, A.P., 30 lbs.

Cooked celery should be white or green in colour, slightly crisp and well-drained.

**METHOD**

1. Cut roots from the heads of celery. Separate the stalks. Save the hearts for salads.
2. Scrub each stalk until perfectly clean.
3. Remove the leaves and set aside all that are fresh, for flavouring soups or for garnish.
4. Remove the coarse strings.
5. Slit the wide part of the stalk lengthwise into 1″ strips.
6. Cut these strips and the narrow part of the stalks crosswise into 1″ or ½″ lengths.
7. Cook in boiling water according to the directions for mild-flavoured vegetables.
8. When tender, drain very thoroughly. Save the stock.
9. Serve with melted butter or Cream Sauce.

**YIELD**

100 3½-oz. servings.

## CREAMED CELERY

**METHOD**

1. Make 1½ gals. thick Cream Sauce using ½ milk and ½ celery stock (page 295).
2. Pour over the hot cooked celery, mix gently.

**VARIATIONS**

1. Add 1 lb. (1 qt.) grated cheese to the cream sauce.
2. Add 1 cup each of finely diced green pepper, finely diced sweet red pepper or pimiento and finely diced sautéed onion.

**YIELD**

100 4½-oz. servings.

## ONIONS

**35 lbs., A.P.**

1. Select onions of uniform size.
2. Pare off outer skin and remove root.
3. Cook according to general method for strong-flavoured vegetables.
4. Serve plain or with cream sauce.

### BAKED ONIONS

**35 lbs., A.P.**

1. Choose small or medium-sized onions.
2. Boil for 10 minutes.
3. Place in a well-greased pan. Brush with melted fat.
4. Bake in a moderate oven until tender. If possible, cover for the first 15 minutes.
5. Baste occasionally after removing the lid.
6. Bake for approximately 1 hour.

## PARSNIPS

**35 lbs.**

1. Scrub thoroughly. Pare. If the parsnips have a woody centre, remove it before cooking, then dice, slice or cut the parsnips into fingers.
2. Cook according to the general method for white vegetables.

### CREAMED PARSNIPS

1. Prepare 25 lbs. parsnips, A.P.
2. Add freshly cooked parsnips to 1½ gallons of cream sauce (page 295).

### DICED PARSNIPS

1. Cut pared parsnips into 1-inch dice.
2. Add ½ lb. butter and salt and pepper to taste.

### MASHED PARSNIPS

1. Mash hot, freshly cooked parsnips.
2. Add ½ lb. butter and salt and pepper to taste. Mix thoroughly.

## BAKED POTATOES

1. Select large or medium-sized potatoes of uniform size.
2. Scrub thoroughly. Remove bruised or cut parts.
3. Place in a hot oven (400°-450°F.) and bake until tender (¾ to 1 hour).
4. As soon as the potato is cooked, make a single cut or a cross on the top to allow the steam to escape.

## BOILED POTATOES

### 50 lbs., A.P.

**METHOD**

1. Choose potatoes of uniform size.
2. Scrub thoroughly and remove bruises.
3. Cook according to the general method for white vegetables.
4. Drain thoroughly.
5. Stand the uncovered pot at the back of the stove for a few minutes to dry the potatoes.

## BROWNED POTATOES I

1. Scrub and pare medium-sized or small potatoes. Cover with cold water.
2. Drain very thoroughly after removing from the cold water.
3. Place in a baking pan containing ¼ inch melted fat. Season with salt and shake the pan over the top of the stove until the potatoes are well coated with the fat. There should be very little extra fat in the pan.
4. Bake in a hot oven (400°-425°F.) until tender (about 1 hour). The potatoes should be turned once.

## BROWNED POTATOES II

1. Scrub and pare medium-sized or small potatoes.
2. Boil until almost tender. Drain.
3. Place in baking pan containing ¼ inch fat. Season with salt and pepper.
4. Bake in a hot oven (450°F.) until tender.
5. Baste occasionally with the fat in the pan. Turn the potatoes once.

## CREAMED POTATOES

|  | Potatoes, A.P. | 40 lbs. |
|---|---|---|
| 1½ gals. | Medium Cream Sauce | 15 lbs. |

**METHOD**

1. Scrub and pare potatoes of uniform size.
2. Boil until tender. Cool and cut into ¾-inch dice.
3. Make the cream sauce according to the method, page 295.
4. Add the diced potatoes to the hot cream sauce and reheat without stirring. The stock pot should be placed in a pan of hot water to prevent scorching.

**YIELD**

100 6-oz. servings.

**VARIATION**

Add 1 qt. (1 lb., 8 oz.) finely diced green pepper and pimiento.


## SCALLOPED POTATOES

| 2 gals. | Medium Cream Sauce | 20 lbs. |
|---|---|---|
| 4 tbsp. | Salt | 2½ oz. |
| 4 gals. | Sliced Raw Potatoes | 24 lbs. |
|  | Melted Butter | 1 lb. |

**METHOD**

1. Make a cream sauce according to the recipe, page 295.
2. Add the 4 tbsp. salt.
3. Grease baking pans.
4. Fill with alternate layers of thinly sliced potato and cream sauce, having sauce on top.
5. Sprinkle with melted butter.
6. Bake in a medium oven (325°-350°F.) until the potatoes are tender (approximately 1½ hours).

**YIELD**

100 6-oz. servings.

**VARIATIONS**

To the recipe for scalloped potatoes, add—
1. 10 lbs. lean corned beef, diced.
2. 2½ lbs. thinly sliced raw onion. Cook in the fat used in making the Cream Sauce.

## MASHED POTATOES

|          | Potatoes, A.P. | 50 lbs. |
|----------|----------------|---------|
| ¾ c.     | Salt           | 8 oz.   |
| 1 c.     | Butter         | 8 oz.   |
| 2 qts.   | Hot Milk       | 5 lbs.  |

**METHOD**

1. Scrub and pare the potatoes. Boil until tender, following the method given for white vegetables.
2. Drain thoroughly. Place the uncovered saucepan over a low heat to dry the potatoes.
3. Mash until free from lumps.
4. Add the butter, heated milk and salt. Beat until the potatoes are creamy.

**YIELD**

100 5-oz. servings.

## DUCHESS POTATOES

|          | Mashed Potatoes<br>(hot or cold) | 36 lbs. |
|----------|----------------------------------|---------|
| 4 gals.  | Beaten Eggs                      | 2 lbs., 10 oz. |
| 1 qt.    | Melted Fat                       |         |

**METHOD**

1. Add the beaten eggs to the mashed potatoes and beat thoroughly.
2. Spread in greased baking pans.
3. Brush the top with melted fat.
4. Reheat in a hot oven (400°-450°F.).

**YIELD**

100 5-oz. servings.

## LYONNAISE POTATOES

**10 lbs. Raw Onions**
**25 lbs. Cooked Potatoes**
**Salt and Pepper**

**METHOD**

1. Peel and cut the onions into thin slices.
2. Cook in a small quantity of fat until tender and golden brown in colour.
3. Peel boiled or steamed potatoes and cut into $\frac{1}{4}$-inch slices.
4. Add to the cooked onion. Season. Cook until the potatoes are thoroughly heated and browned.

**YIELD**

100 5-oz. servings.


## HASHED BROWN POTATOES

**35 lbs. Cooked Potatoes**
**Salt and Pepper**

**METHOD**

1. Use boiled or baked potatoes.
2. Cut into $\frac{1}{2}$-inch dice. Add salt and pepper.
3. Heat in a well-greased pan.
4. When thoroughly heated, press into a cake and brown.
5. Turn and brown on the other side.

**YIELD**

100 5-oz. servings.


## HOME-FRIED POTATOES

**35 lbs. Cooked Potatoes**
**Salt and Pepper**

**METHOD**

1. Peel boiled potatoes and cut into $\frac{1}{4}$-inch slices.
2. Melt a small quantity of fat in a heavy pan. Add the potatoes, salt and pepper. Cook until brown.
3. Turn frequently to prevent burning.

## CHEESE AND POTATO CAKES

|           | Potatoes, A.P.          | 38 lbs. |
| --------- | ----------------------- | ------- |
|           | or                      |         |
| 4 gals.   | Cooked Potatoes         | 28 lbs. |
| ⅓ c.      | Salt                    | 3 oz.   |
| ½ tbsp.   | Pepper                  |         |
| 5 qts.    | Grated Cheese           | 5 lbs.  |

**METHOD**

1. If raw potatoes are used, cook, drain, add the seasonings and mash.
2. Add the grated cheese. Mix thoroughly.
3. Spread about 1 inch thick on greased baking pans.
4. Brown in a fast oven (400°-425°F.) for approximately 20 minutes.
5. Cut into squares and serve hot.

**YIELD**

100 5-oz. servings.


## O'BRIEN POTATOES

|        | Cooked Potatoes                   | 35 lbs. |
| ------ | --------------------------------- | ------- |
| 1 c.   | Diced Pimiento or Sweet Red       |         |
|        | Pepper                            | 5 oz.   |
|        | Salt and Pepper                   |         |

**METHOD**

1. Peel and cut the potatoes into half-inch dice. Add salt, pepper and pimiento.
2. Heat in a well-greased pan. Cook without browning. Turn frequently.
3. Serve very hot.

**YIELD**

100 5-oz. servings.

## POTATOES AU GRATIN

| | | |
|---|---|---|
| 2 qts. | **Grated Cheese** | 2 lbs. |
| 1½ gals. | **Hot Cream Sauce** | 15 lbs. |
| 4 gals. | **Boiled Potatoes** | 28 lbs. |
| ¼ c. | **Salt** | 2½ oz. |

**METHOD**

1. Add the grated cheese to the hot cream sauce.
2. Cut the potatoes into ¾-inch dice.
3. Combine sauce, diced potatoes and salt.
4. Pour into greased baking dishes.
5. Heat in a moderate oven (350°F.).

**NOTE**

1 pint of grated cheese may be kept out and added to 2 quarts of buttered bread crumbs. This may be sprinkled on the top of the pans of potatoes and browned in the oven.

**YIELD**

100 6-oz. servings.

## GLAZED SWEET POTATOES
(FRESH)

|  |  |  |
|---|---|---|
|  | Sweet Potatoes | 35 lbs. |
| ⅓ c. | Salt | 3 oz. |
|  | Boiling Water to cover |  |
|  |  |  |
| 1¾ qt. | Brown Sugar | 3 lbs. |
| ½ gal. | Hot Water | 5 lbs. |
| ¾ pt. | Butter | 15 oz. |
| 1 tsp. | Salt |  |

**METHOD**

1. Scrub the potatoes thoroughly and cook without paring in the boiling salted water—about 20 minutes.
2. Drain, cool.
3. Pare, cut into halves or fingers.
4. Arrange in greased baking pans.
5. Add the butter, sugar and salt to the ½ gal. of hot water and heat until the sugar dissolves and the butter melts.
6. Pour over the potatoes.
7. Bake in a moderate oven (350°F.) until brown (about 30 minutes). The potatoes may have to be turned once.

**YIELD**

100 5-oz. servings.

## SPINACH

**Spinach, A.P., 35 lbs.**

**METHOD**

1. Pick over the spinach and remove the dead leaves and roots. Immerse in a tub of lukewarm water.
2. Lift from this water into a second tub of water of the same temperature—wash thoroughly by moving the leaves up and down.
3. Continue to lift out and re-wash until no sediment can be felt in the bottom of the tub.
4. Lift from the last water into large stock-pots (or steam-jacketed kettles), containing about 1" of boiling salted water. Cover.
5. Cook for 5 to 7 minutes. Turn the spinach over at least once.
6. When tender, lift out and drain thoroughly.
7. Add salt, pepper and butter.

**VARIATION**

Add ¾ tsp. ground nutmeg with the butter and seasonings.

**YIELD**

100 4½-oz. servings.

## CREAMED SPINACH

| | | |
|---|---|---|
| 3 gals. | **Cooked Spinach** | 30 lbs. |
| 3½ c. | **Butter** | 1 lb., 12 oz. |
| 1½ c. | **Finely Chopped Onion** | 7 oz. |
| 3½ c. | **Unsifted Pastry Flour** | 14 oz. |
| 1 gal. | **Milk** | 10 lbs. |
| 4 tsp. | **Salt** | |

**METHOD**

1. Drain the spinach thoroughly. Chop fine.
2. Melt the butter, add the chopped onion and cook until it is tender.
3. Finish as cream sauce.
4. Add the cooked, chopped spinach to the hot sauce. Blend gently, do not stir. Heat for 3 minutes. If the mixture seems to be too thick, add hot milk or hot spinach stock.

**NOTE**

1 qt. of the liquid pressed from the spinach after it has been drained may be used in place of 1 qt. of milk. This improves both colour and flavour.

**YIELD**

100 4½-oz. servings.

**VARIATIONS**

1. Sauté 2 lbs. of sliced mushrooms and add to the cream sauce before adding the spinach.
2. Substitute an equal volume of undiluted Cream of Mushroom soup for the cream sauce.

## BRUSSELS SPROUTS

### Brussels Sprouts A.P., 30 lbs.

**METHOD**

1. Remove discoloured or wilted outside leaves.
2. Trim the stem end and cut the stem across.
3. Wash thoroughly.
4. Soak in cold salted water ($\frac{1}{4}$ cup salt to 1 gal. water) for 20 to 30 minutes. Drain.
5. Boil until tender (12 to 15 minutes). Follow the general method for strong-flavoured vegetables. Drain thoroughly.
6. Add 1 lb. melted butter and serve at once.

**YIELD**

100 3$\frac{1}{2}$-oz. servings.

## CREAMED BRUSSELS SPROUTS

1. Cook Brussels Sprouts as directed.
2. Prepare 1$\frac{1}{2}$ gals. of medium cream sauce.
3. Add to the sauce $\frac{1}{2}$ c. finely chopped parsley and $\frac{1}{2}$ c. finely chopped onions, cooked.
4. Pour over the cooked sprouts.

## BRUSSELS SPROUTS WITH BACON

### 2 lbs. Bacon cut in pieces
### 3 lbs. Grapes, cut in half and seeded
### or
### 3 lbs. Small seedless Grapes

**METHOD**

1. Fry the bacon and grapes until the bacon is crisp.
2. Pour over the sprouts.

## BAKED SQUASH

**35 lbs.**

**METHOD I**

If the squash have tender skins and are not large, cut in halves, scoop out the fibres and seeds. Bake in a moderate oven until tender.

Remove the squash from the shell and mash until free from lumps. Add salt, pepper and butter. Beat thoroughly. Keep hot in the oven until served.

**METHOD II**

1. Cut in halves or large pieces, scoop out the fibres and seeds.
2. Pare and cut into servings.
3. Place in baking pans, sprinkle with salt and pepper, add about $\frac{1}{4}$ inch of water. Cover with another pan.
4. Bake in a moderate oven until tender.
5. Serve in pieces or mash as in Method I.

**METHOD III**

Bake as in Method II without paring the pieces.
Serve without mashing.

## BAKED PEPPER SQUASH

**50 Squash**

**METHOD**

1. Wash thoroughly, cut in half.
2. Remove seeds and strings.
3. Brush with melted butter, season with salt and pepper.
4. Bake as directed above.
5. When tender, serve one-half per person.

**YIELD**

100 servings.

## BAKED SQUASH AND APPLE

| | | |
|---|---|---|
| 3 gals. | Cooked Squash | 30 lbs. |
| 5 qts. | Diced, Raw Apples | 6 lbs. |
| 1½ qts. | Brown Sugar | 2 lbs., 10 oz. |
| 3 c. | Butter or Margarine, | |
| | melted | 1 lb., 8 oz. |
| 2 tbsp. | Salt | |

**METHOD**

1. Arrange the cooked squash and diced apples in layers in greased baking dishes. Sprinkle each layer with the melted fat, sugar and salt. The top layer should be squash.
2. Brush the top with melted fat, sprinkle with brown sugar.
3. Bake in a moderate oven (350°F.) until the apples are tender—approximately 30 to 40 minutes.

**YIELD**

100 6-oz. servings.

**VARIATION**

Cooked sweet potatoes may be substituted for squash.

## TOMATOES

Tomatoes should be used raw but, since they deteriorate very rapidly, it is sometimes necessary to cook them in order to avoid waste.

They may be stewed, baked, scalloped or substituted for canned tomatoes in making tomato sauce, soup or baked beans and tomato.

## CANNED TOMATOES

### 5 #10 tins

1. Open cans just before serving.
2. Whenever possible, serve without heating.
3. When serving hot, bring to the boil quickly. Add salt and pepper to taste and serve at once.

## STEWED TOMATOES

|          | Raw Tomatoes | 35 lbs. |
|----------|--------------|---------|
|          | Butter       | 1 lb.   |
| ¼ c.     | Salt         | 2½ oz.  |
| 1 tbsp.  | Pepper       |         |

**METHOD**

1. Wash tomatoes. Dip in boiling water for 1 minute.
2. Remove skins and any soft spots.
3. Cut into large pieces.
4. Cook over a moderate heat in a covered saucepan until tender.
5. Add butter, salt and pepper.

**YIELD**

100 4-oz. servings.

# TURNIPS

### 35 lbs., A.P.

Turnips are cooked according to the general method for strong-flavoured vegetables.
If over-cooked they will have a disagreeable colour and flavour.
Turnips may be served diced or mashed.

#### OLD TURNIPS

1. Old turnips usually take a very long time to cook unless they are cut into small pieces.
2. To reduce the strong flavour—
   (a) Cook 1½ lbs. whole, pared potatoes with 35 lbs. of diced turnips. Remove the potatoes before serving the turnip.
   (b) Reduce the quantity of turnip to 26 lbs. After mashing them, add 9 lbs. of mashed potatoes and beat the mixture thoroughly.

# MACEDOINE OF VEGETABLES

This is a mixture of two or more diced vegetables. Each vegetable must be boiled separately. They are combined while hot and served with melted fat or butter, salt and pepper.
The vegetables commonly used are:

> Turnip
> Parsnip
> Carrot
> Green Beans
> Green Peas
> Cauliflower (in flowerets)

### PREPARATION OF CANNED VEGETABLES

### 20 #2 tins (20 oz.)

Canned vegetables should be heated in the liquid from the can. They should be cooked only long enough to heat them through. Longer cooking destroys the vitamin content.
After draining the vegetable, save the liquid to use in sauce, soup and gravy.

#### YIELD

100 3-oz. servings.

## CANNED CORN

### 5 #10 tins

Corn can usually be heated without the addition of liquid. Heat the corn slowly, stir frequently, add salt, pepper and butter to taste.
(If there is danger of burning, add a small quantity of milk or cream sauce. The amount required depends on the type and quality of the corn.)

**YIELD**

100 5-oz. servings.

## SCALLOPED CORN

**A**

| 5 #10 tins | Canned Corn | 32 lbs., 8 oz. |
| 2 qts. | Milk | 5 lbs. |
| ¼ c. | Salt | 2½ oz. |
| 1 tbsp. | Pepper | |
| | Fat | 1 lb. |

**B**

| 2 qts. | Buttered Crumbs | 2 lbs. |

**METHOD**

1. Combine A and pour into greased baking pans.
2. Cover with buttered crumbs.
3. Bake in a moderate oven (350°F.) until the corn is hot and the crumbs are brown (20 to 30 minutes).

**YIELD**

100 5-oz. servings.

## TOMATO-JUICE COCKTAIL

**5 #10 tins Canned Tomatoes, or
20 #2 tins Canned Tomatoes
Salt and Pepper
Onion Juice**

**METHOD**

1. Press cold canned tomatoes through a fine sieve until only the seeds remain. Scrape the outside of the sieve to remove all the pulp.
2. If the sieved tomatoes seem too thick to drink, dilute with cold water to the desired consistency.
3. Season to taste with salt, pepper, sugar and onion juice.
4. Chill thoroughly before serving.

**YIELD**

100 5-oz. servings.

## DRIED VEGETABLES

Most dried vegetables must be soaked for several hours before cooking. They should then be cooked in boiling water.

## BOILED BEANS

| 9 qts. | **White or Lima Beans** | 18 lbs. |
| 3 gals. | **Cold Water** | 30 lbs. |

**METHOD**

1. Wash the beans. Pick them over and remove any that are blemished.
2. Place in a large pot and add cold water until it is about 2 inches above the beans—approximately 3 gallons. Soak overnight.
3. Add boiling water to cover. Boil gently or simmer until tender. Add 2½ oz. salt (¼ c.) when the beans are almost cooked.
4. Drain thoroughly.

**YIELD**

100 7-oz. servings.

## QUICK-FROZEN VEGETABLES

Quick-freezing retains the colour, flavour and most of the food value of the fresh vegetable. There is a great saving of labour as no preparation is required for cooking.

To obtain good results, follow these general directions carefully.

### GENERAL RULES

1. Cook all quick-frozen vegetables, except greens such as spinach, without thawing.
2. Break the block of frozen vegetables into four or five pieces before removing from the carton.
3. Drop immediately into boiling water.
4. The quantity of water is the same as for fresh vegetables.
5. The time required for cooking is from $\frac{1}{3}$ to $\frac{1}{2}$ that needed for fresh vegetables.
6. Be very careful not to over-cook.
7. Serve immediately.
8. Save the water for soups and gravies.

### DEFROSTING FROZEN GREENS

1. Consult individual containers for defrosting and cooking instructions.
2. Allow frozen spinach, kale, chard, etc., to stand at room temperature for four to six hours or until it is completely defrosted.
3. Cook immediately, following the method for fresh green vegetables.
4. Serve at once.

## DIRECTIONS FOR COOKING QUICK-FROZEN VEGETABLES
100 PORTIONS)

| | Boiling Salted Water | | | |
|---|---|---|---|---|
| Vegetable | Wt. of Veg. Lbs. | Amt. of Water Gals. | Cooking Time in Minutes (Approx.) | Portion Ounces (Approx.) |
| **Asparagus Cuts** | 25 | 1 | 6 to 9 | 4 to 4½ |
| **Asparagus Spears** | 20 | 1 | 6 to 9 | 4 to 5 stalks |
| **Beans, Green** | 25 | 1 | 8 to 13 | 4 to 4½ |
| **Beans, Lima** | 25 | 1 | 10 to 13 | 4 to 4½ |
| **Beans, Wax** | 25 | 1 | 8 to 13 | 4 to 4½ |
| **Broccoli** | 20 | To cover | 5 to 7 | 4 |
| **Brussels Sprouts** | 25 | To cover | 5 to 6 | 4 to 4½ |
| **Cauliflower** | 20 | To cover | 3 to 5 | 4 |
| **Corn** | 25 | ½ | 5 to 6 | 4 to 4½ |
| **Peas** | 25 | 1 | 4 to 6 | 4 to 4½ |
| **Spinach** | 20 | 1 | 4 to 6 | 4 to 4½ |

# Index